CHILTON'S
REPAIR & TUNE-UP GUIDE

CHEVETTE PONTIAC 1000 1976-84

Covers all Chevrolet Chevette and Pontiac 1000 models

Vice President and General Manager JOHN P. KUSHNERICK
Managing Editor KERRY A. FREEMAN, S.A.E.
Senior Editor RICHARD J. RIVELE, S.A.E.
Editor MARTIN J. GUNTHER

CHILTON BOOK COMPANY
Radnor, Pennsylvania
19089

SAFETY NOTICE

Proper service and repair procedures are vital to the safe, reliable operation of all motor vehicles, as well as the personal safety of those performing repairs. This book outlines procedures for servicing and repairing vehicles using safe, effective methods. The procedures contain many NOTES, CAUTIONS and WARNINGS which should be followed along with standard safety procedures to eliminate the possibility of personal injury or improper service which could damage the vehicle or compromise its safety.

It is important to note that repair procedures and techniques, tools and parts for servicing motor vehicles, as well as the skill and experience of the individual performing the work vary widely. It is not possible to anticipate all of the conceivable ways or conditions under which vehicles may be serviced, or to provide cautions as to all of the possible hazards that may result. Standard and accepted safety precautions and equipment should be used when handling toxic or flammable fluids, and safety goggles or other protection should be used during cutting, grinding, chiseling, prying, or any other process that can cause material removal or projectiles.

Some procedures require the use of tools specially designed for a specific purpose. Before substituting another tool or procedure, you must be completely satisfied that neither your personal safety, nor the performance of the vehicle will be endangered.

Although information in this guide is based on industry sources and is as complete as possible at the time of publication, the possibility exists that the manufacturer made later changes which could not be included here. While striving for total accuracy, Chilton Book Company cannot assume responsibility for any errors, changes, or omissions that may occur in the compilation of this data.

PART NUMBERS

Part numbers listed in this reference are not recommendations by Chilton for any product by brand name. They are references that can be used with interchange manuals and aftermarket supplier catalogs to locate each brand supplier's discrete part number.

ACKNOWLEDGMENTS

Chilton Book Company thanks the Chevrolet Motor Division and the Pontiac Motor Division of the General Motors Corporation for assistance in the preparation of this book.

Information has been selected from Chevette and Pontiac 1000 Service Manuals.

Special tools mentioned in some procedures can be ordered through your Chevrolet or Pontiac dealer or directly through Kent-Moor Tool Division, 28635 Mound Road, Warren, MI., 48092

Chilton's Repair & Tune-Up Guide: Chevette and Pontiac 1000 1976–84
ISBN 0-8019-7457-7 pbk.
Library of Congress Catalog Card No. 83-45300

CONTENTS

Quick Reference Specifications For Your Vehicle

Fill in this chart with the most commonly used specifications for your vehicle. Specifications can be found in Chapters 1 through 3 or on the tune-up decal under the hood of the vehicle.

 Tune-Up

Firing Order_____

Spark Plugs:

    Type_____

    Gap (in.)_____

Point Gap (in.)_____

Dwell Angle (°)_____

Ignition Timing (°)_____

    Vacuum (Connected/Disconnected)_____

Valve Clearance (in.)

    Intake_____   Exhaust_____

Capacities

Engine Oil (qts)

    With Filter Change_____

    Without Filter Change_____

Cooling System (qts)_____

Manual Transmission (pts)_____

    Type_____

Automatic Transmission (pts)_____

    Type_____

Front Differential (pts)_____

    Type_____

Rear Differential (pts)_____

    Type_____

Transfer Case (pts)_____

    Type_____

FREQUENTLY REPLACED PARTS

Use these spaces to record the part numbers of frequently replaced parts.

PCV VALVE

Manufacturer_____

Part No._____

OIL FILTER

Manufacturer_____

Part No._____

AIR FILTER

Manufacturer_____

Part No._____

General Information and Maintenance

HOW TO USE THIS BOOK

Chilton's Repair and Tune-Up Guide for the Chevette/Pontiac 1000 is intended to give you a basic idea of how your car works and how to save money by servicing it yourself. The first two chapters will be the most frequently used, since they contain maintenance and tune-up information and procedures. The following chapters concern themselves with the more complex systems of the Chevette and Pontiac 1000. Operating systems from engine through brakes are coveered to the extent that we feel the average do-it-yourselfer should get involved. Chilton's Chevette/Pontiac 1000 won't explain rebuilding the transmission for the simple reason that the expertise required and the investment in special tools make this task uneconomical. We will tell you how to change your own brake pads and shoes, replace your spark plugs, and do many more jobs that will save you money, give you personal satisfaction, and help you avoid problems.

Before loosening any bolts, please read through the entire section and the specific procedure. This will give you the overall view of what will be required as far as tools, supplies, and you. There is nothing more frustrating than having to walk to the bus stop on Monday morning because you were short one metric bolt during your Sunday afternoon repair. So read ahead and plan ahead.

The sections begin with a brief discussion of the system and what it involves. Adjustments and/or maintenance are then discussed, followed by removal and installation procedures and then repair or overhaul procedures where they are feasible. When repair is considered to be out of your league, we tell you how to remove the part and then how to install the new or rebuilt replacement. In this way you at least save the labor costs. Backyard repair of such components as the alternator are just not practical.

Two basic mechanic's rules should be mentioned here. One, whenever the left side of the car is referred to, it is meant to specify the driver's side of the car. Conversely, the right side of the car means the passenger's side of the car. Second, most screws and bolts are removed by turning counterclockwise and tightened by turning clockwise. Safety is always the most important rule. Constantly be aware of the dangers involved in working on an automobile and take the proper precautions. Use jackstands when working under a raised vehicle. Don't smoke or allow an exposed flame to come near the battery or any part of the fuel system. Always use the proper tool and use it correctly, bruised knuckles and skinned fingers aren't a mechanic's standard equipment. Always take your time and have patience; once you have some experience and gain confidence, working on your car will become an enjoyable hobby.

TOOLS AND EQUIPMENT

Since the Chevette/1000 is built using mainly metric bolts and screws, you're going to need metric tools. Standard wrenches are either too tight or too loose to be used on metric fasteners. With the tools described below you'll be able to perform most of the procedures outlined in this guide.

1. Metric socket wrenches with various length drives.
2. Metric open end wrenches.
3. A ⅝ in. spark plug socket.
4. Round wire spark plug gauge.
5. Slot and phillips head screwdrivers.
6. Timing light.
7. Tachometer.

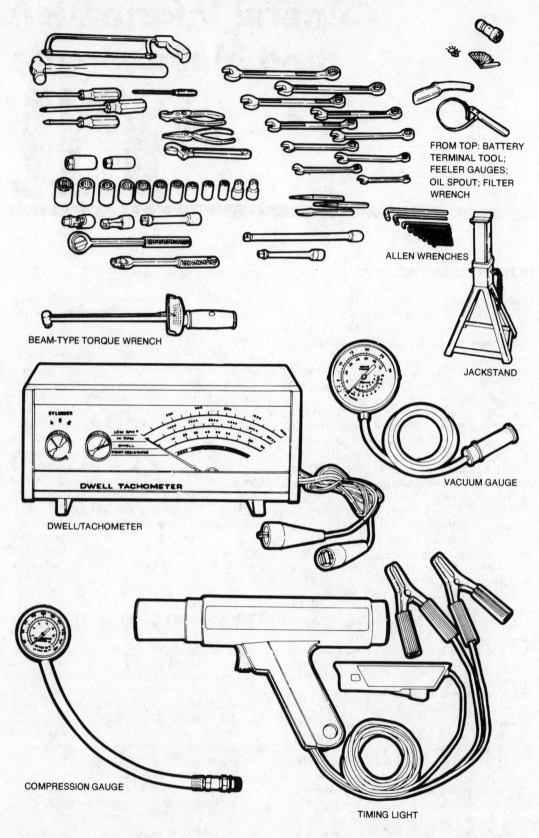

FROM TOP: BATTERY TERMINAL TOOL; FEELER GAUGES; OIL SPOUT; FILTER WRENCH

ALLEN WRENCHES

JACKSTAND

BEAM-TYPE TORQUE WRENCH

DWELL TACHOMETER

DWELL/TACHOMETER

VACUUM GAUGE

COMPRESSION GAUGE

TIMING LIGHT

You need only a basic assortment of hand tools and test instruments for most maintenance and repair jobs

8. Torque wrench. This assures proper tightening pressures and helps avoid stripped threads.

9. Oil filter wrench.

10. Vice-grips.

11. Heavy duty jackstands. Safety is a primary concern when working underneath any car.

HISTORY

The Chevette was introduced in 1976 as Chevrolet's answer to imported cars. When it was first introduced it featured the lightest curb weight, smallest body style and smallest turning circle of any Chevrolet to date.

The first Chevettes came with 1.4 litre, single overhead camshaft engines with 4-speed manual transmissions, 3-speed automatic transmissions were available as an option. The 1.6 litre engine was listed as an option in 1976 but in 1978 it was made standard and the 1.4 was discontinued.

The H.O. (High Output) engine was introduced in 1978. It is the same size as the base 1.6 litre engine but offered more power.

The four door body style was also introduced in 1978. Not only does it increase the leg room and cargo space, but also the wheelbase and overall length of the car.

With 1979 came the introduction of a 2 bbl Holley carburetor to once again boost power and a revised suspension system with softer rate front springs for a more comfortable ride.

Minor changes were made to improve the braking system for 1980.

In 1981 Pontiac introduced its version of the Chevette and called it the T1000. The following year the T was dropped and it was called the 1000. Both the Chevette and the 1000 feature a computer-controlled third-gear converter clutch in the automatic transmission. Also computer-controlled are many other power train functions, including fuel metering and spark timing. Beginning in 1981, Chevette offers an optional 1.8 liter four cylinder diesel engine and a five speed transmission.

SERIAL NUMBER IDENTIFICATION

Vehicle Identification Number (VIN)

The VIN (Vehicle Identification Number) is a 13 (1977–80) or 17 (1981 and later) digit number visible through the windshield on the driver's side of the dash and contains the vehicle and engine identification codes. It can be interpreted in the following charts:

Engine

On the gasoline engines the engine identification number is located on a pad on the right side of the cylinder block below the No. 1 spark plug.

On the diesel engines it is located at the left rear of the engine below the exhaust and manifold.

Transmission

The transmission identification number on the four and five speed manual is centered on a pad on the lower right side of the case. On

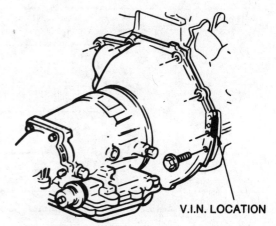

V.I.N. LOCATION

V.I.N. location—automatic transmission

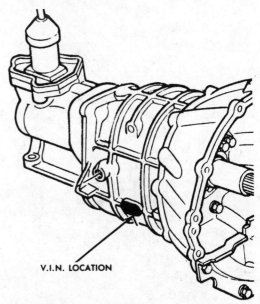

V.I.N. LOCATION

V.I.N. location—4 speed manual transmission

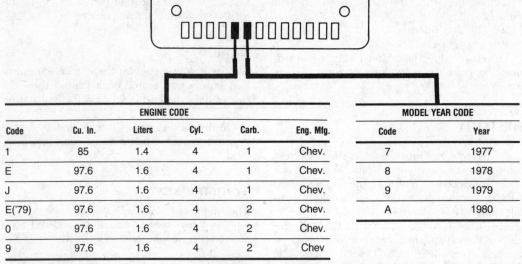

ENGINE CODE						MODEL YEAR CODE	
Code	Cu. In.	Liters	Cyl.	Carb.	Eng. Mfg.	Code	Year
1	85	1.4	4	1	Chev.	7	1977
E	97.6	1.6	4	1	Chev.	8	1978
J	97.6	1.6	4	1	Chev.	9	1979
E('79)	97.6	1.6	4	2	Chev.	A	1980
0	97.6	1.6	4	2	Chev.		
9	97.6	1.6	4	2	Chev		

The thirteen digit Vehicle Identification Number can be used to determine engine application and model year. The 6th digit indicates the model year, and the 5th digit identifies the factory installed engine.

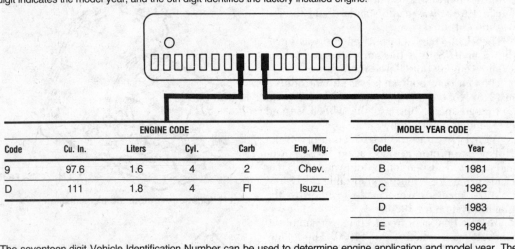

ENGINE CODE						MODEL YEAR CODE	
Code	Cu. In.	Liters	Cyl.	Carb	Eng. Mfg.	Code	Year
9	97.6	1.6	4	2	Chev.	B	1981
D	111	1.8	4	FI	Isuzu	C	1982
						D	1983
						E	1984

The seventeen digit Vehicle Identification Number can be used to determine engine application and model year. The 10th digit indicates the model year, and the 8th digit identifies the factory installed engine.

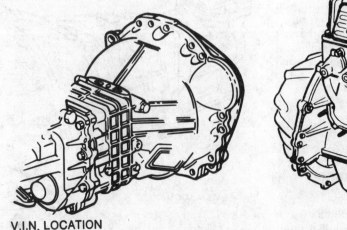

V.I.N. LOCATION

V.I.N. location—5 speed manual transmission

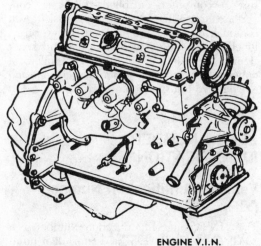

ENGINE V.I.N.

V.I.N. location—1.4 and 1.6 gasoline engine

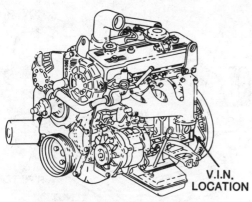

V.I.N.
LOCATION

V.I.N. location—1.8 liter diesel engine

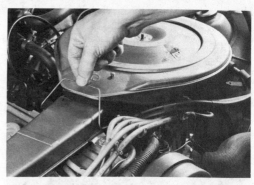

The retaining bail snaps off. Use a screwdriver to pry it off, if it's stubborn

models with automatic transmissions, the number will be found on a tag on the right side of the transmission.

ROUTINE MAINTENANCE

Routine maintenance is preventive medicine. It is the single most important process that can be taken in avoiding repairs and extending the life of any automobile. By taking only a minute or so each day to check oil level, tire pressures and coolant level, you'll be saving yourself time and money in the long run.

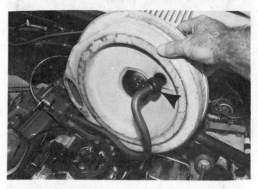

Lift off the old filter and disconnect the hose and grommet (arrow)

Air Cleaner

Gasoline Engines

The 1979–84 models have a removable filter element. It is easily replaced by removing the wing nut on top of the air cleaner and placing the new filter in the same position as the old

The air cleaner wing nut screws off counterclockwise, don't overtighten it when putting it back on

This shield keeps direct road dirt from hitting the filter element. Wipe it clean if you are not replacing the filter

one. GM recommends that the filter be replaced at 50,000 mile intervals when driving under normal conditions. When driving under dusty conditions the filter should be replaced more frequently.

Check the rubber gasket that the air cleaner sits on. If it's in bad shape or missing, replace it

The air cleaner on 1976–78 Chevettes is a welded, non-serviceable unit. GM recommends this filter be changed at 50,000 mile intervals.

To replace the unit:

1. Remove the wing nut from the mounting stud.

2. Pry the retaining bail wire from the air cleaner.

NOTE: *On 1979–84 models, simply remove the air cleaner lid, replace the old filter with a new one and replace the lid. On 1976–78 models, continue as follows.*

3. Disconnect the attaching hose and remove the air cleaner.

4. Position the new air cleaner over the carburetor, attach the hose, reconnect the bail wire, and screw the wing nut back on.

Diesel Engines

GM recommends that the air filter element be replaced at 30,000 mile intervals when driving under normal conditions. When driving under dusty conditions the filter should be changed more frequently.

The air filter element is removed by releasing the four top cover retaining clamps. Lift off the top cover and remove the filter. Install the new filter into the air cleaner then replace the top cover and tighten the retaining clamps.

NOTE: *Make sure all the air intake hoses are connected properly.*

Positive Crankcase Ventilation Valve

Gasoline Engines

PCV valve replacement is recommended at 30,000 miles or 2 year intervals. A clogged PCV

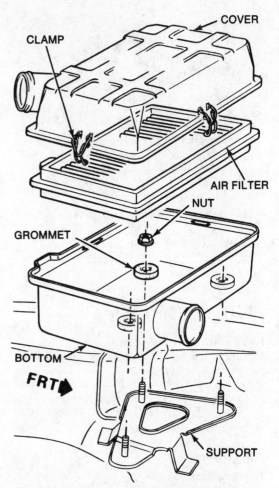

Air cleaner assembly—1.8 liter diesel engine

The PCV valve is located in the valve cover (arrow)

system will cause poor idle and rough running. To replace the valve:

1. Pull the PCV valve from the valve cover, under the air cleaner.

2. Using a pair of pliers, release the valve retaining clip and remove the valve.

3. Install the new valve and insert it into the valve cover.

Finally, remove the valve from the connecting hose. Some are retained by a clip which is released by squeezing with pliers

The valve pulls right out of its grommet in the valve cover

4. Inspect all PCV connecting hoses. Replace any cracked or deteriorated hoses.

Diesel Engines

Periodically check the PCV system for the following:
1. Cracked or plugged hoses.
2. Remove the PCV valve cover and check the diaphragm for deterioration or damage.
3. Broken diaphragm spring.
4. Contamination of the PCV valve body.
5. Make sure the baffle plate located inside the cam cover isn't plugged or contaminated.
To replace the PCV valve:
1. Disconnect the PCV valve connecting hose.
2. Remove the two screws holding the PCV valve to the cam cover.
3. Remove the valve and gasket.

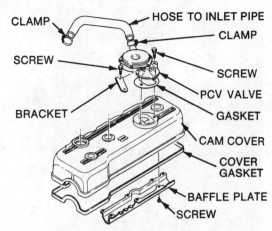

PCV system—1.8 liter diesel engine

4. Clean the cam cover PCV mounting surface.
5. Use a new gasket and reverse the above to install.

Evaporative Canister

On models through 1980 a canister stores carburetor and fuel tank vapors while the engine is off, holding them to be drawn into the engine and burned when the engine is started. The filter mounted on the bottom of the canister requires replacement at 15,000 mile intervals. To replace the filter:
1. Loosen the screw retaining the canister in its bracket.
2. Lift the canister slightly out of the bracket.
3. Remove the old filter from the bottom of the canister.
4. Install the new filter by working it into the retainers on the bottom of the canister.
5. Lower the canister back into its bracket and tighten the screw.
6. Check all connecting hoses and replace any that are suspect.

The evaporative canister is located at the front of the engine compartment on the driver's side

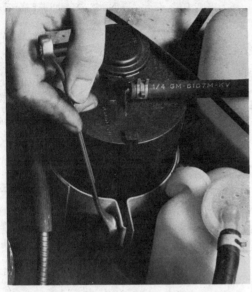

Loosen the bracket retaining screw enough so that you can slip the canister out

Work the old filter out and discard it. The new filter goes in the same way

The filter is located in the bottom of the canister

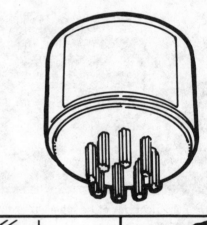

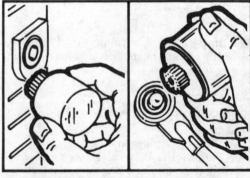

A special tool is available for cleaning the side terminals and clamps

Battery

Although the original equipment battery is a sealed unit and does not require added water, it does need periodic cleaning. Any accumulation of dirt or an acid film on the battery may permit current to flow from one terminal to the other, causing the battery to slowly discharge. Clean the battery regularly with diluted ammonia and rinse with clean water.

The sealed eye on top of the battery is the charge indicator. When the battery is fully charged the eye will be dark green. If the battery requires recharging, the eye will become a lighter green. When the indicator loses its color the battery must be replaced. Do not attempt to recharge a battery with a lightened indicator. It must be replaced.

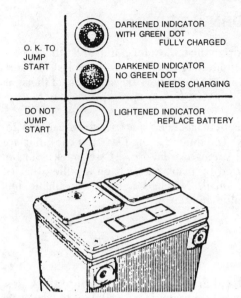

O. K. TO JUMP START — DARKENED INDICATOR WITH GREEN DOT FULLY CHARGED

DARKENED INDICATOR NO GREEN DOT NEEDS CHARGING

DO NOT JUMP START — LIGHTENED INDICATOR REPLACE BATTERY

Battery condition indicator

Belts

TENSION CHECKING, ADJUSTING, AND REPLACEMENT

Push in on the drive belt about midway between the crankshaft pulley and the alternator. Depending on its length, the belt should not deflect more than 1/4–1/2 in. If the belt is frayed or cracked, replace it. Adjust belt tension as follows:

1. Loosen both nuts on the bracket.
2. When replacing the belt, pry the alternator toward the engine and slip the belt from the pulleys.
3. Carefully pry the alternator out with a bar, such as a ratchet handle or broom handle, and then tighten the alternator bracket nuts.
4. Recheck the tension.

The alternator drive belt also operates the water pump. It might be good insurance to carry an extra belt in the trunk.

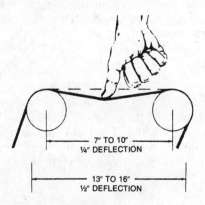

7" TO 10"
1/4" DEFLECTION

13" TO 16"
1/2" DEFLECTION

Allowable fan belt deflection

NOTE: *The optional air conditioning drive belt is adjusted in a similar fashion.*

Air Conditioning

The air conditioner should be turned on and allowed to run for a few minutes every two or three weeks during the winter. This will help the compressor seals stay lubricated and prevent drying and cracking.

This book contains no repair or maintenance procedures for the air conditioning system. It is recommended that any such repairs be left to the experts, whose personnel are well aware of the hazards and who have the proper equipment.

CAUTION: *The compressed refrigerant used in the air conditioning system expands into the atmosphere at a temperature of −21.7°F or lower. This will freeze any surface, including your eyes, that it contacts. In addition, the refrigerant decomposes into a poisonous gas in the presence of flame. Do not open or disconnect any part of the air conditioning system.*

Windshield Wipers

For maximum effectiveness and longest element life, the windshield and wiper blades should be kept clean. Dirt, tree sap, road tar and so on will cause streaking, smearing and blade deterioration if left on the glass. It is advisable to wash the windshield carefully with a commercial glass cleaner at least once a month. Wipe off the rubber blades with the wet rag afterwards.

If the blades are found to be cracked, broken or torn, they should be replaced immediately. Replacement intervals will vary with usage, although ozone deterioration usually limits blade life to about one year. If the wiper pattern is smeared or streaked, or if the blade chatters across the glass, the elements should be replaced. It is easiest and most sensible to replace the elements in pairs.

The wiper blades are retained to the wiper arms by one of two methods. One uses a press-type release tab, which, when depressed, allows the blade to be separated from the arm. The other uses a coil spring retainer. By inserting a screwdriver on top of the spring and pressing downward, the blade can be separated from the arm.

The rubber wiper element can be replaced separately from the blade, which is usually less expensive than replacing both blade and element. As with the blades, two methods are used to retain the rubber element to the blade. On one, a press-type button is used which, when

HOW TO SPOT WORN V-BELTS

V-Belts are vital to efficient engine operation—they drive the fan, water pump and other accessories. They require little maintenance (occasional tightening) but they will not last forever. Slipping or failure of the V-belt will lead to overheating. If your V-belt looks like any of these, it should be replaced.

Cracking or weathering

This belt has deep cracks, which cause it to flex. Too much flexing leads to heat build-up and premature failure. These cracks can be caused by using the belt on a pulley that is too small. Notched belts are available for small diameter pulleys.

Softening (grease and oil)

Oil and grease on a belt can cause the belt's rubber compounds to soften and separate from the reinforcing cords that hold the belt together. The belt will first slip, then finally fail altogether.

Glazing

Glazing is caused by a belt that is slipping. A slipping belt can cause a run-down battery, erratic power steering, overheating or poor accessory performance. The more the belt slips, the more glazing will be built up on the surface of the belt. The more the belt is glazed, the more it will slip. If the glazing is light, tighten the belt.

Worn cover

The cover of this belt is worn off and is peeling away. The reinforcing cords will begin to wear and the belt will shortly break. When the belt cover wears in spots or has a rough jagged appearance, check the pulley grooves for roughness.

Separation

This belt is on the verge of breaking and leaving you stranded. The layers of the belt are separating and the reinforcing cords are exposed. It's just a matter of time before it breaks completely.

HOW TO SPOT BAD HOSES

Both the upper and lower radiator hoses are called upon to perform difficult jobs in an inhospitable environment. They are subject to nearly 18 psi at under hood temperatures often over 280°F., and must circulate nearly 7500 gallons of coolant an hour—3 good reasons to have good hoses.

Swollen hose

A good test for any hose is to feel it for soft or spongy spots. Frequently these will appear as swollen areas of the hose. The most likely cause is oil soaking. This hose could burst at any time, when hot or under pressure.

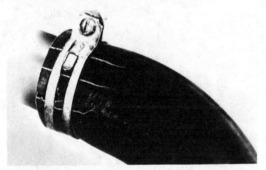

Cracked hose

Cracked hoses can usually be seen but feel the hoses to be sure they have not hardened; a prime cause of cracking. This hose has cracked down to the reinforcing cords and could split at any of the cracks.

Frayed hose end (due to weak clamp)

Weakened clamps frequently are the cause of hose and cooling system failure. The connection between the pipe and hose has deteriorated enough to allow coolant to escape when the engine is hot.

Debris in cooling system

Debris, rust and scale in the cooling system can cause the inside of a hose to weaken. This can usually be felt on the outside of the hose as soft or thinner areas.

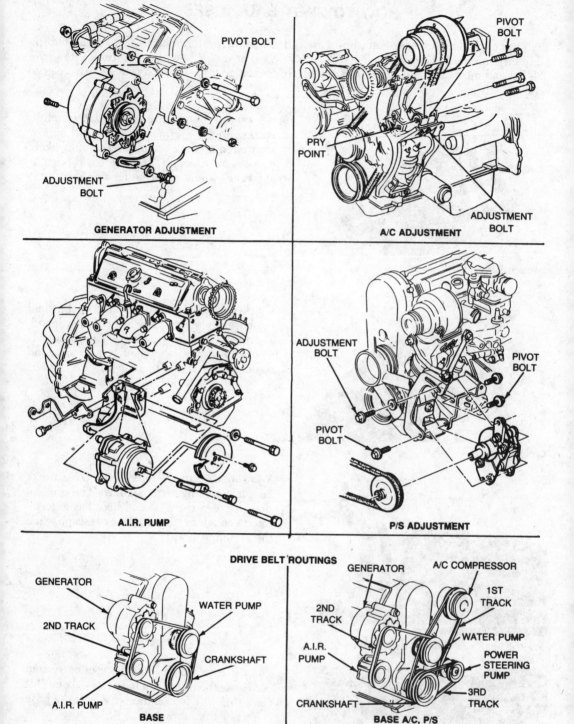

PIVOT BOLT

ADJUSTMENT BOLT

GENERATOR ADJUSTMENT

PIVOT BOLT

PRY POINT

ADJUSTMENT BOLT

A/C ADJUSTMENT

A.I.R. PUMP

ADJUSTMENT BOLT

PIVOT BOLT

PIVOT BOLT

P/S ADJUSTMENT

DRIVE BELT ROUTINGS

GENERATOR

WATER PUMP

2ND TRACK

CRANKSHAFT

A.I.R. PUMP

BASE

GENERATOR

A/C COMPRESSOR

1ST TRACK

2ND TRACK

WATER PUMP

A.I.R. PUMP

POWER STEERING PUMP

CRANKSHAFT

3RD TRACK

BASE A/C, P/S

Gasoline engine drive belt adjustments and routings

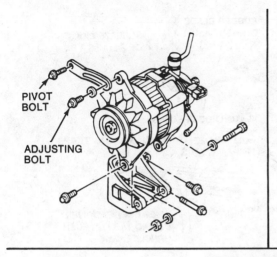

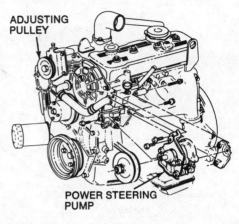

DRIVE BELT ROUTINGS

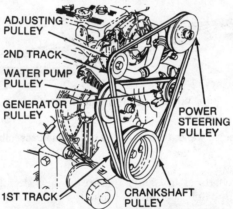

Diesel engine drive belt adjustments and routings

depressed, releases the element, which can be slid off the blade. On the other, a squeeze clip is used; squeezing the clip allows the element to be pulled from the blade. Replacements are simply slid back into place; be sure all the arms are engaged.

Tires

Tires should be checked weekly for proper air pressure. A chart, located at the left front door edge, gives the recommended inflation pressures. Maximum fuel economy and tire life will result if the pressure is maintained at the highest figure given on the chart. The tires should be checked before driving since pressure can increase as much as six pounds per square inch (psi) due to heat buildup. It is a good idea to have your own accurate pressure gauge, because not all gauges on service station air pumps can be trusted. When checking pressures, do not neglect the spare tire. Note that some spare tires require pressures considerably higher than those used in the other tires.

While you are about the task of checking air pressure, inspect the tire treads for cuts, bruises, and other damage. Check the air valves to be sure that they are tight. Replace any missing valve caps.

Check the tires for uneven wear that might indicate the need for front end alignment or tire rotation. Tires should be replaced when a tread wear indicator appears as a solid band across the tread.

When buying new tired, give some thought to the following points, especially if you are considering a switch to larger tires or a different profile series:

1. All four tires should be of the same construction type. Radial, bias, or bias-belted tires should not be mixed.

2. The wheels must be the correct width for

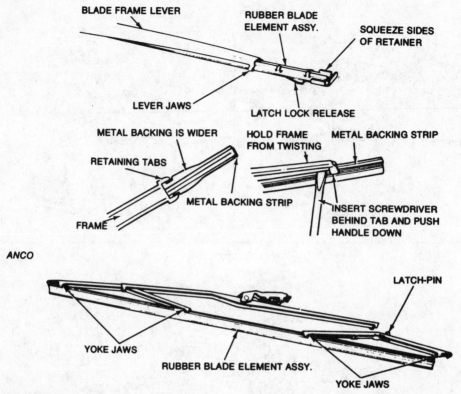

TRICO

BLADE FRAME LEVER

RUBBER BLADE
ELEMENT ASSY.

SQUEEZE SIDES
OF RETAINER

LEVER JAWS

LATCH LOCK RELEASE

METAL BACKING IS WIDER

HOLD FRAME
FROM TWISTING

METAL BACKING STRIP

RETAINING TABS

METAL BACKING STRIP

FRAME

INSERT SCREWDRIVER
BEHIND TAB AND PUSH
HANDLE DOWN

ANCO

LATCH-PIN

YOKE JAWS

RUBBER BLADE ELEMENT ASSY.

YOKE JAWS

The rubber element can be changed without replacing the entire blade assembly; your car may have either one of these types of blades.

the tire. Tire dealers have charts of tire and wheel rim compatibility. A mismatch can cause sloppy handling and rapid tread wear. The tread width should match the rim width (inside bead to inside bead) within an inch. For radial tires, the rim width should be 80% or less of the tire (not tread) width.

3. The height (mounted diameter) of the new tires can change speedometer accuracy, engine speed per given road speed, fuel mileage, acceleration, and ground clearance. Tire manu-

facturers furnish full measurement specifications.

4. The spare tire should be usable, at least for low speed operation, with the new tires.

5. There shouldn't be any body interference

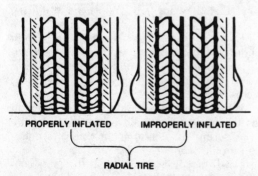

PROPERLY INFLATED   IMPROPERLY INFLATED

RADIAL TIRE

Don't judge a radial tire by its appearance. An improperly inflated radial tire looks similar to a properly inflated one.

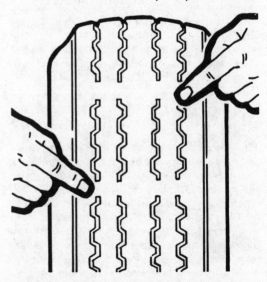

Tread wear indicators will appear as bands across the tread when the tire is due for replacement

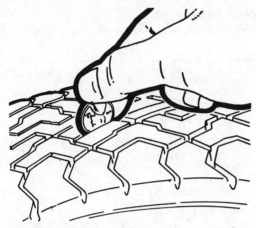

You can use a penny for tread wear checks; if the top of Lincoln's head is visible in two adjacent grooves, the tire should be replaced

Inexpensive gauges are also available for measuring tread wear

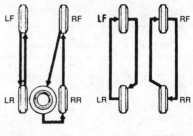

5 WHEEL ROTATION   4 WHEEL ROTATION

RADIAL TIRES

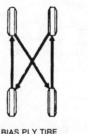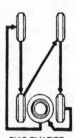

BIAS PLY TIRE 4 WHEEL ROTATION   BIAS PLY TIRE 5 WHEEL ROTATION

BIAS TIRES

Correct rotation patterns for radial and bias/belted tires

when the car is loaded, on bumps or in turning.

All of these problems can be avoided by replacing the tires with new ones of the same type and size. One other thing to remember when buying new tires: always have the dealer install new valve stems. Few things are more aggravating than having a new tire go flat because of an old, leaky valve stem.

TIRE ROTATION

Tire rotation is recommended every 6,000 miles or so, to obtain maximum tire wear. The pattern you use depends on whether or not your car has a usable spare. Radial tires should not be cross-switched (from one side of the car to the other); they last longer if their direction of rotation is not changed. Snow tires sometimes have directional arrows molded into the side of the carcass; the arrow shows the direction of rotation. They will wear very rapidly if their rotation is reversed. Studded tires will lose their studs if their rotational direction is reversed. Mark the wheel position or direction of rota-

tion on radial tires or studded snow tires before removing them to avoid these problems.

Fuel Filter

Gasoline Engine

A paper filter element is located behind the carburetor fuel line inlet nut. The filter should be replaced every 12 months or 12,000 miles whichever occurs first. To replace the filter:

1. Place an absorbent rag beneath the fuel line connection to the carburetor to absorb any spills.

2. Disconnect the small fuel line connection nut, using a flare nut wrench, while holding the large fitting nut with a standard open end wrench.

NOTE: *A flared nut wrench is preferred over a standard open end wrench since it will not slip off and round off the corners of the tubing nut.*

3. Remove the large filter retaining nut from the carburetor. There is a spring behind the filter. Remove the filter and spring.

4. Install the spring and the filter element.

5. Install the new gasket on the retaining nut and screw it into place. Do not overtighten; the threads are rather soft.

6. Install the fuel line.

7. Discard the gas-soaked rag safely.

Vehicle Maintenance Schedule

Interval (Months or miles, whichever occurs first)	Services
SECTION A—Lubrication and General Maintenance	
Every 12 months or 3,750 miles (6,000 km)	Engine oil change (diesel engines) Oil filter change (diesel engines)
Every 12 months or 7,500 miles (12,000 km)	Chassis lubrication Fluid levels check Engine oil change (gasoline engines) Oil filter change (gasoline engines) Tire rotation Rear axle lube change Wheel bearing repack
Every 12 months or 15,000 miles (24,000 km)	Cooling system check
Every 30,000 miles (48,000 km)	Man. transmission fluid change (5 spd.) Auto. transmission fluid change (diesel) Manual steering gear check Clutch cross shaft lubrication
Every 60,000 miles (96,000 km)	Auto. transmission fluid change (1976–78)
Every 100,000 miles (160,000 km)	Auto. transmission fluid change (1979–84)
SECTION B—Safety Maintenance	
Every 12 months or 7,500 miles (12,000 km)	Owner safety checks Tire, wheel and disc brake check Exhaust system check Suspension and steering check Brake and power steering check
Every 12 months or 15,000 miles (24,000 km)	Drive belt check Drum brake and parking brake check Throttle linkage check Underbody flush and check Bumper check
SECTION C—Emission Control Maintenance Gasoline Engines	
At first 6 months or 7,500 miles (12,000 km) Then at 18 month/22,500 miles (36,000 km) Intervals	Thermo. controlled air cleaner check Carburetor choke check Engine idle speed adjustment Vacuum advance system, hoses check
Every 12 months or 15,000 miles (24,000 km)	Fuel filter replacement PCV system check PCV valve and filter replacement
Every 22,500 miles (36,000 km)	Spark plug wire check Idle stop solenoid and/or dashpot check Spark plug replacement Engine timing adjustment and distributor check Carburetor vacuum break adjustment
Every 24 months or 30,000 miles (48,000 km)	Evaporative control system (ECS) check Fuel cap, tank and lines check
Every 50,000 miles	Air cleaner replacement
Diesel Engines	
Every 15,000 miles (24,000 km)	Valve clearance check and adjust
Every 12 months or 15,000 miles (24,000 km)	Fuel cap, fuel lines and fuel tank inspect
Every 30,000 miles (48,000 km)	Adjust engine idle speed Replace air cleaner element Check and adjust fuel injection pump timing

On gasoline engines the fuel filter is located behind the inlet fitting in the carburetor

Hold the fitting while loosening the nut to remove the filter

Diesel Engine

The fuel filter element should be replaced every 30,000 miles. To replace the filter element:
1. Disconnect the negative battery cable.
2. Disconnect the water sensor lead at the

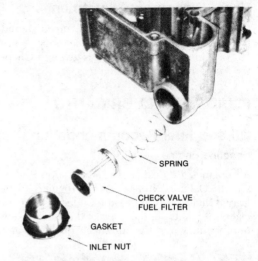

Fuel filter assembly—Gasoline engine

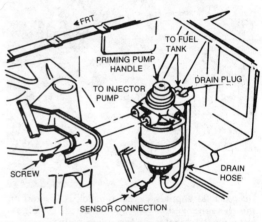

Fuel filter assembly—1.8 liter diesel engine

bottom of the filter, then disconnect the water filter to main body hose.
3. Remove the filter element by turning it counterclockwise using a filter strap wrench. Be careful not to spill any fuel.
4. After draining the filter, unscrew the water sensor from the bottom of the element.
5. Install the sensor in the new filter after applying a thin film of diesel fuel to the sensor O-ring.
6. Clean the filter mounting surface, apply a thin film of diesel fuel to the gasket on the new filter and install the filter. Continue turning the filter an additional ⅔ turn after it contacts the filter main body.
7. Connect the sensor wire. Disconnect the fuel outlet hose from the injector pump and place in a suitable container, then operate the priming pump handle several times to fill the filter with fuel. Reconnect the hose to the injector pump and start the engine to check for leaks.

Valve Clearance Adjustment

On diesel engines the valve clearance should be checked and adjusted if necessary every 15,000 miles. This procedure is given in Chapter 2 under Tune-up Procedures.

FLUIDS AND LUBRICANTS

Oil and Fuel Recommendations

Gasoline Engine

All engines are designed to operate on 91 Research Octane Number fuel (regular). Unleaded fuels only are recommended. The manufacturer points out that fuels of the same octane number may vary in antiknock qualities, and

On gasoline engines the oil dipstick is located on the passenger side as shown above. On diesel engines, it is located on the driver's side

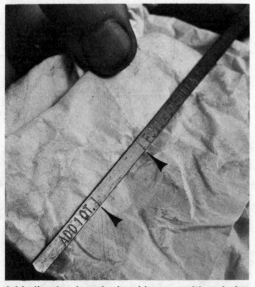

Add oil only when the level is even with or below the "Add 1 qt" mark

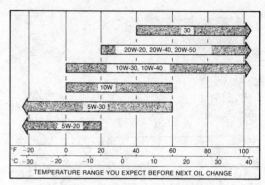

NOTICE: DO NOT USE SAE 5W-20 OILS FOR CONTINUOUS HIGH-SPEED DRIVING. 5W-30 OILS MAY BE USED IN 4-CYLINDER ENGINES UP TO 100°F (38°C)

Engine oil viscosity chart—Gasoline engine

cautions that ". . . continuous or excessive knocking may result in engine damage and constitutes misuse of the engine for which Chevrolet Division is not responsible under the terms of the New Vehicle Warranty."

Only oils labeled SE or SF are approved under warranty. The manufacturer does not recommend the use of oil supplements on a regular basis, but does suggest that a Chevrolet dealer be consulted if a problem exists which can be solved by the temporary use of a specific additive. The accompanying illustration will be helpful in selecting the proper viscosity oil for gasoline engines.

Diesel Engine

The Chevette equipped with a diesel engine is designed to run only on diesel fuel. Number 2-D, which is usually the only diesel fuel available, should be used if you expect the temperatures to be above $-7°C$ (20°F). If temperatures are expected to be below $-7°C$ (20°F) use Number 1-D fuel if available. In some areas a winterized blend also called 2-D is available. Certain additives are also used during the winter months. Check with the service station operator to be sure you get the properly blended fuel.

NOTE: *Do not use number 2-D fuel at tem-*

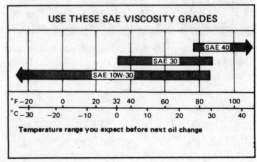

Engine oil viscosity chart—diesel engine

peratures below −7°C (20°F), unless it is winterized either at the service station fuel pump or by use of an additive.

Use only engine oils labeled SF/CC, SF/CD or SE/CC. It does not matter in what order these designations appear on the can as long as one is not missing. The use of engine oil additives is not recommended. Refer to the Engine Oil Viscosity Chart for diesel engines to help select the proper weight oil.

CHANGING OIL AND FILTER

GM recommends that the oil be changed every 6 months or 7500 miles, whichever comes first, for gasoline engines and every 3,750 miles or one year, whichever occurs first, for diesel engines. However, this is only if the car is operated under "normal" conditions. Since many cars are operated beyond the "normal" conditions, the oil should be changed more frequently. It certainly won't do any harm. If your car is used under extreme conditions, such as dusty roads, trailer pulling, or short trips in cold climates, the oil should be changed at least every 3,000 miles or 3 months for gasoline engines and every 2,000 miles or 3 months for diesel engines.

It is also recommended that the oil filter be changed at every oil change. By leaving the old filter in, you are leaving almost a quart of worn oil in the engine which will cause the fresh oil to break down faster than normal.

Always drain the oil when the engine is at operating temperature as the oil will flow easier and more contaminants will be removed.

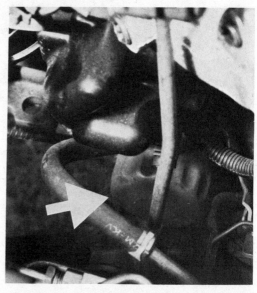

The oil filter on the gasoline engine is located on the driver's side of the engine as shown above. On the diesel engine, it is located on the passenger's side

You'll need a draining pan capable of holding at least 5 quarts.

Change the oil as follows:

1. Run the engine until it reaches normal operating temperature.

2. Jack up the front of the car and support it on safety stands.

3. Slide a drain pan of at least 5 quarts capacity under the oil pan.

4. Loosen the drain plug. Turn the plug

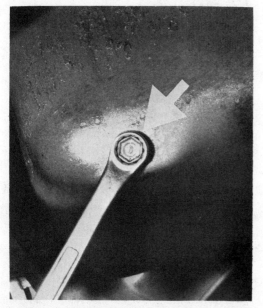

The oil drain plug on the gasoline engine is a 12mm hex head bolt

Bottom view of the oil filter on a gasoline engine. It will be easier to remove the filter from beneath the car

Lightly coat the filter gasket with fresh oil

out by hand. By keeping an inward pressure on the plug as you unscrew it, oil won't escape past the threads and you can remove it without being burned by hot oil.

5. Allow the oil to drain completely and then install the drain plug. Don't overtighten the plug, or you'll be buying a new pan.

6. Using a strap wrench, remove the oil filter. Keep in mind that it's holding about one quart of dirty, hot oil.

7. Empty the old filter into the drain pan and dispose of the filter.

8. Using a clean rag, wipe off the filter adapter on the engine block. Be sure that the rag doesn't leave any lint which could clog an oil passage.

9. Coat the rubber gasket on the filter with fresh oil. Spin it onto the engine *by hand;* when the gasket touches the adapter surface give it another ½–¾ turn. No more, or you'll squash the gasket and it will leak.

10. Refill the engine with four quarts of oil.

11. Start the car. If the oil pressure light does not turn off or the oil pressure gauge shows no pressure after a few seconds, shut off the engine and locate the problem.

12. If the oil pressure is OK and there are no leaks, shut the engine off and lower the car.

Transmission

FLUID RECOMMENDATION AND LEVEL CHECK

Manual

Check the level of the lubricant in the transmission at 7,500 mile intervals or every 6 months. The lubricant should be maintained at the level of the filler plug. To check the level, remove the square-headed plug from the side of the transmission case. A slight amount of fluid may run out (indicating the transmission is full) or you can use your finger to determine if the

lubricant is at the filler plug. If not, top it up with SAE 80 or 80–90 gear oil in all four speed transmissions. Cars operated in Canada and equipped with a four speed transmission should use the SAE 80 all year.

All Diesel engines equipped with five speed transmissions use SAE 5W-30, type SF engine oil. All Gasoline engines with five speed transmissions use SAE 80 or 80–90 gear oil.

Automatic

Check the automatic transmission fluid level whenever you check the engine oil. It is even more important to check the fluid level when you are pulling a trailer or driving in a mountainous area. Automatic transmission fluid that smells burned or has a dark brown appearance is a signal of impending problems.

Check the fluid level with the car parked on

Manual transmission drain plug

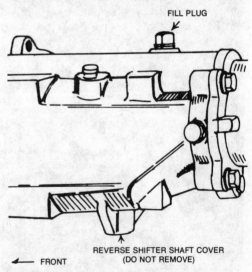

Bottom view of the 4-speed manual transmission. The fill plug is located on the driver's side of the transmission case

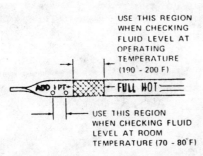

USE THIS REGION WHEN CHECKING FLUID LEVEL AT OPERATING TEMPERATURE (190 - 200 F)

ADD 1 PT — FULL HOT

USE THIS REGION WHEN CHECKING FLUID LEVEL AT ROOM TEMPERATURE (70 - 80°F)

Automatic transmission dipstick markings

a level spot, shift lever in Park, and with the engine running and warmed up.

1. Remove the dipstick, which is located in the engine compartment on the passenger's side.

2. Carefully touch the end of the dipstick to determine whether the fluid is cool, warm, or hot.

3. Use a clean rag to wipe off the dipstick.

4. Fully reinsert the dipstick until the cap at the top is firmly seated.

5. Remove the dipstick and take your reading. If the fluid felt cool, the level should be about 3 mm–10 mm (⅛–⅜ in.) below the "Add" mark. There are two raised dots below the "Add" mark to denote this range. If the fluid was warm, the fluid should be right around the "Add" mark. The level should be between the "Add" and "Full" marks if the fluid was hot to the touch.

NOTE: *One pint will raise the fluid level from "Add" to "Full" when the transmission is hot. Be careful not to overfill the transmission, as this is just as bad as running with the fluid low.*

If it is necessary to top up the transmission fluid use DEXRON® II aut?mtic transmission fluid only.

DRAIN AND REFILL

Manual Transmission

4 SPEED AND 5 SPEED (GASOLINE ENGINE)

The manufacturer states that the transmission lubricant need never be changed. However, persons buying a used vehicle or those subjecting their cars to heavy-duty use may wish to change the lubricant. This may be done by removing the drain plug and draining off the old lube. Dispose of this in the same manner as you would used oil. Reinstall the drain plug. Using a suction gun or squeeze bulb filler, fill the transmission to the level of the filler plug. Use SAE 80–90 or 90 GL-5 gear lubricant

5-SPEED (DIESEL ENGINE)

The manufacturer recommends that the fluid be changed at the first 7,500 miles then every 30,000 miles. The lubricant should be filled to the level of the filler plug hole. Use SAE 5W-30 SF engine oil.

Automatic Transmission

The manufacturer recommends that the automatic transmission oil pan should be drained, the screen cleaned, and fresh fluid added every 60,000 miles (1976–78), 100,000 miles (1979–84 gasoline engines), 30,000 miles (1981–84 diesel engines). If you're frequently pulling a trailer, you should perform this service every 15,000 miles.

1. Jack up the front of the car and support the transmission with a jack at the vibration damper.

2. Place a drain pan under the transmission.

3. Remove the oil pan retaining bolts at the front and sides of the pan.

4. Loosen the rear pan retaining bolts about four turns.

5. Using a screwdriver, pry the transmission pan loose and let the fluid drain into the drain pan. Be careful not to gouge the pan mating surface on the transmission.

6. Remove the remaining bolts and remove the oil pan and its gasket. Throw the old gasket away.

7. Drain off all the fluid from the pan.

8. Clean the pan with solvent and let it dry.

9. Remove the two screen-to-valve body bolts, screen, and gasket. Throw the gasket away.

10. Give the screen a good cleaning in solvent and let it dry.

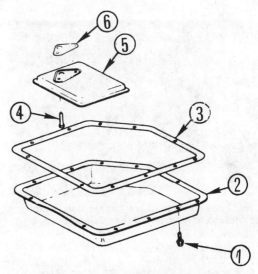

1. Oil pan bolt	4. Filter screen bolt
2. Pan	5. Filter screen
3. Gasket	6. Gasket

Automatic transmission oil pan and filter

11. Install a new gasket on the screen and replace the two bolts. Tighten the two bolts to 6–10 ft. lbs. (8–14 Nm) 1976–77, 13–15 ft. lbs. 1978–84.

12. Install a new gasket on the oil pan and install the oil pan. Tighten the bolts to 10–13 ft. lbs. (14–18 Nm) 1976–77, 7–10 ft. lbs. 1978–84.

13. Lower the car and add the correct amount of DEXRON® II automatic transmission fluid through the filler tube. (See capacities chart). A long neck funnel is handy for this operation.

14. Place the selector in Park, apply the parking brake, start the engine and let it idle normally.

15. Shift the selector through each transmission range, place it in Park, and then check the fluid level.

16. Add fluid as necessary.

Differential (Drive Axle)
FLUID RECOMMENDATION AND LEVEL CHECK

It is recommended that the rear axle lubricant level be checked at each engine oil change interval. The proper lubricant is SAE 80 or 90 GL-5 gear lubricant. The filler plug is removed with a ⅜ in. drive ratchet and short extension. When the unit is cold, the level should be ½ in. below the filler plug hole; when it is hot, it should be even with the hole. Lubricant may be added by a suction gun.

You'll need a ⅜ in. drive ratchet handle and an extension to remove the rear axle plug

Coolant
COOLANT RECOMMENDATION AND LEVEL CHECK

Once a month, the engine coolant level should be checked. This is quickly accomplished by

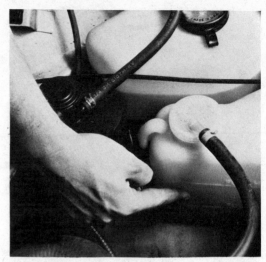

Coolant level should be at the lower mark when cold, higher mark when hot

observing the level of coolant in the recovery tank, which is the translucent tank mounted to the right of the radiator, and connected to the radiator filler neck by a length of hose. As long as coolant is visible in the tank between the "Full Cold" and "Full Hot" marks, the coolant level is OK.

If coolant is needed, a 50/50 mix of ethylene glycol-based antifreeze and clear water should always be used for additions, both winter and summer. This is imperative on cars with air conditioning; without the antifreeze, the heater core could freeze when the air conditioning is used. Add coolant to the recovery tank through the capped opening; make additions only when the engine is cool.

The radiator hoses, clamps, and radiator cap should be checked at the same time as the coolant level. Hoses which are brittle, cracked, or swollen should be replaced. Clamps should be checked for tightness (screwdriver tight only—do not allow the clamp to cut into the hose or crush the fitting). The radiator cap gasket should be checked for any obvious tears, cracks, or swelling, or any signs of incorrect seating in the radiator neck.

CAUTION: *To avoid injury when working with a hot engine, cover the radiator cap with a thick cloth. Wear a heavy glove to protect your hand. Turn the radiator cap slowly to the first stop, and allow all the pressure to vent (indicated when the hissing noise stops). When the pressure has been released, press down and remove the cap the rest of the way.*

DRAIN SYSTEM, FLUSH AND REFILL

The cooling system should be drained, flushed and refilled every two years or 30,000 miles, according to the manufacturer's recommenda-

You can use an inexpensive tester to check anti-freeze protection

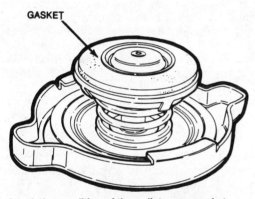

Check the condition of the radiator cap gasket

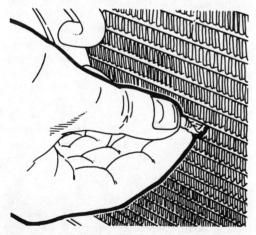

Clean the front of the radiator of any bugs, leaves or other debris at every yearly coolant change

tions. However, many mechanics prefer to change the coolant every year; it is cheap insurance against corrosion, overheating or freezing.

1. Remove the radiator cap when the engine is cool. See the preceding "CAUTION" about removing the cap.

2. With the radiator cap removed, run the engine until heat can be felt in the upper hose, indicating that the thermostat is open. The heater should be turned on to its maximum heat position, so that the core is flushed out.

3. Shut off the engine and open the drain cock in the bottom of the radiator.

4. Close the drain cock and fill the system with clear water. A cooling system flushing additive can be added, if desired.

5. Run the engine until it is hot again.

6. Drain the system, then flush with water until it runs clear.

7. Clean out the coolant recovery tank: remove the cap leaving the hoses in place. Remove the tank and drain it of any coolant. Clean it out with soap and water, empty it, and install it.

8. Close the drain cock and fill the radiator with a 50/50 mix of ethylene glycol base antifreeze and water to the base of the radiator filler neck. Fill the coolant recovery tank with the same solution to the "Full Hot" mark. Install the recovery tank cap.

9. Run the engine until the upper radiator hose is hot again (radiator cap still off). With the engine idling, add the 50/50 mix of antifreeze and water to the radiator until the level reaches the bottom of the filler neck. Shut off the engine and install the radiator cap, aligning the arrows with the overflow tube. Turn off the heater.

Master Cylinder

FLUID RECOMMENDATION AND LEVEL CHECK

The master cylinder is in the left rear side of the engine compartment, on the firewall. To check the fluid level as recommended at each engine oil change interval:

1. Clean off the area around the cap. Very small particles of dirt can cause serious difficulties in the brake system.

2. Pry the two wire retaining clips off the cap and to one side with a screwdriver. Take off the cover.

3. The proper level in each of the two reservoirs is within ¼ in. of the top. Add fluid as necessary.

4. Replace the cover and snap the retaining wire back in place.

NOTE: *Use only high-quality brake fluid specifically designated for disc brake systems. (DOT-3) Ordinary fluid will boil during heavy braking, causing complete loss of braking power.*

Master cylinder retaining clips (arrows)

After prying the retaining wires back, lift off the cover

Power Steering Pump

LEVEL CHECK

The power steering hydraulic fluid level is checked with a dipstick inserted into the pump reservoir. The dipstick is attached to the reservoir cap. The level can be checked with the fluid either warm or cold; the car should be parked on a level surface. Check the fluid level every 12 months or 7,500 miles, whichever comes first.

1. With the engine off, unscrew the dipstick and check the level. If the engine is warm, the level should be between the "Hot" and "Cold"

marks. If the engine is cold, the level should be between the "Add" and "Cold" marks.

2. If the level is low, add power steering fluid until correct. Be careful not to overfill, which will cause fluid loss and seal damage.

Steering Gear

There is no filler plug on the steering gear box. The unit is factory filled. It should be checked for leakage every 36,000 miles. An oily film is not evidence of leakage. Leakage is the actual loss of grease.

Chassis Greasing

The proper grease to be used is water-resistant EP chassis lubricant. A hand grease gun is satisfactory.

NOTE: *Ball joints must not be lubricated at temperatures below 10°F.*

1. There are two steering linkage grease fittings, all reached from under the car. A grease gun with a flexible extension will allow you to reach all the fittings. Wipe off the fittings, install the gun, and pump in grease until it leaks out around the rubber seals. Wipe off the excess and the grease fitting.

2. There is a grease fitting above both upper ball joints and below both lower ball joints, four in all. Grease these as in Step 1.

3. Rub a little grease on the steering stops riveted to the lower control arms. Rub a little grease on the parking brake cable guides under the rear of the car.

Body Lubrication and Maintenance

Door, Hood and Trunk Hinges

Use a heavy grease or silicone lubricant on the hinges to avoid binding conditions. After the initial application, exercise the hinge a few times to assure proper lubrication.

Door Locks

Apply graphite through the key slot. Insert the key and operate the lock several times to make sure the graphite has worked into the mechanism.

Windshield Washers

Fill the windshield washer tank with a cleaning solution. Do not use antifreeze as it may cause damage to the paint.

PUSHING AND TOWING

Do not attempt to push start a Chevette or a Pontiac 1000, whether it's equipped with an

Capacities

Year	Engine No. Cyl Displacement liters	Engine Crankcase Add ½ Qt For New Filter	Transmission Pts to Refill After Draining 4-Speed Manual	Transmission Pts to Refill After Draining 5-Speed Manual	Transmission Pts to Refill After Draining Automatic	Drive Axle (pts)	Fuel Tank (gals)	Cooling System (qts) With Heater	Cooling System (qts) With A/C
1976–77	4-1.4	4	3	—	7	2.8	13	8.5	9
	4-1.6	4	3	—	7	2.8	13	8.5	9
1978	4-1.6	4	3	—	10	2	12.5	8.5	9
1979–84	4-1.6	4	3.4	4	③	1.75	12.5	9	9.25
1981–84	4-1.8 (diesel)	5②	—	3¼	③	1.75	12.5	9	①

① Not available
② 6 qts with new oil filter
③ 180c trans.—10
   200c trans—7

automatic or manual transmission. Under certain conditions this may damage the catalytic converter or other parts of the car.

The car should not be towed to start, since there is a chance of the towed vehicle ramming the tow car. A Chevette or a Pontiac 1000 may be towed with its rear wheels on the ground at speeds under 35 mph for distances up to 50 miles. If the car must be towed farther or faster, the driveshaft must be disconnected or the car must be towed on its front wheels.

Manual transmission models can be towed on all four wheels at freeway speeds for extensive distances, provided that the transmission is overfilled by about a quart of gear oil and a sturdy tow bar is used.

NOTE: *Whenever the car is towed with all four wheels on the ground, the steering column must not be locked.*

JUMP STARTING

Jump starting is the only way to start a Chevette and Pontiac 1000 with a weak battery. The following method is recommended by the manufacturer.

NOTE: *Do not attempt this procedure on a frozen battery. It will very likely explode. If your Chevette or T1000 is equipped with a Delco Freedom battery and the charge indicator is light, do not attempt to jump start the car.*

1. Turn off all electrical equipment. Place the automatic transmission in Park and the manual unit in neutral. Set the handbrake.

2. Make sure that the two vehicles are not contacting each other. It is a good idea to keep the engine running in the booster vehicle.

3. Remove all vent caps from both batteries and cover the openings with cloths.

4. Attach one end of a jumper cable to the positive (+) terminal of the booster battery. The

To jump start a side terminal battery, you'll need adapters (which are readily available) which attach under the retaining bolts (arrows)

red cable is normally used. Attach the other end to the positive (+) terminal of the discharged battery.

5. Attach one end of the other cable (the black one) to the negative (−) terminal of the booster battery. Attach the other end to a ground point on the engine of the car being started. An ideal point is the engine lift bracket located between two of the spark plugs. Do not connect it to the battery.

NOTE: *Be careful not to lean over the battery while making this last connection.*

6. If the engine will not start, disconnect the batteries as soon as possible. If this is not done, the two batteries will soon reach a state of equilibrium, possibly with both of them too weak to start an engine. This should be no problem if the engine of the booster vehicle is left running fast enough to keep up the charge.

7. Reverse the procedure exactly to remove the jumper cables. Discard the rags, because they may have acid on them.

NOTE: *To jump start a Maintenance Free® battery, you must first check the charge indicator on top of the battery. If the green dot is visible or the indicator is dark, you may jump the battery. If the indicator is light, under no circumstances should you jump the battery. The battery then must be replaced.*

JACKING AND HOISTING

The bumper jack supplied with the car should never be used for any service operation other than tire changing. NEVER get under the car while it is supported by a bumper jack. If the jack should slip or tip over, as bumper jacks often do, it would be exceedingly difficult to raise the car again while pinned underneath. Always block the wheels when changing tires.

The service operations in this book often require that one end or the other, or both, of the car be raised and supported safely. The best arrangement is a grease pit or a vehicle hoist. The illustrations show the contact points for various types of lift equipment. A hydraulic floor jack is also referred to. It is realized that these items are not often found in the home garage, but there are reasonable and safe substitutes. Small hydraulic, screw, or scissors jacks are satisfactory for raising the car. Heavy wooden blocks or adjustable jackstands should be used to support the car while it is being worked on.

Drive-on trestles, or ramps, are a handy and safe way to raise the car. These can be bought or constructed from suitable heavy timbers or steel.

In any case, it is always best to spend a little extra time to make sure that the car is lifted and supported safely.

NOTE: *Concrete blocks are not recom-*

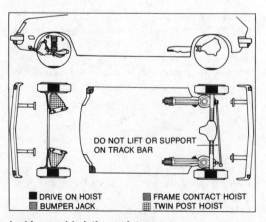

DO NOT LIFT OR SUPPORT ON TRACK BAR

■ DRIVE ON HOIST ▦ FRAME CONTACT HOIST
▨ BUMPER JACK ▦ TWIN POST HOIST

Jacking and hoisting points

mended. They may break if the load is not evenly distributed.

HOW TO BUY A USED CAR

Many people believe that a two or three year old used car is a better buy than a new car. This may be true; the new car suffers the heaviest depreciation in the first two years, but is not old enough to present a lot of costly repair problems. Whatever the age of the used car you might want to buy, this section and a little patience will help you select one that should be safe and dependable.

Tips

1. First decide what model you want, and how much you want to spend.

2. Check the used car lots and your local newspaper ads. Privately owned cars are usually less expensive, however you will not get a warranty that, in most cases, comes with a used car purchased from a lot.

3. Never shop at night. The glare of the lights make it easy to miss faults on the body caused by accident or rust repair.

4. Try to get the name and phone number of the previous owner. Contact him/her and ask about the car. If the owner of the lot refuses this information, look for a car somewhere else.

A private seller can tell you about the car and maintenance. Remember, however, there's no law requiring honesty from private citizens selling used cars. There is a law that forbids the tampering with or turning back the odometer mileage. This includes both the private citizen and the lot owner. The law also requires that the seller or anyone transferring ownership of the car must provide the buyer with a signed statement indicating the mileage on the odometer at the time of transfer.

5. Write down the year, model and serial number before you buy any used car. Then dial 1-800-424-9393, the toll free number of the National Highway Traffic Safety Administration, and ask if the car has ever been included on any manufacturer's recall list. If so, make sure the needed repairs were made.

6. Use the "Used Car Checklist" in this section and check all the items on the used car you are considering. Some items are more important than others. You know how much money you can afford for repairs, and, depending on the price of the car, may consider doing any needed work yourself. Beware, however, of trouble in areas that will affect operation, safety or emission. Problems in the "Used Car Checklist" break down as follows:

1-8: Two or more problems in these areas

indicate a lack of maintenance. You should beware.

9-13: Indicates a lack of proper care, however, these can usually be corrected with a tune-up or relatively simple parts replacement.

14-17: Problems in the engine or transmission can be very expensive. Walk away from any car with problems in both of these areas.

7. If you are satisfied with the apparent condition of the car, take it to an independent diagnostic center or mechanic for a complete check. If you have a state inspection program, have it inspected immediately before purchase, or specify on the bill of sale that the sale is conditional on passing state inspection.

8. Road test the car—refer to the "Road Test Checklist" in this section. If your original evaluation and the road test agree—the rest is up to you.

Used Car Checklist

NOTE: *The numbers on the illustrations refer to the numbers on this checklist.*

1. *Mileage:* Average mileage is about 12,000 miles per year. More than average mileage may indicate hard usage. 1975 and later catalytic converter equipped models may need converter service at 50,000 miles.

2. *Paint:* Check around the tailpipe, molding and windows for overspray indicating that the car has been repainted.

3. *Rust:* Check fenders, doors, rocker panels, window moldings, wheelwells, floorboards, under floormats, and in the trunk for signs of rust. Any rust at all will be a problem. There is no way to check the spread of rust, except to replace the part or panel.

4. *Body appearance:* Check the moldings, bumpers, grille, vinyl roof, glass, doors, trunk lid and body panels for general overall condition. Check for misalignment, loose holdown clips, ripples, scratches in glass, rips or patches in the top. Mismatched paint, welding in the trunk, severe misalignment of body panels or ripples may indicate crash work.

5. *Leaks:* Get down and look under the car. There are no normal "leaks", other than water from the air conditioning condenser.

6. *Tires:* Check the tire air pressure. A common trick is to pump the tire pressure up to make the car roll easier. Check the tread wear, open the trunk and check the spare too. Uneven wear is a clue that the front end needs alignment. See the troubleshooting chapter for clues to the causes of tire wear.

7. *Shock absorbers:* Check the shock absorbers by forcing downward sharply on each corner of the car. Good shocks will not allow the car to bounce more than twice after you let go.

8. *Interior:* Check the entire interior. You're looking for an interior condition that agrees with the overall condition of the car. Reasonable wear is expected, but be suspicious of new seatcovers on sagging seats, new pedal pads, and worn armrests. These indicate an attempt to cover up hard use. Pull back the carpets and look for evidence of water leaks or flooding. Look for missing hardware, door handles, control knobs

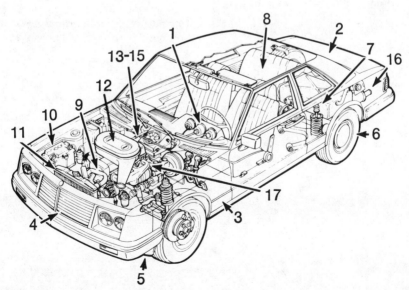

You should check these points when buying a used car. The "Used Car Checklist" gives an explanation of the numbered items

etc. Check lights and signal operations. Make sure all accessories (air conditioner, heater, radio etc.) work. Check windshield wiper operation.

9. *Belts and Hoses:* Open the hood and check all belts and hoses for wear, cracks or weak spots.

10. *Battery:* Low electrolyte level, corroded terminals and/or cracked case indicate a lack of maintenance.

11. *Radiator:* Look for corrosion or rust in the coolant indicating a lack of maintenance.

12. *Air filter:* A dirty air filter usually means a lack of maintenance.

13. *Ignition Wires:* Check the ignition wires for cracks, burned spots, or wear. Worn wires will have to be replaced.

14. *Oil level:* If the oil level is low, chances are the engine uses oil or leaks. Beware of water in the oil (cracked block), excessively thick oil (used to quiet a noisy engine), or thin, dirty oil with a distinct gasoline smell (internal engine problems).

15. *Automatic Transmission:* Pull the transmission dipstick out when the engine is running. The level should real "Full", and the fluid should be clear or bright red. Dark brown or black fluid that has distinct burnt odor, signals a transmission in need of repair or overhaul.

16. *Exhuast:* Check the color of the exhaust smoke. Blue smoke indicates, among other problems, worn rings; black smoke can indicate burnt valves or carburetor problems. Check the exhaust system for leaks; it can be expensive to replace.

17. *Spark Plugs:* Remove one of the spark plugs (the most accessible will do). An engine in good condition will show plugs with a light tan or gray deposit on the firing tip. See the color Tune-Up tips section for spark plug conditions.

Road Test Check List

1. *Engine Performance:* The car should be peppy whether cold or warm, with adequate power and good pickup. It should respond smoothly through the gears.

2. *Brakes:* They should provide quick, firm stops with no noise, pulling or brake fade.

3. *Steering:* Sure control with no binding, harshness, or looseness and no shimmy in the wheel should be expected. Noise or vibration from the steering wheel when turning the car means trouble.

4. *Clutch (Manual Transmission):* Clutch action should give quick, smooth response with easy shifting. The clutch pedal should have about 1–1½ inches of free-play before it disengages the clutch. Start the engine, set the parking brake, put the transmission in first gear and slowly release the clutch pedal. The engine should begin to stall when the pedal is one-half to three-quarters of the way up.

5. *Automatic Transmission:* The transmission should shift rapidly and smoothly, with no noise, hesitation, or slipping.

6. *Differential:* No noise or thumps should be present. Differentials have no "normal" leaks.

7. *Driveshaft, Universal Joints:* Vibration and noise could mean driveshaft problems. Clicking at low speed or coast conditions means worn U-joints.

8. *Suspension:* Try hitting bumps at different speeds. A car that bounces has weak shock absorbers. Clunks mean worn bushings or ball joints.

9. *Frame:* Wet the tires and drive in a straight line. Tracks should show two straight lines, not four. Four tire tracks indicate a frame bent by collision damage. If the tires can't be wet for this purpose, have a friend drive along behind you and see if the car appears to be traveling in a straight line.

Tune-Up and Performance Maintenance

2

TUNE-UP PROCEDURES

Keeping a car in tune should be considered by the owner as routine maintenance. By tuning the car regularly you will not only be improving the power and performance of the automobile but at the same time you'll be increasing the life-span of the car. It will also greatly aid the car in meeting with federal specifications for emission control. The best pollution control device is a well tuned car.

Spark Plugs

GM recommends replacing the spark plugs at 22,500–30,000 mile intervals. They should, however, be removed and checked before that figure. Chapter 10 provides illustrations of correct and incorrect spark plug conditions and what causes them to burn incorrectly. This chart will enable you to locate any developing problems and make the necessary adjustments to possibly prevent a major repair.

1. Remove each spark plug wire by pulling on the rubber cap, not on the wire. The wires have a carbon core to suppress radio static, and this core is easily separated if the wire is roughly handled.

2. Wipe the wires clean with a cloth dampened in kerosene and wipe them dry. If the wires appear to be cracked, they should be replaced.

3. Blow or brush the dirt away from each of the spark plugs. Sometimes this is done by loosening the plugs and cranking the engine with the starter.

4. Remove each spark plug with a ⅝ in. spark plug socket. Be careful that the socket is all the way down on the plug to prevent it from slipping and cracking the porcelain insulator.

5. Refer to Chapter 10 for details on evaluating the condition of the plugs. In general, a tan or medium gray color on the business end

of the plug indicates normal combustion conditions. The manufacturer states that the spark plug's useful life is from 22,500 to 30,000, depending on the year, miles. This being the case, it would be wise to replace the plugs if it had been more than the mileage interval since the last tune-up or if the mileage interval will be reached before the next tune-up. Refer to the "Tune-Up Specifications" chart for the proper spark plug type.

6. If the plugs are to be reused, file the center and side electrodes with a small, fine file. Check the gap between the two electrodes with a spark plug gap gauge. The round wire type is the most accurate. If the gap is incorrect, use the adjusting device on the wire gauge to correct the error. Be careful not to bend the electrode too far, because excessive bending may cause it to weaken and possibly fall off into the engine. This would require cylinder head removal to reach the broken piece, and could result in cylinder wall and ring damage.

Carefully pull the spark plug boot off. Don't yank on the wire

Gasoline Engine Tune-Up Specifications

When analyzing compression test results, look for uniformity among cylinders rather than specific pressures.

Year	Eng V.I.N. Code	Engine No. Cyl Displacement liters	HP	Spark Plugs Type	Gap (in.)	Distributor Point Dwell (deg)	Point Gap (in.)	Ignition Timing (deg) Man. Trans	Auto Trans	Fuel Pump Pressure (psi)	Idle Speed (rpm) Man. Trans	Auto Trans
1976–77	I	4-1.4	52①	R43TS	.035	Electronic		10B	10B	5–6.5	800(1000)	800(850)
	E	4-1.6	60②	R43TS	.035	Electronic		8B	10B	5–6.5	800(1000)	800(850)
1978	E	4-1.6	63③	R43TS	.035	Electronic		8B	8B	5–6.5	800(800)	800(800)
1979	E	4-1.6	70	R42TS	.035	Electronic		12B	18B(16B)	5–6.5	800(800)	750(750)
	O	4-1.6	74	R42TS	.035	Electronic		12B	18B(12B)	5–6.5	800(800)	750(750)
1980	9	4-1.6	70	R42TS	.035	Electronic		12B	18B	5–6.5	800	750(800)
	O	4-1.6	74	R42TS	.035	Electronic		12B	18B	5–6.5	800	750
1981	9	4-1.6	70	R42TS	.035	Electronic		18	18	5–6.5	800	700
1982–84	9	4-1.6	70	R42TS	.035	Electronic		④	④	5–6.5	800	700

Figures in parenthesis are for California
B Before Top Dead Center
① 59 for 1977
② 62 for 1977
③ Optional H.O. engine rated at 68 bhp V.I.N. code J
④ See underhood specification sticker
NOTE: The underhood specifications sticker occasionally reflects tune-up specification changes made in production. Sticker information must be followed if it disagrees with data supplied here.
Part numbers in this chart are not recommendations by Chilton for any product by brand name.

Diesel Tune-Up Specifications

Year	Engine No. Cyl. Displacement (liters)	Static Injection Timing	Fuel Injection Order	Compression (lbs)	Injection Nozzle Opening Pressure (psi)	Intake Valve Opens (deg)	Idle Speed ▲ (rpm) Man.	Idle Speed ▲ (rpm) Auto.
'81–'82	4-(1.8)	18°B	1-3-4-2	441 ①	1707	32	625	725
'83–'84	4-(1.8)	11°B	1-3-4-2	441 ①	1707	32	620	720

NOTE: *The underhood specifications sticker often reflects changes made in production. Sticker figures must be used if they disagree with those in the above chart.*
▲ See underhood sticker for fast idle speed.   ① At 200 rpm

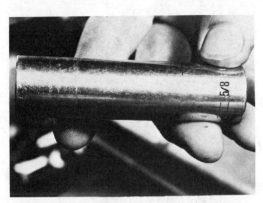
You'll need a ⅝ in. spark plug socket, not the more common ¹³/₁₆ in. variety

The plug can usually be unscrewed by hand once it's loosened

Use a round wire gauge to check spark plug gap

Turn the wrench counterclockwise to remove the spark plug

7. Clean the plug threads with a wire brush. Crank the engine with the starter to blow out any dirt particles from the cylinder head threads.

8. Screw the plugs in finger tight. Tighten them with the plug socket. If a torque wrench is available, tighten them to 15 ft. lbs.

9. Reinstall the wires. If there is any doubt as to their proper locations, refer to the "Firing Order" illustration in Chapter 3.

Ignition System

Gasoline Engine

All gasoline engine Chevette and Pontiac 1000 models are equipped with High Energy Ignition (HEI). This is a pulse triggered, transistor-controlled, inductive discharge ignition system

All of the HEI system components are housed in the distributor, except the coil

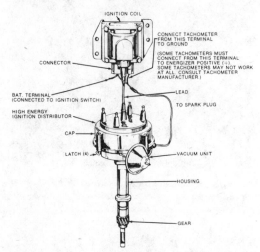

HEI system—This illustration is a representative schematic and does not depict actual component location

To remove the distributor cap, push down on the screw latches and release them by turning

No regular maintenance is necessary with HEI, but an occasional check of cap and rotor condition is a good idea. Look for pitting and burning

that uses no breaker points. The HEI distributor contains a pick-up assembly and an electronic module which perform the function of breaker points. Centrifugal and vacuum advance mechanisms are basically the same as those in breaker point distributors. 1981 and later models are equipped with EST (Electronic Spark Timing) distributors which have no mechanical or vacuum advance mechanisms. The ignition coil is mounted externally, on the left side of the engine, beneath the intake manifold, and is not visible on A/C equipped cars. The coil has a plastic cover.

The voltage delivered by this system is also far greater than the conventional system, enabling longer spark plug life as the hotter plug won't be as susceptible to fouling. There is no

regular servicing of the distributor other than checking the distributor cap and rotor for burning and pitting.

HEI SYSTEM TACHOMETER HOOKUP

Connect the positive tachometer lead to the coil terminal that is connected to the distributor. Connect the negative lead to a good ground. Please note, however, that some tachometers must connect to the coil terminal and the bat-

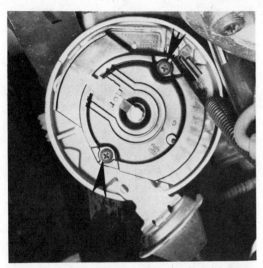

Unscrew the two phillips head screws (arrows) to remove the rotor

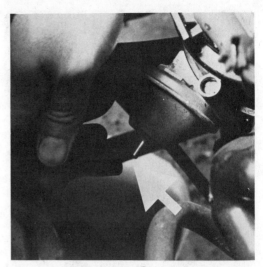

Disconnect and plug the distributor vacuum line

If the tip of the rotor is burned or pitted, replace it

tery positive terminal. Check the tachometer manufacturer's instructions.

CAUTION: *Never ground the coil terminal as the HEI electronic module could be damaged.*

Diesel Engine

A conventional ignition system is not needed on the diesel engine, because it uses compression heat rather than a manufactured spark to ignite its air/fuel mixture. An electrically operated glow plug system is used on the diesel engine to pre-heat the combustion chambers for easy cold startup.

Ignition Timing

1. Bring the engine to normal operating temperature. Stop the engine and connect a tachometer. Disconnect and plug the PCV hose

at the vapor canister and the vacuum hose at the distributor vacuum advance unit.

NOTE: *Use an adapter to make timing light connections at the distributor No. 1 terminal.*

NOTE: *On 1981 and later models with the Electronic Spark Timing (EST) distributor, the four lead wiring harness from the distributor must be disconnected before timing is set.*

Start the engine and check curb idle speed. Adjust as necessary on cars without both automatic transmission and air conditioning by turning the idle solenoid in or out. On cars with both automatic transmission and air conditioning, make sure that the wire connected to the solenoid is green with a double white strip NOT a brown wire. Switch wires if necessary. With automatic transmission in Drive and air conditioning off, turn the 1/8 in. hex screw in the end of the solenoid in until fully bottomed. Turn the solenoid assembly to obtain 950 rpm and turn the hex screw out to obtain the necessary rpm. (See tune-up specifications chart.)

2. Stop the engine, clean the timing marks and mark them with chalk. Connect a timing light.

3. Start the engine and aim the timing light at the timing marks. If the marks align, stop the engine, remove the timing light.

4. If adjustment is necessary, loosen the distributor clamp and rotate the distributor to align the marks. Tighten the clamp and recheck the timing.

NOTE: *Air conditioned models require removal of the compressor, bracket, and belt to reach the distributor clamp.*

5. Reset the curb idle speed if necessary, stop the engine, and remove the tachometer and

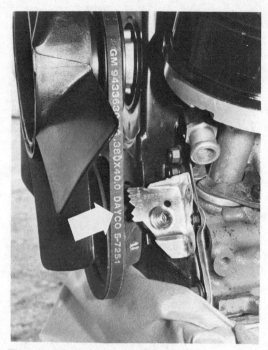

The arrow indicates the timing scale

The flash of the timing light will "stop" the timing marks which allows you to see if they align. Be careful that the timing light wires don't dangle into the fan or its belt

timing light. Reconnect the PCV and vacuum hoses.

Valve Lash

Gasoline Engine

All gasoline engines are equipped with a hydraulic valve system which requires no adjustment or maintenance.

Diesel Engine

NOTE: *The rocker arm shaft bracket bolts and nuts should be tightened to 20 ft. lbs. before adjusting the valves.*

1. Unscrew the retaining bolts and remove the cylinder head cover.

2. Rotate the crankshaft until the No. 1 or No. 4 piston is at TDC of the compression stroke.

3. Start with the intake valve on the NO. 1 cylinder and insert a feeler gauge of the correct thickness (intake—0.01 in., exhaust—0.014 in.) into the gap between the valve stem cap and the rocker arm. If adjustment is required, loosen the lock nut on top of the rocker arm and turn the adjusting screw clockwise to decrease the gap and counterclockwise to increase it. When the proper clearance is reached, tighten the lock nut and then recheck the gap. Adjust the remaining three valves in this step (see illustration) in the same manner.

4. Rotate the crankshaft one complete revolution and then adjust the remaining valves accordingly.

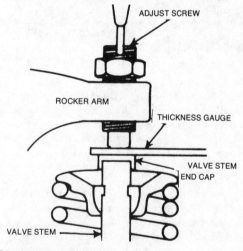

Diesel engine valve adjustment

Carburetor

IDLE SPEED ADJUSTMENT

1976–78

Two idle speeds are controlled by a solenoid on models without both automatic transmis-

You'll need a tachometer and ⅛ in. allen wrench to adjust the idle speed. Leave the air cleaner on, it's removed here for clarity

sion and air conditioning. One is normal curb idle speed (solenoid energized). The other is base idle speed (solenoid de-energized), which is 200 rpm lower than curb idle speed and prevents dieseling when the ignition is turned off. On cars with air conditioning the solenoid is energized when the air conditioning is on to maintain curb idle speed.

1. With the engine at normal operating temperature, air cleaner on, choke open, and the air conditioner off, attach a tachometer to the engine. Apply the parking brake, block the rear wheels, disconnect and plug the PCV hose at the vapor cannister and the vacuum advance hose at the distributor.

2. For cars without automatic transmission and air conditioning, turn the idle solenoid in or out to obtain the curb idle speed stated in the tune-up specification chart, then disconnect the wire from the solenoid.

3. With the automatic transmission in Drive or the manual transmission in Neutral, set the base idle speed to 200 rpm lower than the curb idle speed by turning the ⅛ in. hex screw located in the end of the solenoid. Reconnect the wire to the solenoid.

4. Cars with both automatic transmission and air conditioning must have a green wire with double white stripe connected to the idle solenoid, NOT a brown wire. Correct this if necessary.

5. With the air conditioning off and the automatic transmission in Drive, turn the ⅛ in.

hex screw in the end of the solenoid until fully bottomed.

6. Turn the entire solenoid assembly to obtain 950 rmp.

7. Adjust the curb idle speed by turning the hex screw out to obtain the correct rpm. (See tune-up specifications chart.)

8. Check the ignition timing and adjust if necessary. Readjust the solenoid assembly and curb idle speed if necessary.

9. Stop the engine, remove the tachometer, and connect the PCV and vacuum hoses.

1979–80

Refer to the Vehicle Emission Control Information sticker on the vehicle for the latest specification information and idle speed adjustment procedure.

1981 and Later

On these models, the carburetor mixture and idle speed are adjusted by the Computer Command Control (CCC) System. It is possible to adjust the basic idle speed—however, this procedure requires special knowledge and tools and should be performed by a qualified technician.

See Chapter Four for an explanation of the (CCC) System.

IDLE MIXTURE ADJUSTMENT

Carburetor idle mixture is preset at the factory and a plastic limiter cap is mounted on the idle mixture screw. The cap limits the mixture screw

The adjustment screw is at the center of the solenoid

Cut the tab and remove the limiter cap

The arrow points to the idle mixture screw

to approximately one turn leaner (clockwise) without breaking the cap. Idle mixture should be adjusted at major carburetor overhaul. Before suspecting the carburetor as the cause of poor performance or rough idle, check the ignition system thoroughly, including the distributor, timing, spark plugs and wires. Also be sure to check the air cleaner, evaporative emission system, PCV system, EGR valve and engine compression. Check the intake manifold, vacuum hoses and other connections for leaks and cracks.

NOTE: *On 1978–80 models, change was made on some General Motors carburetors*

to limit the range of idle mixture adjustment on the rich side. In other words, backing out the adjustment screw will not make an appreciable difference. The new procedure requires the use of artificial enrichment through the addition of propane. Since it is not feasible to buy a tank of propane for one or two carburetor adjustments, the procedure for cars from 1978–80 on is not covered here. On 1981–1984 models, the idle mixture is adjusted by the CCC system and requires no manual adjustment.

1976–77

1. With engine at normal operating temperature, air cleaner on, choke open, and air conditioning off, attach a tachometer to the engine. Apply parking brake, block the rear wheels, and disconnect and plug the PCV hose at vapor canister and vacuum advance hose at the distributor.

2. Start the engine and check ignition timing. Adjust timing as necessary. Replace vacuum advance hose.

3. Place automatic transmission in Drive or manual transmission in Neutral.

NOTE: *If the mixture screw is removed from the carburetor, gently seat it, then back it out 3 turns. Continue with Step 4.*

4. Remove the air cleaner, cut the tab off the limiter cap and remove the cap from the screw. Replace the air cleaner. Obtain the maximum idle speed by turning the mixture screw clockwise (leaner) or counterclockwise (richer).

5. Turn the idle speed solenoid in or out to obtain the higher idle speed stated on the underhood tune-up specifications sticker.

6. While turning the idle mixture screw clockwise (leaner), watch the tachometer to ob-

tain the lower idle speed stated on the underhood specifications sticker.

7. Stop engine, remove the tachometer, and replace the PCV and vacuum advance hoses.

Diesel Engine Idle Speed Adjustment

1. Set the parking brake and block the wheels.

2. Place the transmission in Neutral. Connect a tachometer as per the manufacturer's instructions.

3. Start the engine and allow it to reach normal operating temperature.

4. Loosen the lock nut on the idle speed adjusting screw and turn the screw to obtain the correct idle speed (see underhood specifications sticker).

5. Tighten the lock nut, turn the engine off and disconnect the tachometer.

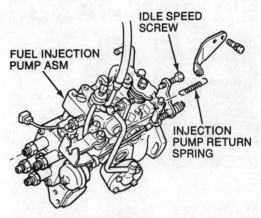

Base idle screw—diesel engine

Engine and Engine Rebuilding

3

ENGINE ELECTRICAL

HEI Distributor

All Chevette and Pontiac 1000 models are equipped with High Energy Ignition (HEI). This is a pulse triggered, transistor-controlled, inductive discharge ignition system that uses no breaker points. The HEI distributor contains a pick-up assembly and an electronic module which perform the function normally done by breaker points. The unit automatically controls the dwell period, stretching it with the increased speed of the engine. No dwell adjustment is necessary. On models through 1980, centrifugal and vacuum advance mechanisms are basically the same as those in breaker point distributors. 1981 and later models are equipped with EST (Electronic Spark Timing) distributors which have no mechanical or vacuum advance mechanisms. The capacitor in the distributor only serves to reduce radio noise. The ignition coil is mounted externally of the distributor.

Distributor mounting is at the front of the engine on the left-side.

REMOVAL AND INSTALLATION

1. If the car is air conditioned: disconnect the electrical lead at the air conditioning compressor, remove the compressor mounting through bolt and two adjusting bolts. Remove the two bolts and remove the upper compressor mounting bracket. Raise the car and remove the two bolts securing the lower compressor mounting bracket. Pull the bracket outward for clearance and lower the car.

2. Remove the air cleaner.

3. Remove the distributor cap and place it out of the way.

4. Remove the ignition coil cover by prying on the flat located on the front edge of the cover.

5. Remove the coil mounting bracket bolts.

6. Disconnect the electrical connector with red and brown wires that go from the coil to the distributor.

7. Remove the fuel pump, gasket, and push rod, making a note of which direction the push rod is installed. It's important that the push rod be installed in exactly the same direction as removed.

8. Scribe a mark on the engine in line with the rotor. Note the approximate position of the distributor housing in relation to the engine.

HEI connections are difficult to reach on the Chevette/1000. The distributor is fairly accessible (except on models with A/C) but the ignition coil is hidden under the intake manifold

9. Remove the distributor hold down bolt and clamp.

10. Remove the distributor.

11. Install the distributor in reverse order of removal, making sure that the distributor is fully seated.

INSTALLATION—ENGINE DISTURBED

1. Remove the No. 1 spark plug and place a finger over the spark plug hole. Turn the engine until compression is felt in the No. 1 cylinder.

2. Install the distributor with the distributor body scribe mark aligned with the mark on the engine and with the rotor pointing toward the distributor cap No. 1 spark plug tower.

3. Install the hold-down clamp and nut, but do not tighten them securely.

4. Install the distributor cap by aligning the tab in the cap with the notch in the housing and securing the four latches.

5. Connect the wiring harness connector to the terminals on the side of the cap. The connector will attach one way only. Reconnect the vacuum advance line.

6. Check and adjust the ignition timing. Securely tighten the distributor hold-down clamp.

FIRING ORDER

To avoid confusion replace spark plug wires one at a time.

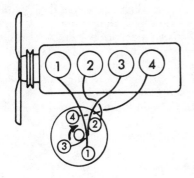

The arrow points to the distributor hold-down bolt

Alternator

A Delcotron 10-S1 series alternator is used. This unit also contains a solid state, integrated circuit voltage regulator. The alternator is non-adjustable and requires no periodic maintenance.

The diesel Chevette is fitted with an Hitachi alternator, which is equipped with an IC regulator and drives a vacuum pump mounted at its rear.

ALTERNATOR PRECAUTIONS

The following are a few precautions to observe in servicing the Delcotron (AC) generator and the regulator.

1. When installing a battery, be certain that the ground polarity of the battery and the ground polarity of the generator and regulator are the same.

2. When connecting a booster battery, be sure to connect the correct battery terminals together.

Alternator and Regulator Specifications

	Alternator			Regulator		
Year	Manufacturer	Output (amps)		Manufacturer	Type	Volts @ 85°
1976–80	Delco Remy	32		Delco Remy	Integral	13.8–14.8
1981–84	Delco Remy	42		Delco Remy	Integral	—
1981–84	Hitachi	55 ①		Hitachi	Integral	—

① 1983–84—50

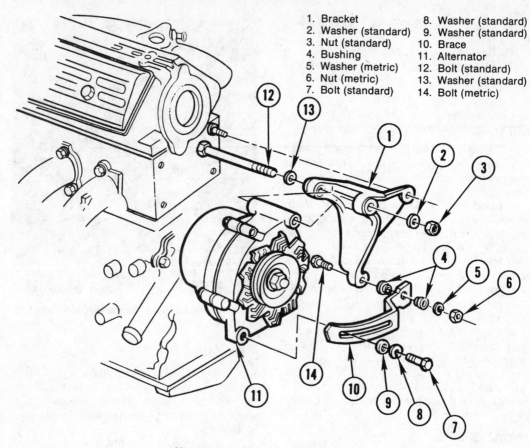

1. Bracket
2. Washer (standard)
3. Nut (standard)
4. Bushing
5. Washer (metric)
6. Nut (metric)
7. Bolt (standard)
8. Washer (standard)
9. Washer (standard)
10. Brace
11. Alternator
12. Bolt (standard)
13. Washer (standard)
14. Bolt (metric)

Alternator mounting—gasoline engine

3. When hooking up a charger, connect the correct leads to the battery terminals.

4. Never operate the car on an open circuit. Be sure all battery, alternator and generator connections are tight.

5. Do not short across or ground any of the terminals on the generator or regulator.

6. Never polarize an AC system.

7. Do not use test lamps of more than 12 volts for checking diode continuity.

8. Avoid long soldering times when replacing diodes or transistors, as prolonged heat will damage them. Always use a heat sink.

9. Always disconnect the battery ground terminal when servicing any AC system. This will prevent accidentally reversing polarity.

10. Always disconnect the battery and AC generator if electric arc welding equipment is being used on the car.

11. Never "jump" a battery for starting purposes with more than 12 volts.

REMOVAL AND INSTALLATION

1. Disconnect the negative battery cable.

2. Disconnect the alternator wiring. On the Chevette diesel, remove the fan shroud and fresh air duct, then disconnect the oil and vacuum lines at the vacuum pump.

3. Remove the brace bolt and the drive belt.

4. Support the alternator, remove the mounting bolt, and remove the alternator.

NOTE: *On the diesel, the mount bolts are removed from below the car.*

5. Installation is the reverse of removal. Adjust drive belt deflection to ½ in. under moderate thumb pressure.

Regulator

The regulator is a micro circuit unit built in to the alternator. The unit requires no voltage adjustment.

Starter

Engine cranking is accomplished by a solenoid-actuated starter motor powered by the vehicle battery. The motor on the gasoline engine is a Delco-Remy unit similar to previous Chevrolet starters. No periodic lubrication of the motor or solenoid is necessary.

The Chevette diesel is equipped with an Hi-

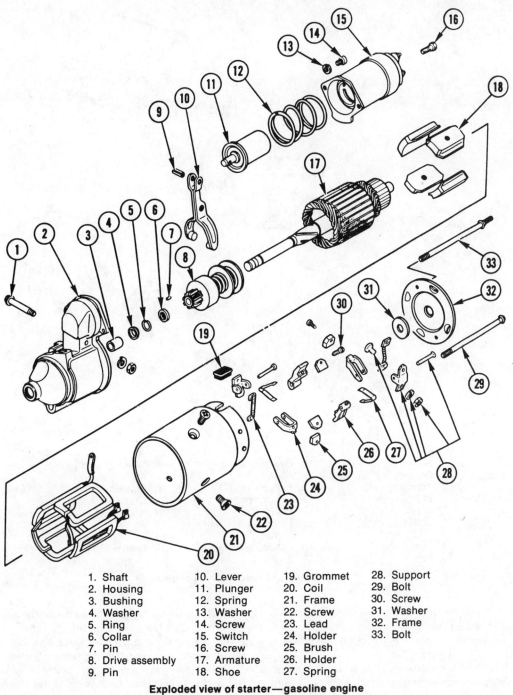

1. Shaft	10. Lever	19. Grommet	28. Support
2. Housing	11. Plunger	20. Coil	29. Bolt
3. Bushing	12. Spring	21. Frame	30. Screw
4. Washer	13. Washer	22. Screw	31. Washer
5. Ring	14. Screw	23. Lead	32. Frame
6. Collar	15. Switch	24. Holder	33. Bolt
7. Pin	16. Screw	25. Brush	
8. Drive assembly	17. Armature	26. Holder	
9. Pin	18. Shoe	27. Spring	

Exploded view of starter—gasoline engine

tachi reduction gear starter motor which is solenoid activated.

REMOVAL AND INSTALLATION— GASOLINE ENGINE

Cars Without Power Brakes—1976–79

1. Disconnect the negative battery cable and remove the air cleaner.

2. Disconnect the electrical connector from the oil pressure sending unit and remove the sending unit.

NOTE: *The oil pressure sending unit has a harness lock. To disconnect the electrical connector, lift the tab on the collar of the lock and remove the lock assembly.*

3. Disconnect the wires from the starter solenoid.

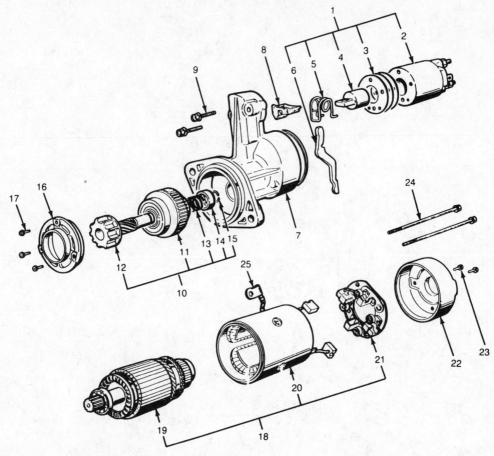

1. Solenoid assembly	10. Pinion assembly	18. Motor assembly
2. Solenoid	11. Clutch	19. Armature
3. Adjusting plate	12. Pinion shaft	20. Frame
4. Plunger	13. Return spring	21. Brush holder
5. Torsion spring	14. Pinion stop retainer	22. Rear cover
6. Shift lever	15. Pinion stop retainer	23. Screw
7. Gear case	clip	24. Through bolt
8. Dust cover	16. Bearing retainer	25. Lead wire
9. Bolt	17. Screw	

Exploded view of starter—diesel engine

4. Remove the brace screw from the bottom of the starter housing.

5. Remove the two starter-to-flywheel housing mounting screws.

6. Hold the starter with both hands and tip it past the engine mount bracket, then upward between the intake manifold and wheel arch.

7. Installation is the reverse of removal.

Cars Without Power Brakes—1980 and Later

1. Disconnect the battery ground cable.

2. Remove the air cleaner.

3. Disconnect the gas line at the carburetor and move to one side.

4. Disconnect the vacuum hoses at the carburetor.

5. Remove the splash shield from the distributor coil and move to one side.

6. Using a 6 in. and 12 in. extension with a universal socket, remove the upper starter bolt.

7. Remove the lower starting bolt and move the starter as necessary to disconnect the starter wiring.

8. Remove the master cylinder mounting nuts to gain access for removing the starter.

9. Installation is the reverse of removal.

Cars With Power Brakes (Without Air Conditioning)—1976–79

1. Disconnect the battery negative cable and remove the air cleaner.

2. Remove the distributor cap and place it aside.

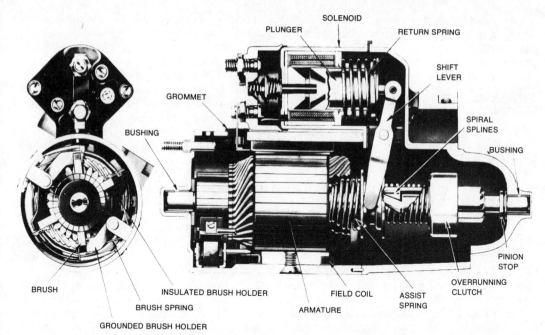

SOLENOID

PLUNGER

RETURN SPRING

SHIFT LEVER

GROMMET

SPIRAL SPLINES

BUSHING

BUSHING

PINION STOP

BRUSH

INSULATED BRUSH HOLDER

FIELD COIL

ASSIST SPRING

OVERRUNNING CLUTCH

BRUSH SPRING

ARMATURE

GROUNDED BRUSH HOLDER

Cross section view of the starter motor—gasoline engine

3. Remove the fuel line from the fuel pump to the carburetor.

4. Disconnect the electrical connector from the ignition coil. Remove the three coil bracket retaining screws and remove the coil with bracket.

5. Disconnect the vacuum hose to the distributor vacuum advance unit.

6. Disconnect the electrical connector from the oil pressure sending unit and remove the sending unit. See the preceding "Note" concerning the oil pressure sender harness lock.

7. Disconnect the wires from the starter solenoid.

8. Remove the brace screw from the bottom of the starter housing.

9. Remove the two starter-to-flywheel housing mounting screws.

10. Hold the starter with both hands and remove it by sliding it toward the front of the car.

11. Installation is the reverse of removal.

Cars With Power Brakes And Air Conditioning—1976–79

1. Disconnect the negative battery cable and remove the air cleaner.

2. Remove the upper starter-to-flywheel housing mounting screw.

3. Remove the two steering column lever cover screws.

4. Remove the mast jacket lower bracket screw.

5. Remove the upper steering column mounting bracket.

6. Disconnect the four electrical connectors from the steering column.

7. Raise the car.

8. Disconnect the flexible coupling (rag joint) and push it aside.

9. Disconnect the wires from the starter solenoid.

10. Remove the brace screw from the bottom of the starter housing.

11. Remove the lower starter-to-flywheel housing mounting screw.

12. To gain clearance, raise the engine ½ in. with a jack placed under the left-side of the engine.

13. Remove the starter by lowering it through the opening at the bottom of the engine.

14. Installation is the reverse of removal.

Cars With Power Brakes—1980 and Later

1. Disconnect the battery ground cable.

2. Remove the air cleaner.

3. Disconnect the gas line at the carburetor and move to one side.

4. Remove the splash shield from the distributor coil and move to one side.

5. Using a 6 in. and 12 in. extension with a universal socket, remove the upper starter bolt.

6. Remove the steering column cover screws and remove the cover.

7. Remove the steering column upper nuts and toe pan screw.

8. Raise the front of the car and make sure it is supported securely.

9. Remove the steering shaft from the steering coupling. Lower the vehicle and move the steering column from inside of the car to gain access to the starter.

10. Installation is the reverse of removal.

REMOVAL AND INSTALLATION—DIESEL ENGINE

1. Disconnect the negative battery cable.

2. Disconnect the starter wiring after labeling. The starter is located at the right rear of the engine.

3. Remove the upper mounting nut and the lower mounting bolt, then remove the starter.

4. Installation is the reverse of removal.

STARTER DRIVE REMOVAL AND INSTALLATION—GASOLINE ENGINE

1. Disconnect the field coil connector(s) from the starter solenoid terminal and remove the starter through-bolts.

2. Remove the commutator end frame, field frame assembly, and the armature from the drive housing.

3. Remove the starter drive by sliding the two-piece thrust collar off the armature shaft. Install a ½ in. pipe coupling or other suitable cylinder onto the shaft to butt against the edge of the retainer. Using a hammer, tap the coupling to force the retainer toward the armature end of the snap-ring.

4. Use pliers to remove the snap-ring from the groove in the shaft. If the snap-ring becomes distorted, use a new one upon assembly. Remove the retainer and starter drive from the armature.

Inspect all parts, replacing where necessary. Do not use grease dissolving solvent when cleaning starter parts—the drive mechanism and internal electrical insulation will be damaged.

To install:

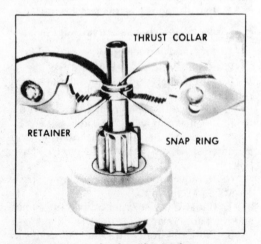

Forcing the snap-ring into the retainer

5. Apply silicone lubricant to the drive end of the armature and slide the drive assembly onto the armature with the pinion outward. Install the retainer on the armature with its cupped surface facing away from the pinion.

6. Install the snap-ring on the shaft by standing the armature on a wood surface (commutator end down), placing the snap-ring on the end of the shaft held in position with a wood block, and tapping the wood block with a hammer. Slide the snap-ring into its groove on the shaft. Place the thrust collar on the shaft with its shoulder against the snap-ring.

7. With the armature on a flat surface, place the retainer and thrust collar next to the snap-ring. Using pliers on both sides of the shaft at the same time, grip the retainer and thrust collar and squeeze until the snap-ring is forced into the retainer.

8. Apply silicone lubricant to the drive housing bushing. With the thrust collar in place against the snap-ring and retainer, slide the armature and starter drive assembly into the drive housing. Engage the solenoid shift lever with the drive assembly.

9. Place the field frame over the armature and apply sealing compound between the frame and the solenoid case. Using care to avoid damage to the brushes, position the field frame against the drive housing.

10. Use silicone lubricant to lubricate the commutator end frame bushing. Install the leather washer onto the armature shaft and slide the commutator end frame onto the armature shaft.

11. Install the through-bolts and reconnect the field coil connector(s) to the starter solenoid terminal.

Battery

REMOVAL AND INSTALLATION

To remove the battery simply remove the hold down bolts and loosen and remove the cable ends at the battery.

Make sure the carrier is in sound condition and is capable of holding the battery firmly and keeping it level. To prevent the battery from shaking in its carrier, the hold-down bolts should be relatively tight, not tight enough, however, to place a severe strain on the battery case or cover.

Be sure to replace the battery terminals on the proper posts.

ENGINE MECHANICAL

All gasoline engine models are powered by a 1.4 or 1.6 liter, in line four cylinder, overhead

General Engine Specifications

Year	Engine No. Cyl Displacement (cu in.) liters	Carburetor Type	Horsepower @ rpm	Torque @ rpm (ft. lbs.)	Compression Ratio	Oil Pressure @ 2000 rpm
1976–77	4-1.4 (85)	1 bbl	52 ① @ 5300	67 @ 3400	8.5:1	39–46
	4-1.6 (98)	1 bbl	60 ② @ 5300	77 @ 3200	8.5:1	39–46
1978	4-1.6 (98)	1 bbl	63 @ 4800	82 @ 3200	8.6:1	34–42
	4-1.6 HO (98)	1 bbl	68 @ 5000	84 @ 3200	8.6:1	34–42
1979–80	4-1.6 (98)	2 bbl	70 @ 5200	82 @ 2400	8.6:1	55
	4-1.6 HO (98)	2 bbl	74 @ 5200	88 @ 2800	8.6:1	55
1981	4-1.6 (98)	2 bbl	70 @ 5200	88 @ 2400	8.5:1	55
1982–84	4-1.6 (98)	2 bbl	65 @ 5200	80 @ 3200	9.4:1	57 ③
1981–84	4-1.8 (111) Diesel	Fuel Injection	51 @ 5000	72 @ 2000	22.0:1	64 ④

① 57 for 1977
② 63 for 1977
③ @ 1200 rpm
④ @ 5000 rpm

N.A. Not Available
Bore and stroke for all 1.4 engines is 82 x 66.2 mm
Bore and stroke for all 1.6 engines is 82 x 75.7 mm

camshaft engine. These engines are either 85 or 98 cu. in., respectively.

The cylinder block is made of cast iron. Each cylinder has individual intake and exhaust ports. The valve lifters are mounted in the head, next to their respective valves and are operated by lobes on the camshaft.

The camshaft is belt driven and housed on the top of the cylinder head. It is supported by five bearings in a "cam carrier". Bearing inserts are not used.

The crankshaft is also supported by five main bearings. It is lubricated through oil holes which lead from the main oil supply on the left side of the block. Number five bearing is the end thrust bearing.

The pistons are made of a cast aluminum alloy and incorporate the use of two compression rings and one oil control ring.

The crankshaft also drives, by way of a gear, the distributor and the oil pump. A cam on the shaft of the distributor drives the fuel pump.

Beginning in 1981, the Chevette offers an optional diesel engine. This is a 1.8 liter inline four-cylinder overhead camshaft engine on which the belt-driven camshaft rides in five bearings. The valves are operated by direct acting rocker arms, while adjustment is manually obtained through lash adjusters on the opposite end of each rocker arm. The cast iron, cross-flow cylinder head incorporates a pre-combustion chamber which adds to smooth performance and easy startup characteristics.

The injection pump and the oil pump are also driven off of a cog belt by means of the crankshaft. The crankshaft is supported in the cast iron cylinder block by five main bearings with the thrust being taken on the center bearing.

Understanding the Engine

The basic piston engine is a metal block containing a series of chambers. The upper engine block is usually an iron or aluminum alloy casting, consisting of outer walls, which form hollow jackets around the cylinder walls. The lower block provides a number of rigid mounting points for the bearings which hold the crankshaft in place, and is known as the crankcase. The hollow jackets of the upper block add to the rigidity of the engine and contain the liquid coolant which carries the heat away from the cylinders and other engine parts. The block of an air cooled engine consists of a crankcase which provides for the rigid mounting of the crankshaft and for studs whicgh hold the cylinders in place. In a water-cooled engine, only the cylinder head is bolted to the top of the block. The water pump is mounted directly to the block.

The crankshaft is a long, iron or steel shaft mounted rigidly in the bottom of the crankcase, at a number of points (usually 4–7). The crankshaft is free to turn and contains a number of counterweighted crankpins (one for each cylinder) that are offset several inches from the center of the crankshaft and turn in a circle as the crankshaft turns. The crankpins are centered under each cylinder. Pistons with circular rings to seal the small space between the pistons and wall of the cylinders are connected to the crankpins by steel connecting rods. The rods connect the pistons at their upper ends with the crankpins at their lower ends.

When the crankshaft spins, the pistons move up and down in the cylinders, varying the volume of each cylinder, depending on the position of the piston. Two openings in each cylinder head (above the cylinders) allow the intake of the air/fuel mixture and the exhaust of burned gasses. The volume of the combustion chamber must be variable for the engine to compress the fuel charge before combustion, to makes use of the expansion of the burning gasses and to exhaust the burned gasses and take in a fresh fuel mixture. As the pistons are forced downward by the expansion of burning fuel, the connection rods convert the reciprocating (up and down) motion of the pistons into rotary (turning) motion of the crankshaft. A round flywheel at the rear of the crankshaft provides a large, stable mass to smooth out the rotation.

The cylinder heads form tight covers for the tops of the cylinders and contain machined chambers into which the fuel mixture is forced as it is compressed by the pistons reaching the upper limit of their travel. Each combustion chamber contains one intake valve, one exhaust valve and one spark plug per cylinder. The spark plugs are screwed into holes in the cylinder head so that the tips protrude into the combustion chambers. The valve in each opening in the cylinder head is opened and closed by the action of the camshaft. The camshaft is driven by the crankshaft through a chain or belt at $\frac{1}{2}$ crankshaft speed (the camshaft gear is twice the size of the crankshaft gear). The valves are operated either through rocker arms and pushrods (overhead valve engine) or directly by the camshaft (overhead cam engine).

Lubrication oil is stored in a pan at the bottom of the engine and is force fed to all parts of the engine by a gear type pump, driven from the crankshaft. The oil lubricates the entire engine and also seals the piston rings, giving good compression.

Engine Removal and Installation

1. Remove the hood from the car.
CAUTION: *Do not discharge the air conditioning compressor or disconnect any air conditioning lines. Damage to the air conditioning system or personal injury could result.*
2. Disconnect the battery cables.
3. Remove the battery cable clips from the frame rail.
4. Drain the cooling system. Disconnect the radiator hoses from the engine and the heater hoses at the heater
5. Tag and disconnect any wires leading from the engine.
6. Remove the radiator upper support and remove the radiator and engine fan. On the diesel, you must also remove the oil cooler.
7. Remove the air cleaner assembly.
8. Disconnect the following items:
   a. Fuel line at the rubber hose along the left frame rail. On the diesel, disconnect and plug the fuel lines at the injector pump and position them out of the way.
   b. Automatic transmission throttle valve linkage.
   c. Accelerator cable.
9. On air conditioned cars, remove the compressor from its mount and lay it aside. If equipped with power steering, remove the power steering pump and bracket and lay it aside.
10. Raise the car and support it with jackstands.
11. Remove the engine strut (shock-type) on the diesel.
12. Disconnect the exhaust pipe at the exhaust manifold.
13. Remove the flywheel dust cover on manual transmission cars or the torque converter underpan on automatic transmission cars.
14. On automatic transmission cars, remove the torque converter-to-flywheel bolts.
15. Remove the converter housing or flywheel housing-to-engine retaining bolts and lower the car.
16. Position a floor jack or other suitable support under the transmission.
17. Remove the safety straps from the front engine mounts and remove the mount nuts.
18. Remove the oil filter on the diesel.
19. Install the engine lifting apparatus.
20. Remove the engine by pulling forward to clear the transmission while lifting slowly. Check to make sure that all necessary disconnections have been made and that proper clearance exists with surrounding components. Remove the lifting apparatus.
To install the engine:
21. Install the engine lifting apparatus and install guide pins in the engine block.
22. Install the engine in the car by aligning the engine with the transmission housing.
23. Install the front engine mount nuts and safety straps.
24. Raise the car and support it with jackstands.
25. Install the engine-to-transmission housing bolts. Tighten to 25 ft. lbs.
26. On automatic transmission cars, install

Valve Specifications

Year	Engine No. Cyl Displacement liters	Seat Angle (deg)	Face Angle (deg)	Spring Test Pressure Nm @ mm (lbs. @ in.)	Spring Installed Height (mm)	Stem to Guide Clearance mm (in.)		Stem Diameter mm (in.)	
						Intake	Exhaust	Intake	Exhaust
1976–84	4-1.4	46	45	284 @ 32 (68 @ 1.26)	32 (1.26 in.)	.015–.045 ① (.0006–.0017 in.)	.035–.065 ② (.0014–.0025 in.)	7.97 (.3138 in.)	7.95 (.3130 in.)
	4-1.6	45 ③	46 ③	284 @ 32 (68 @ 1.26)	32 (1.26 in.)	.015–.045 ① (.0006–.0017 in.)	.035–.065 ② (.0014–.0025 in.)	7.97 (.3138 in.)	7.95 (.3130 in.)
1981–84	4-1.8 Diesel	45	45	140 @ 31.5 (108 @ 1.24) ③	40.9 (1.61)	.0038–.0711 (.0015–.0028)	.0457–.0762 (.0018–.0030)	7.94– 7.96 (.3128– .3134)	7.94– 7.95 (.3126– .3132)

① 1976—.0018–.0021   ② 1976—.0026–.0029   ③ 1976–77—Seat angle 46, Face angle 45

Crankshaft and Connecting Rod Specifications
All measurements are given in inches

Year	Engine No. Cyl Displacement liters	Crankshaft				Connecting Rod		
		Main Brg Journal Dia	Main Brg Oil Clearance	Shaft End-Play	Thrust on No.	Journal Diameter	Oil Clearance	Side Clearance
1976	4-1.4	2.0075–2.0085	.0009–.0025	.004–.008	4	1.809–1.810	.0014–.0030	.004–.012
	4-1.6	2.0075–2.0085	.0009–.0025	.004–.008	4	1.809–1.810	.0014–.0030	.004–.012
1977	4-1.4	2.0078–2.0088	.0009–.0026	.004–.008	4	1.809–1.810	.0014–.0031	.004–.012
1977–84	4-1.6	2.0078–2.0088	①	.004–.008	4	1.809–1.810	.0014–.0031	.004–.012
1981–84	4-1.8 Diesel	2.2019	.0015–.0031	.0024–.0094	3	1.927–1.928	.0016–.0032	N.A.

① 1976–78—All .0009–.0026
1979–84—#1 thru 4—.0005–.0018
#5—.0009–.0026

Ring Side Clearance

All measurements are given in mm except engine displacement, inches are given in parenthesis

Year	Engine No. Cyl Displacement liters	Top Compression	Bottom Compression	Oil Control
1976–84	4-1.4	.305–.686 (.0012–.0027 in.)	.305–.813 (.0012–.0032 in.)	.000–.127 (.0000–.0050 in.)
	4-1.6	.305–.686 (.0012–.0027 in.)	.305–.813 (.0012–.0032 in.)	.000–.127 (.0000–.0050 in.)
1982	4-1.8 Diesel	.089–.125 (.0035–.0049)	.036–.051 (.0014–.0020)	.031–.071 (.0012–.0028)
1983–84	4-1.8 Diesel	.089–.125 (.0035–.0049)	.05–.085 (.0019–.0033)	.031–.071 (.0012–.0028)

Ring Gap

All measurements are given in mm except engine displacement, inches are given in parentheses

Year	Engine No. Cyl Displacement liters	Top Compression	Bottom Compression	Oil Control
1976–84	4-1.4, 1.6	.229–.483 (.009–.019 in.)	.203–.452 (.008–.018 in.)	.381–1.397 (.015–.055 in.)
1981–84	4-1.8 Diesel	.198–.399 (.0078–.0157)	.198–.399 (.0078–.0157)	.198–.399 (.0078–.0157)

Piston Clearance

All measurements are in mm except engine displacement, inches are given in parenthesis

Year	Engine No. Cyl Displacement liters	Piston to Bore Clearance (mm)
1976–84	4-1.4	.020–.040 (.0008–.0016 in.) ①
	4-1.6	.020–.040 (.0008–.0016 in.) ①
1981–82	4-1.8 Diesel	.0152–.0356 (.006–.0014)
1983–84	4-1.8 Diesel	.025–.050 (.0002–.0017)

① Measured 48 mm (1½ in.) from top of piston

the torque converter to the flywheel. Torque the bolts to 35 ft. lbs.

27. Install the flywheel dust cover or torque converter underpan as applicable.

28. Install the engine strut on the diesel.

29. Install the exhaust pipe to the exhaust manifold and lower the car.

30. Install the air conditioning compressor or the power steering pump if necessary, and adjust drive belt tension.

31. Connect the following items:

   a. Fuel lines.

   b. Automatic transmission throttle valve linkage.

   c. Accelerator cable.

32. Install the air cleaner.

33. Install the engine fan, radiator, and radiator upper support. Install the oil cooler if so equipped.

34. Connect all wires previously disconnected.

35. Connect the radiator and heater hoses and fill the cooling system.

36. Install the battery cable clips along the frame rail.

37. Install the engine hood.

38. Connect the battery cables, start the engine and check for leaks.

Camshaft Cover

REMOVAL AND INSTALLATION

Gasoline Engine

1. Disconnect the negative battery cable.

2. Remove the air cleaner, PCV valve and heat stove assembly.

3. Remove the spark plug wiring harness from the cam cover.

Torque Specifications
All readings in Nm, ft. lbs. given in parentheses

Year	Engine No. Cyl Displacement liters	Cylinder Head Bolts	Rod Bearing Bolts	Main Bearing Bolts	Crankshaft Pulley or Damper Bolt	Flywheel to Crankshaft Bolts	Manifold	
							Intake	Exhaust
1976–77	4-1.4, 1.6	95–100 (70–80)	46–54 (34–40)	54–75 (40–52)	90–115 (65–85)	54–75 (40–52)	18–24 (13–18)	①
1978–84	4-1.6	100 (75)	54 (40)	68 (50)	100 (75)	68 (50)	20 (15)	①,②
1981–84	4-1.8 Diesel	③	84.5 (65)	97.5 (75)	N/A	N/A	39 (30)	N/A

① Center bolts—18–24 (13–18); end bolts—26–34 (19–25)
② 1983–84, all bolts—18 (25)
③ First tighten to 21–36 ft. lbs. then retighten to 83–98 (new bolt), 90–105 (reused bolt)

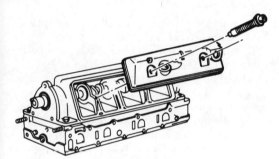

Camshaft cover—gasoline engine

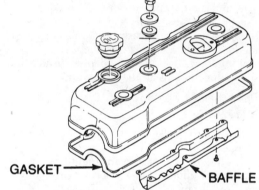

Rocker arm cover—diesel engine

4. Remove the accelerator support and lay aside.

5. Remove the bolts retaining the cover to the cam carrier

NOTE: *The original sealer may be hard to break loose. Be careful not to bend the seal face of the cover or nick the seal face of the carrier.*

6. Installation is the reverse of removal. Clean and degrease the mating surfaces and apply a bead of RTV sealant. Install the retaining nut and gasket assemblies and torque to 15 lb. in.

Rocker Arm Cover
REMOVAL AND INSTALLATION
Diesel Engine

1. Disconnect the negative battery cable.
2. Remove the fresh air hose.
3. Remove the PCV Valve and move aside.
4. Move the wire harness from the retainers.
5. Drain the coolant.
6. Remove the heater hose at the left hand insulator.
7. Disconnect the wire at the defogger relay, if so equipped.

8. Remove the rocker arm cover nuts and remove the cover.

9. Installation is the reverse of removal. Refill the cooling system and torque the cover nuts to 7 ft. lbs.

Valve Stem Oil Seal and Valve Spring Replacement
Gasoline Engine

NOTE: *A special valve spring compressor is necessary for this procedure. (Tool No. J-25477)*

1. Remove the rocker arm from the valve to be serviced.

2. Remove the spark plug from the cylinder to be serviced.

3. Install an air hose adapter in the spark plug hole and apply air pressure to hold the valve in place.

4. Using the spring compressor, compress the valve spring, remove the rocker arm guide, valve locks, caps, and valve spring.

5. Remove the valve stem oil seal.

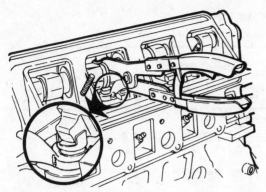

Valve spring compressing tool—gasoline engine

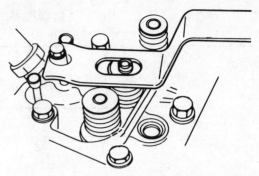

Valve spring compressing tool—diesel engine

6. Install the new valve stem oil seal.

7. Compress the valve spring and cap and install the valve locks and rocker arm guide.

8. Release the compressor while making sure that the locks seat correctly in the upper groove of the valve stem. Grease can be used to hold the locks while releasing the compressor.

9. Remove the air hose adapter, install the spark plug, and install the rocker arm.

Diesel Engine

REMOVAL

1. Remove rocker arm cover as previously outlined.

2. Remove rocker arm shaft and bracket assembly as outlined under Rocker Arm removal and Installation.

3. Rotate engine to T.D.C. for cylinder being serviced.

4. Remove valve stem end caps.

5. Compress valve spring using tool J-29760. Remove valve collets and remove valve spring upper seat and valve springs.

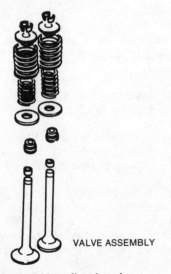

VALVE ASSEMBLY

Valve assembly—diesel engine

6. Remove valve stem oil seal.

7. Remove valve spring lower seat.

INSTALLATION

1. Lubricate valve stem and valve spring lower seat with clean engine oil.

2. Install new seal over valve stem and onto valve guide. Check that projection on inner face of oil seal fits into the groove in the valve guide.

3. Install inner and outer springs and upper seat. Compress valve springs using Spring Compressing Tool J-29760 and install valve spring retainers. Remove tool and inspect to make sure retainers are fully seated in the valve stem groove.

4. Apply valve stem end caps with clean engine oil and install stem and caps.

5. Reinstall rocker arm shaft and bracket assembly.

Rocker Arm

REMOVAL AND INSTALLATION

Gasoline Engine

NOTE: *A special valve spring compressor is necessary for this procedure. Also prelubricate new rocker arms with Molykote® or its equivalent.*

1. Remove the camshaft cover.

2. Using the special valve spring compressor, compress the valve springs and remove the rocker arms. Keep the rocker arms and guides in order so that they can be installed in their original locations.

3. To install the rocker arms, compress the valve springs and install the rocker arm guides.

4. Position the rocker arms in the guides and on the valve lash adjusters.

5. Install the camshaft cover.

Diesel Engine

1. Disconnect the negative battery cable.

2. Remove the cylinder head cover.

3. Remove the rocker arm shaft bracket bolts and nuts in sequence. Loosen them in this or-

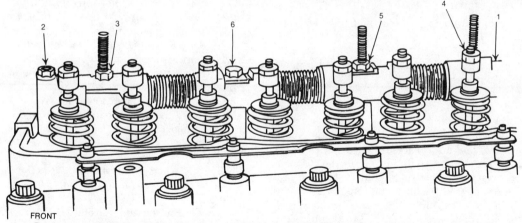

Rocker arm shaft bracket bolt and nut loosening and tightening sequence—diesel engine

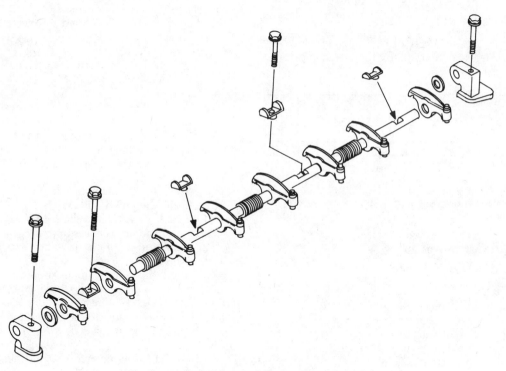

Rocker arms, bracket and shaft—diesel engine

der: 6-1-2-5-4-3. Remove the rocker arm shaft bracket and the rocker arm assembly.

4. Remove the rocker arms.

5. Apply a generous amount of clean engine oil to the rocker arm shaft, rocker arms and the valve stem end caps.

6. Install the rocker arm shaft assembly and then tighten the bolts to 20 ft. lbs. in the sequence given in Step 3.

7. Adjust the valves as previously detailed and reinstall the cylinder head cover.

Valve Adjustment

Gasoline Engine

Adjustment of the hydraulic valve lash adjusters is not possible.

Cleanliness should be exercised when handling the valve lash adjusters. Before installation of lash adjusters, fill them with oil and check the lash adjuster oil hole in the cylinder head to make sure that it is free of foreign matter.

Diesel Engine

NOTE: *The rocker arm shaft bracket bolts and nuts should be tightened to 20 ft. lbs. before adjusting the valves.*

1. Unscrew the retaining bolts and remove the cylinder head cover.

2. Rotate the crankshaft until the No. 1 or No. 4 piston is at TDC of the compression stroke.

3. Start with the intake valve on the NO. 1 cylinder and insert a feeler gauge of the correct thickness (intake—0.01 in., exhaust—0.014 in.) into the gap between the valve step cap and the rocker arm. If adjustment is required, loosen the lock nut on top of the rocker arm and turn the adjusting screw clockwise to decrease the gap and counterclockwise to increase it. When the proper clearance is reached, tighten the lock nut and then recheck the gap. Adjust the remaining three valves in this step (see illustration) in the same manner.

4. Rotate the crankshaft one complete revolution and then adjust the remaining valves accordingly.

CYLINDER NO.		1		2		3		4
VALVES	I	E	I	E	I	E	I	E
STEP. 1	○	○	○			○		
STEP. 2				○	○		○	○

I : INTAKE VALVE
E: EXHAUST VALVE

Valve adjustment torque sequence—diesel engine

Intake Manifold

GASOLINE ENGINE

Removal

1. Disconnect negative battery cable.
2. Drain cooling system.
3. Remove air cleaner.
4. Disconnect upper radiator and heater hoses at intake manifold.
5. Remove the EGR valve, located on the intake manifold.
6. Disconnect all electrical wiring vacuum hoses and the accelerator linkage from the carburetor. Remove the fuel line from the carburetor.
7. If vehicle is equipped with air conditioning, perform the following operations before continuing.

   a. Remove raidator upper support.

   b. Remove the generator and A/C drive belts, including the two A/C adjusting bolts.

   c. Remove fan blade and pulley.

   d. Remove timing belt cover.

   e. Move the compressor so it is out of the

way. CAUTION: *Do not disconnect any of the tubing in the air conditioning system as personal injury may result*

   f. Raise the vehicle and remove the lower A/C compressor bracket.

   g. Lower the vehicle and remove the upper A/C compressor bracket.

8. Remove the coil and set aside.

9. Remove the intake manifold bolts and remove manifold.

Installation

NOTE: *If a new intake manifold is being installed, transfer the following parts from the old one.*
- Thermostat and housing
- Carburetor
- Vacuum fittings and plugs

1. With the new gasket, and gasket surface well cleaned, install the new manifold.

2. Install manifold bolts and torque to 20 N·m (15 lb. ft.)

3. Remount the coil.

4. For vehicles equipped with air conditioning, the following steps must be completed before continuing.

   a. Install the upper A/C compressor bracket.

   b. Raise the vehicle and install the lower A/C compressor bracket.

   c. Lower the vehicle and install the A/C compressor.

   d. Install the timing bolt cover

   e. Install the pulley and fan blades.

   f. Install the A/C drive belt, two adjusting bolts and adjust as necessary.

   g. Install the generator drive belt and adjust as necessary.

   h. Install the radiator upper support.

5. Connect all electrical wiring, vacuum hoses and accelerator linkage to the carburetor. Install the fuel line to the carburetor.

6. Install the EGR valve. Torque to 13–18 ft. lbs.

7. Connect the upper radiator and heater hoses to intake manifold.

8. Refill the cooling system.

9. Install the air cleaner.

10. Connect the battery cable, start the engine and check for leaks.

DIESEL ENGINE

Removal and Installation

1. Disconnect the negative battery cable.

2. Disconnect the fresh air hose and the vent hose. Remove the fuel separator.

3. Tag and disconnect all electrical connectors, the accelerator linkage and the glow plug wires.

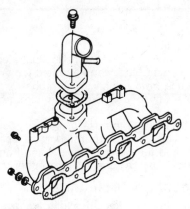

Intake manifold—diesel engine

4. Disconnect the injector lines at the injection pump and at the injector nozzles. Remove the injector lines and the hold-down clamps.

5. Remove the glow plug line at the cylinder head.

6. If equipped with power steering, remove the drive belt, the idler pulley and the bracket.

7. Remove the upper half of the front cover and the bracket.

8. Unscrew the mounting bolts and remove the intake manifold.

9. Place a new gasket over the mounting studs on the cylinder head and install the manifold. Tighten the bolts to 30 ft. lbs.

10. Installation of the remaining components is in the reverse order of removal.

Exhaust Manifold

GASOLINE ENGINE

Removal

1. Remove the negative battery cable.

2. Raise the vehicle and disconnect the exhaust pipe from the manifold.

3. Lower the vehicle and remove the carburetor heat tube.

4. On California models, remove the pulse air injection tubing.

5. Remove the exhaust manifold bolts and manifold.

Installation

1. Install the manifold and manifold bolts. Install the inner upper bolts first as these are guide bolts.

NOTE: *Exhaust manifold center bolts must be torqued to 20 N·m (15 ft. lbs.). The end legs must be torqued to 30 N·m (22 ft. lbs.).*

2. On California models, install the pulse air injection tubing.

3. Install the carburetor heat tube.

4. Raise the vehicle and connect the exhaust pipe to the manifold.

5. Lower the vehicle and connect the battery cable. Start the engine and check for leaks.

DIESEL ENGINE

Removal

1. Disconnect the negative battery cable.

2. Raise the vehicle and support it safely.

3. Disconnect the exhaust pipe from the exhaust manifold.

4. Remove the power steering belt, flex hose and pump.

5. Remove the exhaust manifold bolts and remove the manifold.

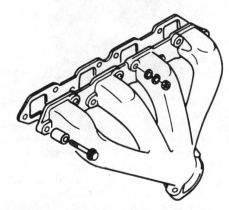

Exhaust manifold—diesel engine

Installation

1. Installation is the reverse of removal.

2. Clean all mating surfaces and install a new gasket.

3. Tighten the bolts a little at a time starting with the inner bolts and working outward.

Cylinder Head

GASOLINE ENGINE

Removal

NOTE: *In order to complete the rocker arm removal a special tool (#J-25477) is necessary.*

1. Disconnect battery negative cable.

2. Remove the accessory drive belts.

3. Remove the engine fan.

4. Remove the timing belt upper cover retaining screws and nuts and remove the cover.

5. Loosen the idler pulley and remove the timing belt from the camshaft drive sprocket.

6. Remove the air cleaner and silencer assembly.

7. Drain the cooling system. Disconnect the upper radiator hose at the thermostat and the heater hose at the intake manifold.

ENGINE OVERHAUL

Most engine overhaul procedures are fairly standard. In addition to specific parts replacement procedures and complete specifications for your individual engine, this chapter also is a guide to accepted rebuilding procedures. Examples of standard rebuilding practice are shown and should be used along with specific details concerning your particular engine.

Competent and accurate machine shop services will ensure maximum performance, reliability and engine life. Procedures marked with the symbol shown above should be performed by a competent machine shop, and are provided so that you will be familiar with the procedures necessary to a successful overhaul.

In most instances it is more profitable for the do-it-yourself mechanic to remove, clean and inspect the component, buy the necessary parts and deliver these to a shop for actual machine work.

On the other hand, much of the rebuilding work (crankshaft, block, bearings, pistons, rods, and other components) is well within the scope of the do-it-yourself mechanic.

Tools

The tools required for an engine overhaul or parts replacement will depend on the depth of your involvement. With a few exceptions, they will be the tools found in a mechanic's tool kit (see Chapter 1). More in-depth work will require any or all of the following:
 • a dial indicator (reading in thousandths) mounted on a universal base
 • micrometers and telescope gauges
 • jaw and screw-type pullers
 • scraper
 • valve spring compressor
 • ring groove cleaner
 • piston ring expander and compressor
 • ridge reamer
 • cylinder hone or glaze breaker

 • Plastigage®
 • engine stand

Use of most of these tools is illustrated in this chapter. Many can be rented for a one-time use from a local parts jobber or tool supply house specializing in automotive work.

Occasionally, the use of special tools is called for. See the information on Special Tools and the Safety Notice in the front of this book before substituting another tool.

Inspection Techniques

Procedures and specifications are given in this chapter for inspecting, cleaning and assessing the wear limits of most major components. Other procedures such as Magnaflux and Zyglo can be used to locate material flaws and stress cracks. Magnaflux is a magnetic process applicable only to ferrous materials. The Zyglo process coats the material with a flourescent dye penetrant and can be used on any material. Check for suspected surface cracks can be more readily made using spot check dye. The dye is sprayed onto the suspected area, wiped off and the area sprayed with a developer. Cracks will show up brightly.

Overhaul Tips

Aluminum has become extremely popular for use in engines, due to its low weight. Observe the following precautions when handling aluminum parts:
 • Never hot tank aluminum parts (the caustic hot-tank solution will eat the aluminum)
 • Remove all aluminum parts (identification tag, etc.) from engine parts prior to hot-tanking.
 • Always coat threads lightly with engine oil or anti-seize compounds before installation, to prevent seizure.
 • Never over-torque bolts or spark plugs, especially in aluminum threads.

Stripped threads in any component can be repaired using any of several commercial repair kits (Heli-Coil, Microdot, Keenserts, etc.)

When assembling the engine, any parts that will be in frictional contact must be pre-lubed to provide lubrication at initial start-up. Any product specifically formulated for this purpose can be used, but engine oil is not recommended as a pre-lube.

When semi-permanent (locked, but removable) installation of bolts or nuts is desired, threads should be cleaned and coated with Loctite® or other similar, commercial non-hardening sealant.

Repairing Damaged Threads

Several methods of repairing damaged threads are available. Heli-Coil® (shown here), Keenserts® and Microdot® are among the most widely used. All involve basically the same principle—drilling out stripped threads, tapping the hole and installing a prewound insert—making welding, plugging and oversize fasteners unnecessary.

Two types of thread repair inserts are usually supplied—a standard type for most Inch Coarse, Inch Fine, Metric Coarse and Metric Fine thread sizes and a spark plug type to fit most spark plug port sizes. Consult the individual manufacturer's catalog to determine exact applications. Typical thread repair kits will contain a selection of prewound threaded inserts, a tap (corresponding to the outside diameter threads of the insert) and an installation tool. Spark plug inserts usually differ because they require a tap equipped with pilot threads and a combined reamer/tap section. Most manufacturers also supply blister-packed thread repair inserts separately in addition to a master kit containing a variety of taps and inserts plus installation tools.

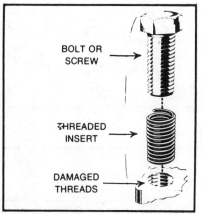

Damaged bolt holes can be repaired with thread repair inserts

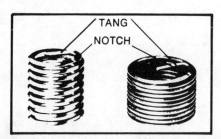

Standard thread repair insert (left) and spark plug thread insert (right)

Before effecting a repair to a threaded hole, remove any snapped, broken or damaged bolts or studs. Penetrating oil can be used to free frozen threads; the offending item can be removed with locking pliers or with a screw or stud extractor. After the hole is clear, the thread can be repaired, as follows:

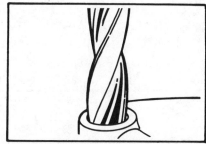

Drill out the damaged threads with specified drill. Drill completely through the hole or to the bottom of a blind hole

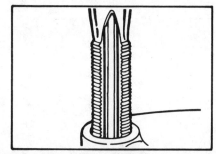

With the tap supplied, tap the hole to receive the thread insert. Keep the tap well oiled and back it out frequently to avoid clogging the threads

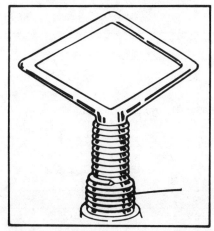

Screw the threaded insert onto the installation tool until the tang engages the slot. Screw the insert into the tapped hole until it is ¼–½ turn below the top surface, After installation break off the tang with a hammer and punch

Standard Torque Specifications and Fastener Markings

In the absence of specific torques, the following chart can be used as a guide to the maximum safe torque of a particular size/grade of fastener.
- There is no torque difference for fine or coarse threads.
- Torque values are based on clean, dry threads. Reduce the value by 10% if threads are oiled prior to assembly.
- The torque required for aluminum components or fasteners is considerably less.

U.S. Bolts

SAE Grade Number	1 or 2			5			6 or 7		
Number of lines always 2 less than the grade number.									
Bolt Size (Inches)—(Thread)	**Maximum Torque**			**Maximum Torque**			**Maximum Torque**		
	Ft./Lbs.	Kgm	Nm	Ft./Lbs.	Kgm	Nm	Ft./Lbs.	Kgm	Nm
¼—20	5	0.7	6.8	8	1.1	10.8	10	1.4	13.5
—28	6	0.8	8.1	10	1.4	13.6			
5/16—18	11	1.5	14.9	17	2.3	23.0	19	2.6	25.8
—24	13	1.8	17.6	19	2.6	25.7			
⅜—16	18	2.5	24.4	31	4.3	42.0	34	4.7	46.0
—24	20	2.75	27.1	35	4.8	47.5			
7/16—14	28	3.8	37.0	49	6.8	66.4	55	7.6	74.5
—20	30	4.2	40.7	55	7.6	74.5			
½—13	39	5.4	52.8	75	10.4	101.7	85	11.75	115.2
—20	41	5.7	55.6	85	11.7	115.2			
9/16—12	51	7.0	69.2	110	15.2	149.1	120	16.6	162.7
—18	55	7.6	74.5	120	16.6	162.7			
⅝—11	83	11.5	112.5	150	20.7	203.3	167	23.0	226.5
—18	95	13.1	128.8	170	23.5	230.5			
¾—10	105	14.5	142.3	270	37.3	366.0	280	38.7	379.6
—16	115	15.9	155.9	295	40.8	400.0			
⅞—9	160	22.1	216.9	395	54.6	535.5	440	60.9	596.5
—14	175	24.2	237.2	435	60.1	589.7			
1—8	236	32.5	318.6	590	81.6	799.9	660	91.3	894.8
—14	250	34.6	338.9	660	91.3	849.8			

Metric Bolts

Relative Strength Marking	4.6, 4.8			8.8		
Bolt Markings						
Bolt Size Thread Size x Pitch (mm)	**Maximum Torque**			**Maximum Torque**		
	Ft./Lbs.	Kgm	Nm	Ft./Lbs.	Kgm	Nm
6 x 1.0	2–3	.2–.4	3–4	3–6	.4–.8	5–8
8 x 1.25	6–8	.8–1	8–12	9–14	1.2–1.9	13–19
10 x 1.25	12–17	1.5–2.3	16–23	20–29	2.7–4.0	27–39
12 x 1.25	21–32	2.9–4.4	29–43	35–53	4.8–7.3	47–72
14 x 1.5	35–52	4.8–7.1	48–70	57–85	7.8–11.7	77–110
16 x 1.5	51–77	7.0–10.6	67–100	90–120	12.4–16.5	130–160
18 x 1.5	74–110	10.2–15.1	100–150	130–170	17.9–23.4	180–230
20 x 1.5	110–140	15.1–19.3	150–190	190–240	26.2–46.9	160–320
22 x 1.5	150–190	22.0–26.2	200–260	250–320	34.5–44.1	340–430
24 x 1.5	190–240	26.2–46.9	260–320	310–410	42.7–56.5	420–550

Timing belt cover retaining screws—gasoline engine

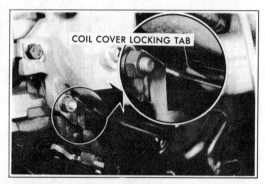

Coil cover locking tab location

Location of the coil bracket fasteners

8. Remove the accelerator cable support bracket.

9. Remove the spark plug wires from the cam cover.

10. Disconnect the electrical connections at:
   a. Idle solenoid
   b. Choke

Depressing valve spring—gasoline engine

   c. Temperature sending unit
   d. Alternator

11. Raise the car and disconnect the exhaust pipe at the manifold.

12. Lower the car and remove the bolt holding the dipstick tube bracket to the exhaust manifold.

13. Disconnect the fuel line at the carburetor.

14. Remove the coil cover and disconnect the secondary voltage wire from the coil.

15. Remove the coil bracket fasteners and lay the coil aside.

16. Remove the cam cover as follows:
   a. Remove the PCV valve.
   b. Remove the heat stove assembly.
   c. Remove the spark plug wiring harness from cam cover.

17. Remove the rocker arms by depressing the valve spring with tool #J-25477. Place the rocker arms and guides in a rack so they may be installed in the same location.

18. Remove the nut and gasket assemblies from the studs in the camshaft carrier. Remove the studs and cam carrier. It may be necessary to use a sharp wedge to separate the carrier from the cylinder head. Be careful not to damage the mating surfaces.

19. Remove the cylinder head and manifold assembly.

Installation

1. Install the cylinder head gasket over the dowel pins with the note "This Side Up" facing up.

2. Replace the cylinder head and manifold.

3. Replace the cam carrier. Apply a thin, continuous coat of Loctite #75® (or equivalent) to both surfaces (head and cam carrier). Wipe the excess sealer from the cylinder head. Coat the threads of the cylinder head bolts with sealing compound and install bolts finger tight.

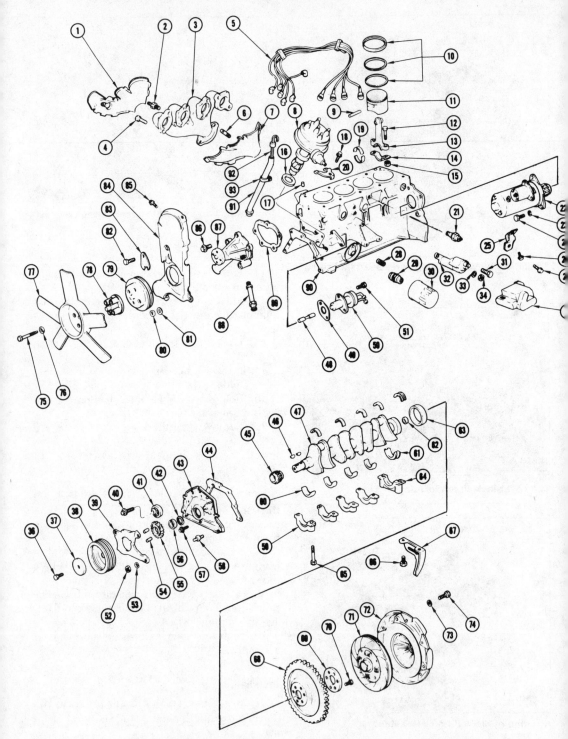

Exploded view of the cylinder head, oil pan and related parts—gasoline engine

Tighten bolts to 100 N·m (75 lb. ft.) in the proper sequence.

4. Install cam cover attaching studs.

5. Install rocker arms and apply Molycoat® or equivalent.

6. Replace camshaft cover gasket. Clean surfaces on camshaft cover and cam carrier with degreaser. Place a ⅛ in. bead of RTV sealer all around the cam cover sealing area. Install covers and torque retaining nut assemblies to 1.6 N·m (15 lb. in.) while the sealer is still wet.

7. Install accelerator support.

8. Install spark plug wiring harness and heat stove assembly.

9. Install PCV valve.

10. Install coil bracket bolt. Torque to 20 N·m (15 lb. ft.).

11. Connect fuel line to carburetor.

12. Replace dipstick tube bracket to manifold.

13. Raise vehicle and attach exhaust pipe to manifold.

14. Lower vehicle and make the electrical connections at:

    a. Idle solenoid

    b. Choke

    c. Temperature sending switch

    d. Generator

15. Connect spark plug wires.

16. Connect air cleaner and silencer assembly.

17. Connect upper radiator hose and heater hose at the inlet manifold.

18. Replace engine coolant.

19. Replace timing belt.

DIESEL ENGINE

Removal

1. Disconnect the negative battery cable.

2. Drain the cooling system.

3. Remove the cylinder head cover.

4. Disconnect the bypass hose. Remove the upper half of the front cover.

5. Loosen the tension pulley bolts and slide the timing belt off of the two upper gears.

6. Unscrew the bearing cap bolts and then remove the camshaft as detailed later in this section.

7. Tag and disconnect the glow plug resistor wire.

8. Disconnect the injector lines at the injector pump and at the injector nozzles and then remove the injector lines. Disconnect and plug the fuel leak-off hose.

9. Disconnect the exhaust pipe at the manifold.

10. Remove the oil feed pipe from the rear of the cylinder head.

11. Disconnect the upper radiator hose and position it out of the way.

12. Remove the head bolts in the sequence shown and then remove the cylinder head with the intake and exhaust manifolds installed.

1. Stove	32. Coil	63. Seal
2. Stud	33. Washer	64. Cap
3. Manifold	34. Nut	65. Bolt
4. Bolt	35. Shield	66. Bolt
5. Wires	36. Bolt	67. Deflector
6. Stud	37. Washer	68. Flywheel
7. Stove	38. Pulley	69. Retainer
8. Distributor	39. Cover	70. Bolt
9. Piston pin	40. Bolt	71. Plate
10. Piston ring	41. Pulley	72. Clutch cover and pressure plate
11. Piston	42. Seal	73. Lockwasher
12. Bolt	43. Cover	74. Bolt
13. Rod	44. Gasket	75. Bolt
14. Cap	45. Gear	76. Lockwasher
15. Nut	46. Key	77. Fan
16. Gasket	47. Crankshaft	78. Spacer
17. Pin	48. Fuel pump pushrod	79. Pulley
18. Bolt	49. Gasket	80. Nut
19. Connecting rod bearing	50. Fuel pump	81. Washer
20. Clamp	51. Bolt	82. Bolt
21. Switch	52. Nut	83. Cover
22. Motor and switch	53. Washer	84. Cover
23. Washer	54. Pin	85. Bolt
24. Bolt	55. Sprocket	86. Bolt
25. Brace	56. Spacer	87. Water pump
26. Bolt	57. Bolt	88. Nipple
27. Bolt	58. Stud	89. Gasket
28. Valve	59. Cap	90. Engine Cylinder Block
29. Connector	60. Bearing	91. Tube
30. Element	61. Bearing	92. Gauge
31. Bolt	62. Bearing	93. Clamp

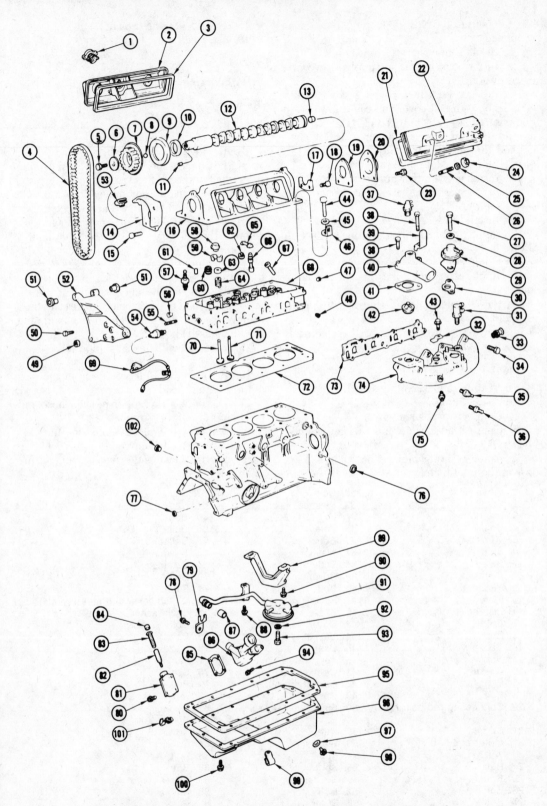

Exploded view of the cylinder block and related parts—gasoline engine

1. Cap
2. Cover
3. Gasket
4. Bolt
5. Bolt
6. Washer
7. Sprocket
8. Ball
9. Guide
10. Seal
11. Pin
12. Camshaft
13. Plug
14. Cover
15. Bolt
16. Housing
17. Retainer
18. Bolt
19. Gasket
20. Cover
21. Gasket
22. Cover
23. Bolt
24. Nut
25. Gasket
26. Stud
27. Bolt
28. Lockwasher
29. Valve
30. Gasket
31. Fitting
32. Support
33. Nipple
34. Bolt

35. Gauge
36. Stud
37. Switch
38. Bolt
39. Support
40. Outlet
41. Gasket
42. Thermostat
43. Bolt
44. Bolt
45. Washer
46. Bracket
47. Plug
48. Plug
49. Nut
50. Bolt
51. Bushing
52. Bracket
53. Nut
54. Switch
55. Stud
56. Plug
57. Plug
58. Cap
59. Key
60. Seal
61. Pin
62. Guide
63. Seal
64. Spring
65. Arm
66. Adjuster
67. Extension
68. Head

69. Wire
70. Valve
71. Valve
72. Cylinder head gasket
73. Intake manifold gasket
74. Intake manifold
75. Fitting
76. Plug
77. Plug
78. Screw
79. Clamp
80. Screw
81. Cover
82. Valve
83. Spring
84. Plug
85. Gasket
86. Oil pump
87. Seal
88. Bolt
89. Support
90. Screw
91. Pipe
92. Washer
93. Bolt
94. Bolt
95. Gasket
96. Pan
97. Gasket
98. Screw
99. Clip
100. Screw
101. Clip
102. Plug

1. Plate
2. Spring
3. Mount
4. Screw
5. Nut
6. Washer
7. Washer
8. Bracket
9. Adapter

10. Bolt
11. Mounting assembly
12. Support
13. Washer
14. Bolt
15. Nut
16. Washer
17. Nut
18. Washer

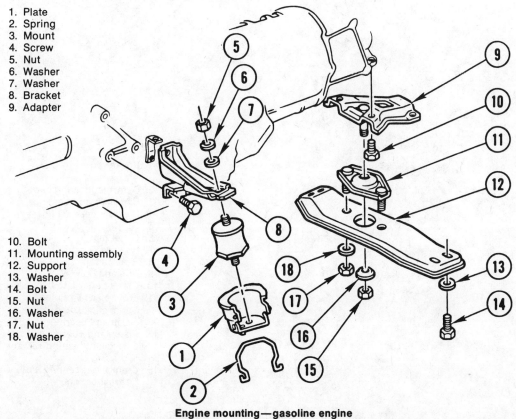

Engine mounting—gasoline engine

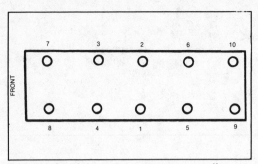

Cylinder head torque sequence—gasoline engine

Installation

NOTE: *The gasket surfaces on both the head and the block must be clean of any foreign matter and free of nicks or heavy scratches. Cylinder bolt threads in the block and on the bolt must also be clean.*

13. Place a new gasket over the dowel pins with the word "TOP" facing up.

14. Apply engine oil to the threads and the seating face of the cylinder head bolts, install them and then tighten them in the proper sequence.

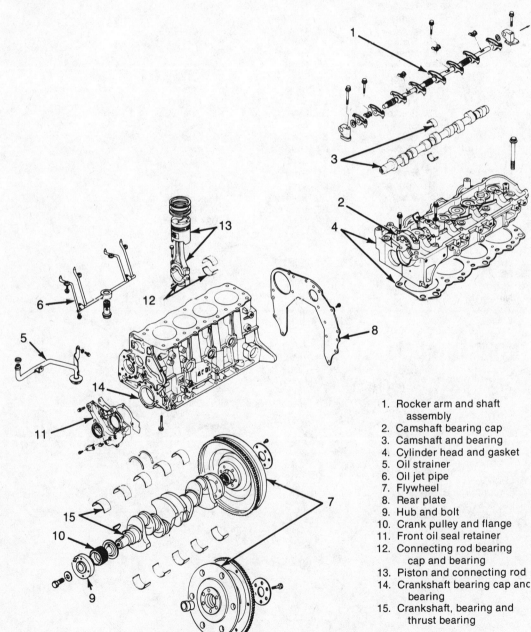

1. Rocker arm and shaft assembly
2. Camshaft bearing cap
3. Camshaft and bearing
4. Cylinder head and gasket
5. Oil strainer
6. Oil jet pipe
7. Flywheel
8. Rear plate
9. Hub and bolt
10. Crank pulley and flange
11. Front oil seal retainer
12. Connecting rod bearing cap and bearing
13. Piston and connecting rod
14. Crankshaft bearing cap and bearing
15. Crankshaft, bearing and thrust bearing

Exploded view of cylinder block—diesel engine

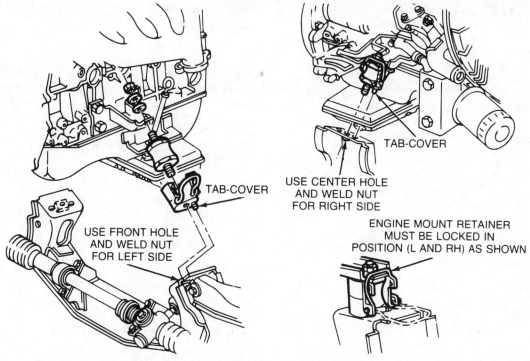

TAB-COVER

USE CENTER HOLE
AND WELD NUT
FOR RIGHT SIDE

TAB-COVER

USE FRONT HOLE
AND WELD NUT
FOR LEFT SIDE

ENGINE MOUNT RETAINER
MUST BE LOCKED IN
POSITION (L AND RH) AS SHOWN

Engine mounting—diesel engine

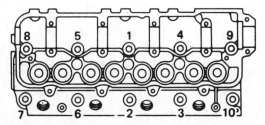

Cylinder head torque sequence—diesel engine

15. Install the camshaft and rocker arm assembly. Loosen the adjusting screws so that the entire rocker arm assembly is held in a free state.

16. Reinstall the timing belt as outlined later in this section.

17. Connect the upper radiator hose and the oil feed pipe.

18. Connect the exhaust pipe to the manifold.

19. Install the fuel leak-off hose. Connect the injector lines.

20. Connect the glow plug resistor wire.

21. Adjust the valve clearance as previously detailed. Install the cylinder head cover.

22. Refill the cooling system.

DISASSEMBLY GASOLINE ENGINE

NOTE: *For ease in servicing cylinder head, remove generator mounting bracket, ex-*haust manifold and intake manifold before continuing.*

1. Using tool J-8062 or equivalent, compress valve spring and remove valve locks.

2. Release compressor tool and remove spring cap, spring and valve stem seal.

3. Remove valves from cylinder head, placing them in a rack so they may be returned to their original position.

CLEANING AND INSPECTION

1. Clean all carbon from combustion chambers and valve ports using tool J-8089 or equivalent.

2. Thoroughly clean valve guides using tool J-8101.

3. Clean valve stems and heads on a buffing wheel.

4. Clean carbon deposits from head gasket mating surface.

5. Inspect the cylinder head for cracks in the exhaust ports, combustion chambers, or external cracks to the water chamber.

6. Inspect the valves for burned heads, cracked faces or damaged stems.

NOTE: *Excessive valve stem to bore clearance will cause excessive oil consumption and may cause valve breakage. Insufficient clearance will result in noisy and sticky functioning of the valve and disturb engine smoothness.*

7. Measure valve stem clearance as follows: Clamp a dial indicator on one side of the cylinder head locating the indicator so that movement of the valve stem from side to side (crosswise to the head) will cause a direct movement of the indicator stem. The indicator stem must contact the side of the valve stem just above the valve guide. With the valve head dropped about 2.0mm off the valve seat; move the stem of the valve from side to side using light pressure to obtain a clearance reading. If clearance exceeds specifications it will be necessary to ream valve guides for oversize valves as outlined. Oversize valves are available in: .075 mm, .150mm and .300mm.

8. Check valve spring tension with Tool J-8056 spring tester. Springs should be compressed to the specified height and checked against the specifications chart. Springs should be replaced if not within 10 lbs. (44N) of the specified load.

ASSEMBLY GASOLINE ENGINE

1. Insert valve in proper port.
2. Check installed height of valve. If necessary, grind the tip of the valve to obtain a dimension of 18mm above the head. This is required to assure correct operation of the valve lash adjusters.
NOTE: *Do not grind more than .75mm from any valve tip, otherwise interference between the rocker arm and valve cap may occur.*
3. Install valve stem oil seal.
NOTE: *Two valve stem oil seals are used. The intake is identified by the letters "IN" on the seal. The exhaust is identified by "EX" and a color coded retainer. DO NOT MIX SEALS ON INSTALLATION.*
4. Place valve spring and cap over valve stem and compress with tool J-8062.
5. Install valve locks and release compressor tool. Make sure that the locks seat properly in the groove on the valve stem. Grease may be used to hold the locks in place while releasing the compressor tool.
6. Install remaining valves in the same manner.
7. Check the installed height of the valve springs. Measure from the top of the spring seat, or shim, to the top of the spring. If out of specification, add shim(s) to correct.

DISASSEMBLY DIESEL ENGINE

NOTE: *See Rocker Arm Removal and Installation procedure previously outlined.*

Valve Guides
Gasoline Engine

Valves with oversize stems are available. Remove the cylinder head and remove the camshaft from the cylinder head. Remove the valves and ream the valve guides with an appropriate oversize reamer.

Diesel Engine

Check the amount of wear in valve guide to determine the clearance between valves.
1. Drive out the valve guide with tool J-26512 fitted against the valve guide from lower face of the cylinder head.
2. Apply engine oil to the outer circumference of the valve guide. Set the installer (J-26512) to the valve guide, then drive the guide into position from the upper face of the cylinder head using a hammer. The valve guide should always be replaced together with the valve as a set.

Hot Plug Replacement
Diesel Engine

1. Remove the hot plug in the following manner. Insert a suitable round bar sizing 3 to 5 mm (0.12 to 0.20 in.) in diameter into nozzle holder fitting hold to touch the hot plug, then drive out the hot plugs using a hammer.
2. Install lock ball into groove in hot plug. Drive the hot plug into cylinder head by aligning lock ball in hot plug with groove in cylinder head.
3. Press the hot plug into position by applying 4500 to 5000 kg (9922.5 to 11025 lbs.) pressure using a bench press with a piece of metal fitted against the hot plug face for protection. After installation, grind the face of hot plug flush with the face of the cylinder head.

Valve Seat Insert Replacement
Diesel Engine

Check valve seat contact width, condition of seat contact, scores, dents, etc.
Check the amount of valve seat depression (from lower face of cylinder head to valve face) using a depth gage with a falve fitted into cylinder head.
Arc-weld excess metal around inner face of the valve seat insert and allow to cool off a few minutes, then pry off the valve seat insert with screw drivers.
Press a new valve seat insert into the bore using a bench press. After installation of the valve seat insert, grind finish the seating face with a seat grinder carefully noting the seating angle, contact width and depression. Lap the valve and seat as the final step.

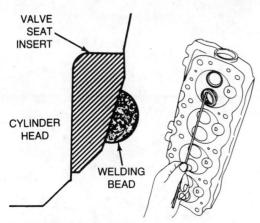

Valve seat insert replacement—diesel engine

Timing Cover, Belt and Camshaft

TIMING BELT COVER REMOVAL AND INSTALLATION

Upper Front Cover All Engines

1. Disconnect the negative battery cable. Remove the radiator upper mounting panel or fan shroud.

2. Remove the engine accessory drive belts on the gasoline engine. Remove the bypass hose on the diesel engine.

3. Remove the engine fan.

4. Remove the cover retaining screws and nuts and remove the cover.

To install the cover:

5. Align the screw slots on the upper and lower parts of the cover.

6. Install the cover retaining screws and nuts.

7. Install the engine fan.

8. Install the engine accessory drive belts or the bypass hose.

9. Connect the negative battery cable.

Lower Front Cover—All Engines

1. Disconnect the negative battery cable.

2. Loosen the alternator and the A/C compressor bolts, if so equipped. Remove the drive belt.

3. Remove the damper pulley-to-crankshaft bolt and washer and remove the pulley.

4. Remove the upper front timing belt cover as outlined previously.

5. Remove the lower cover retaining nut (gasoline) or bolts (diesel). Remove the lower cover.

6. To install the cover, align the cover with the studs on the engine block.

7. Install the lower front cover retaining nut or bolts.

8. Install the upper front timing belt cover.

9. Install the crankshaft damper pulley. Torque the retaining bolt to the specified torque.

10. Install the drive belt and tighten the alternator and compressor mounting bolts.

11. Connect the negative battery cable.

Upper Rear Cover Gasoline Engine

1. Disconnect the negative battery cable.

2. Remove the upper and lower front cover, the timing belt, and the camshaft timing sprocket.

3. Remove the three screws retaining the camshaft sprocket cover to the camshaft carrier.

4. Inspect the condition of the cam seal.

5. Position and align a new gasket over the end of the camshaft and against the camshaft carrier.

6. Install the three camshaft sprocket cover retaining screws.

7. Install the camshaft sprocket, timing belt, and upper and lower front covers.

8. Connect the negative battery cable.

Timing Belt and Sprockets

GASOLINE ENGINE

Removal

CAUTION: *Do not discharge the air conditioner compressor or disconnect any air conditioning lines. Damage to the air conditioning system or personal injury could result.*

NOTE: *A belt tension gauge is necessary for the completion of this procedure.*

1. Rotate the engine so the timing mark on the camshaft pulley is at 0°, #1 cylinder is at Top Dead Center. With #1 cylinder at TDC, a 1/8 in. drill rod may be inserted inserted through a hole in the timing belt upper rear cover into a hole in the camshaft drive sprocket.

Mark the location of the rotor in No. 1 spark plug firing position on the distributor housing—gasoline engine

A ½ in. drill rod should go through the hole in the rear of the upper rear timing belt cover and the hole in the camshaft sprocket—gasoline engine

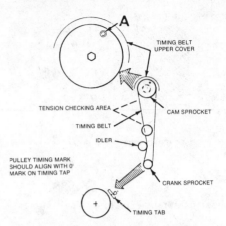

QUICK CHECK HOLE (IN SPROCKET) SHOULD ALIGN WITH HOLE IN TIMING BELT UPPER COVER (A) WHEN #1 CYL. IS AT T.D.C.

Camshaft alignment and timing belt tension check—gasoline engine.

BELT SIZE	ACCEPTABLE OPERATING RANGE	ADJUSTMENT SPECIFICATION
19mm	222 - 356N (50–80 LB.)	311±31N (70±7 LB.)

Timing belt adjustment specifications

This is provided to verify camshaft timing and to facilitate installation of the belt.

2. Remove timing belt lower cover.

3. Loosen the idler pulley retaining bolt and allow idler to rotate clockwise.

4. Remove the timing belt from camshaft and crankshaft sprockets.

5. Remove the distributor cap and mark the location of the rotor at #1 cylinder firing position. For vehicles equipped with A/C, remove the A/C compressor and the lower compressor bracket. DO NOT disconnect any lines!

6. Remove timing belt sprocket bolt and washer.

7. Remove camshaft sprocket.

8. Remove crankshaft sprocket.

Installation

1. Place crankshaft sprokcet on end of crankshaft. Be sure that the locating tabs face outward.

2. Align the dowel in the camshaft sprocket with the locating hole in the end of the camshaft.

3. Apply Loctite® sealer or equivalent to the threads of the bolt and install bolt and washer. Torque to 100 N·m (75 ft. lbs.).

4. Install belt on camshaft and crankshaft sprockets.

5. Using a ¼ in. allen wrench, rotate the idler pulley counterclockwise on its attaching bolt until all the slack is taken out of the belt. Tighten the bolt.

6. To facilitate the installation of the timing belt, #1 cylinder should be at TDC. If necessary, rotate the crankshaft clockwise a minimum of one revolution. Stop when #1 cylinder reaches TDC. DO NOT reverse direction.

7. Install a belt tension gauge between the camshaft sprocket and the idler pulley on the slack side. (see illus.)

8. Adjust to the proper tension by loosening the idler attaching bolt. Using the ¼ in. allen wrench, rotate the idler pulley until the proper tension is attained. Torque the attaching bolt to 20 N·m (15 ft. lbs.).

9. Install the timing belt lower cover and front cover.

10. Replace the distributor cap.

11. For vehicles with A/C, replace the lower compressor bracket and the A/C compressor.

12. Attach the negative battery cable.

DIESEL ENGINE

Removal and Installation

NOTE: *In order to complete this procedure you will need three special tools. A gear puller (J-22888), a fixing plate (J-29761) and a belt tension gauge (J-26486).*

1. Disconnect the negative battery cable.

2. Drain the cooling system.

3. Remove the fan shroud, cooling fan and the pulley.

4. Disconnect the bypass hose and then remove the upper half of the front cover.

5. With the No. 1 piston at TDC of the compression stroke, make sure that the notch mark on the injection pump gear is aligned with the index mark on the front plate. If so, thread

a lock bolt (8mm × 1.25) through the gear and into the front plate.

6. Remove the cylinder head cover and install a fixing plate (J-29761) in the slot at the rear of the cam. This will prevent the cam from rotating during the procedure.

7. Remove the crankshaft damper pulley and check to make sure that the No. 1 piston is still at TDC.

8. Remove the lower half of the front cover and then remove the timing belt holder from the bottom of the front plate.

9. Remove the tension spring behind the front plate, next to the injection pump.

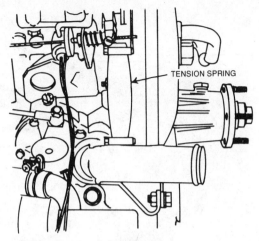

Tension spring—diesel engine

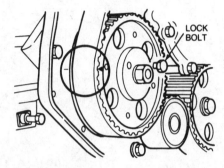

Injector gear setting mark—diesel engine

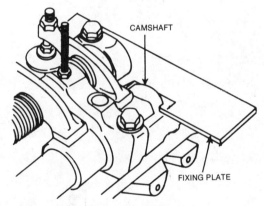

Camshaft fixing plate—diesel engine

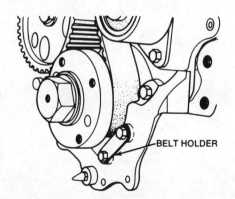

Timing belt holder—diesel engine

10. Loosen the tension pulley and slide the timing belt off the pulleys.

11. Remove the camshaft gear retaining bolt, install a gear puller and remove the gear.

To Install:

12. Reinstall the cam gear loosely so that it can be turned smoothly by hand.

13. Slide the timing belt back over the gears and note the following: the belt should be properly tensioned between the pulleys, the cogs and the belt and the gears should be properly engaged, the crankshaft should not be turned and the belt slack should be concentrated at the two tension pulleys. Push the tension pulley in with your finger and install the tension spring.

14. Partially tighten the tension pulley bolts in sequence (top first, bottom second) so as to prevent any movement of the pulley.

15. Tighten the camshaft gear retaining bolt to 45 ft. lbs. Remove the injection pump gear lock bolt.

16. Remove the fixing plate from the end of the cam.

17. Install the crankshaft damper pulley and then check that the No. 1 piston is still at TDC. *Do not try to adjust it by moving the crankshaft.*

18. Check that the marks on the injection pump gear and the front plate are still aligned and that the fixing plate still fits properly into the slot on the camshaft.

19. Loosen the tensioner pulley and plate bolts, concentrate the looseness of the timing belt around the tensioner and then tighten the bolts.

20. Belt tension should be 46–63 lbs., checked at a point midway between the upper two pulleys.

21. Remove the damper pulley again and

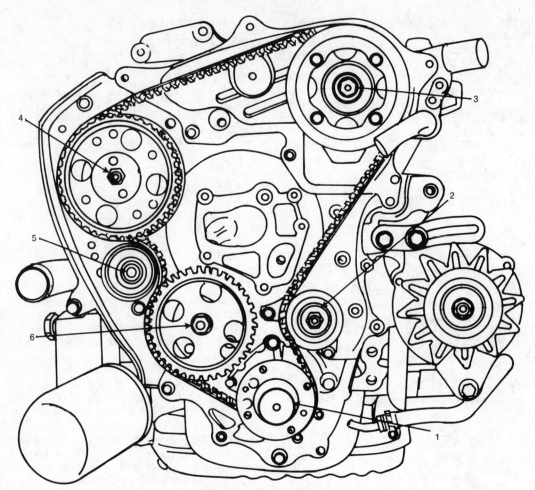

Timing belt installation sequence—diesel engine

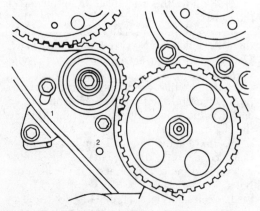

Tightening the tension pulley bolts in sequence—top first, bottom second

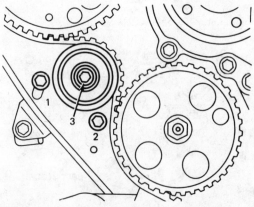

Final tightening sequence of the tension pulley and plate bolts—diesel engine

install the belt holder in position away from the timing belt.

22. Installation of the remaining components is in the reverse order of removal.

Crankcase Front Cover
REMOVAL AND INSTALLATION
Gasoline Engine

NOTE: *A special oil seal alignment tool is required for this procedure.*

1. Disconnect the negative battery cable.
2. Remove the upper and lower front timing belt covers, crankshaft pulley, idler pulley, timing belt, and the crankshaft timing sprocket.
3. Remove the three oil pan bolts and the cover attaching bolts.
4. Remove the old cover, gasket and the front portion of the oil pan gasket.
5. Inspect the crankshaft front oil seal and replace if necessary.

To install:

6. Replace the crankcase cover gasket, cut the front portion of the oil pan gasket, and apply RTV sealer or its equivalent to the cut-off portion of the oil pan gasket.
7. Using the special oil seal alignment tool, install the front cover. Torque the cover bolts to 75–110 in. lbs.
8. Install the crankshaft timing sprocket, timing belt, idler and crankshaft pulleys. Adjust timing belt tension using all parts of Step 19 in "Timing Belt and Sprockets Removal and Installation." Install the upper and lower front timing belt covers.
9. Connect the negative battery cable.

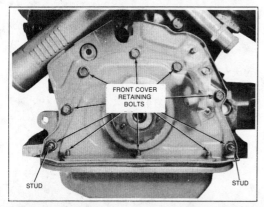

Crankcase front cover retaining bolts—gasoline engines

Camshaft
REMOVAL AND INSTALLATION

NOTE: *The camshaft is supported on five bearings surfaces in the cam carrier, located on top of the cylinder head. Bearing inserts are not used.*

Gasoline Engine

NOTE: *A special valve spring compressor is necessary for this procedure. Also, if replacing camshaft or rocker arms, prelube new parts with Molykote or its equivalent.*

1. Disconnect the negative battery cable.
2. Remove engine accessory drive belts.
3. Remove the engine fan and pulley.
4. Remove the upper and lower front timing belt covers.
5. Loosen the idler pulley and remove the timing belt from the camshaft sprocket.
6. Remove the camshaft sprocket attaching bolt and washer and remove the camshaft sprocket.
7. Remove the camshaft covers. Using the special valve spring compressor, remove the valve rocker arms and guides. Keep the rocker arms and guides in order so that they can be installed in their original locations.
8. Remove any components necessary to gain working clearance.

NOTE: *The heater assembly will probably have to be removed from the firewall to gain working clearance.*

9. Remove the camshaft carrier rear cover.
10. Remove the camshaft thrust plate bolts. Slide the camshaft slightly to the rear and remove the thrust plate.
11. Remove the engine mount nuts and wire retainers.
12. Using a floor jack, raise the engine.
13. Remove the camshaft from the camshaft carrier.

To install:

14. Install the camshaft into the camshaft carrier.
15. Lower the engine.
16. Install the engine mount nuts and attach the retaining wires.
17. Slide the camshaft to the rear and install thrust plate. Slide the camshaft forward.
18. Position and align a new gasket over the end of the camshaft, against the camshaft carrier. Using RTV sealer, install the camshaft carrier rear cover.
19. Position and align a new gasket over the end of the camshaft, against the camshaft carrier, and install the upper rear timing belt cover.
20. Install any components which were removed to gain working clearance.
21. Install the valve rocker arms and guides in their original locations using the special valve spring compressor. Install the camshaft covers.
22. Align the dowel in the camshaft sprocket

with the hole in the end of the camshaft and install the sprocket.

23. Apply Loctite® sealer or its equivalent to the sprocket retaining bolt threads and install the bolt and washer. Torque the sprocket retaining bolt to 65–85 ft. lbs.

24. Turn the crankshaft counterclockwise to bring the #1 cylinder to top dead center. Check to make sure the distributor rotor is in firing position from #1 cylinder. Place a ⅛ in. drill rod through the cam sprocket quick check hole into the hole in the upper timing belt cover. If the holes do not line up, loosen the timing belt and rotate the camshaft until it is properly aligned.

25. Adjust timing belt tension as outlined in "Timing Belt and Sprocket Removal and Installation."

26. Install the upper and lower front timing belt covers.

27. Install the engine fan and pulley.

28. Install the engine accessory drive belts.

29. Connect the negative battery cable.

Diesel Engine

NOTE: *In order to complete this procedure you will need a gear puller (J-22888) and a fixing plate (J-29761).*

1. Remove the cylinder head cover.

2. Remove the timing belt as previously detailed. Remove the plug.

3. Install the fixing plate into the slot at the rear of the camshaft.

4. Remove the camshaft gear retaining bolt and then use a puller to remove the cam gear.

5. Remove the rocker arms and shaft as previously detailed.

6. Unscrew the bolts attaching the front head plate and then remove the plate.

7. Unscrew the camshaft bearing cap retaining bolts and remove the bearing caps with the cap side bearings.

8. Lift out the camshaft oil seal and then remove the camshaft.

9. Coat the cam and cylinder head journals with clean engine oil.

10. Position the camshaft back in the cylinder head with a new oil seal.

11. Apply a suitable liquid gasket to the cylinder head face of the No. 1 camshaft bearing cap.

12. Install the remaining bearing caps. Install the rocker arm shaft assembly leaving the adjusting screws loose.

13. Install the front head plate.

14. Install the timing belt as previously detailed.

15. Adjust the valve clearance to specifications and then install the cylinder head cover.

Pistons and Connecting Rods (Gasoline Engine)

REMOVAL

1. Remove oil pan, oil pump and cylinder head as previously outlined.

2. For the cylinder being serviced, turn crankshaft until piston is at bottom of the stroke. Place a cloth on top of piston.

3. Use a ridge reamer to remove any ridge and/or deposits from the upper end of cylinder bore.

4. Turn crankshaft until piston is at top of stroke and remove cloth and cuttings.

5. Remove connecting rod cap, and cover the studs with plastic tubing or other similar devices. Remove assembly.

DISASSEMBLY

1. Remove connecting rod bearings from connecting rods and caps. If bearings are being reused, place them in a rack so they may be reinstalled in their original position.

2. Remove piston rings by expanding and sliding them off the pistons. Tool J-25220 is available for this purpose.

3. Place connecting rod and piston assembly on Tool J-24086-20. Using an arbor press and piston pin remover, J-24086-8, press the piston pin out of connecting rod and piston.

NOTE: *The above special tools or their equivalents may be used.*

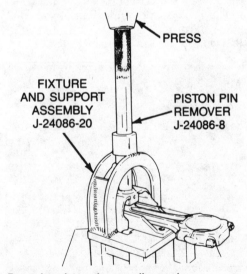

Removing piston pin—gasoline engine

CLEANING AND INSPECTION

Connecting Rods

1. Wash connecting rods in cleaning solvent and dry with compressed air.

2. Check for twisted or bent rods and in-

spect for nicks or cracks. Replace connecting rods that are damaged.

Pistons

1. Clean varnish from piston skirts and pins with a cleaning solvent. Clean the ring grooves with a groove cleaner and make sure oil ring holes and slots are clean.

NOTE: *Do not wire brush any part of the piston.*

2. Inspect the piston for cracked ring lands, skirts or pin bosses, wavy or worn ring lands, scuffed or damaged skirts, eroded areas at top of the piston. Replace pistons that are damaged or show signs of excessive wear.

Inspect the grooves for nicks or burrs that might cause the rings to hang up.

Piston Pins

The piston pin clearance is designed to maintain adequate clearance under all engine operating conditions. Because of this, the piston and piston pin are a matched set and not serviced separately.

Inspect piston pin bores and piston pins for wear. Piston pin bores and piston pins must be free of varnish or scuffing when being measured. The piston pin should be measured with a micrometer and the piston pin bore should be measured with a dial bore gage or an inside micrometer. If clearance is in excess of the .026mm wear limit, the piston and piston pin assembly should be replaced.

Piston Selection

1. Check used piston to cylinder bore clearance as follows:

    a. Measure the cylinder bore diameter with a telescope gage.

    b. Measure the piston diameter (at skirt across centerline of piston pin).

    c. Subtract piston diameter from cylinder bore diameter to determine piston-to-bore clearance.

    d. Compare piston-to-bore clearance obtained with those clearances recommended in specifications section, and determine if piston-to-bore clearance is in acceptable range.

2. If used piston is not acceptable, check piston size and determine if a new piston can be selected to fit cylinder bore.

3. If cylinder bore must be reconditioned, measure new piston diameter (across center line of piston pin) then hone cylinder bore to obtain preferable clearance.

4. Select new piston and mark piston to identify the cylinder for which it was fitted.

ASSEMBLY

1. Lubricate piston pin holes in piston and connecting rod to facilitate installation of pin.

2. Place connecting rod in piston and hold in place with piston pin guide and piston pin. Place assembly on fixture and support assembly.

3. Using piston pin installer, J-24086-9, press the piston pin into the piston and connecting rod.

NOTE: *After installer hub bottoms on support assembly, do not exceed 5000 psi pressure, as this could cause structural damage to the tool.*

4. Remove piston and connecting rod assembly from tool and check piston for freedom of movement on piston pin.

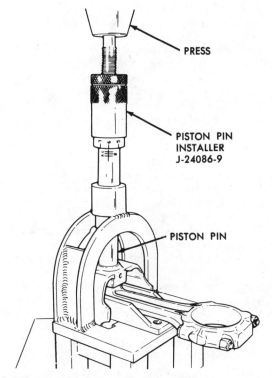

Installing piston pin—gasoline engine

Piston Rings

All compression rings are marked on the upper side of the ring. When installing compression rings, make sure the marked side is toward the top of the piston. The top ring is treated with molybdenum for maximum life.

The oil control rings are of the three piece type, consisting of two segments (rails) and a spacer.

1. Select rings comparable in size to the piston being used.

2. Slip the compression ring in the cylinder

bore; then press the ring down into the cylinder bore about 6mm (above ring travel). Be sure ring is square with cylinder wall.

3. Measure the space or gap between the ends of the ring with a feeler gage.

4. If the gap between the ends of the ring is below specifications, remove the ring and try another for fit.

5. Fit each compression ring to the cylinder in which it is going to be used.

6. If the pistons have not been cleaned and inspected as outlined, do so.

7. Slip the outer surface of the top and second compression ring into the respective piston ring groove and roll the ring entirely around the groove to make sure that the ring is free. If binding occurs at any point the cause should be determined, and if caused by ring groove, remove by dressing with a fine cut file. If the binding is caused by a distorted ring, check a new ring.

8. Install piston rings as follows:

a. Install oil ring spacer in groove.

b. Hold spacer ends buttled and install lower steel oil ring rail with gap properly located.

c. Install upper steel oil ring rail with gap properly located.

d. Flex the oil ring assembly to make sure ring is free. If binding occurs at any point the cause should be determined, and if caused by ring groove, remove by dressing groove with a fine cut file. If binding is caused by a distorted ring, check a new ring.

e. Install second compression ring with gaps properly located.

f. Install top compression ring with gap properly located.

9. Proper clearance of the piston ring in its piston ring groove is very important to provide proper ring action and reduce wear. Therefore, when fitting new rings, the clearances between the surfaces of the ring and groove should be measured.

INSTALLATION

Cylinder bores must be clean before piston installation. This may be accomplished with a hot water and detergent wash. After cleaning, the bores should be swabbed several times with light engine oil and a clean dry cloth.

1. Lubricate connecting rod bearings and install in rods and rod caps.

2. Lightly coat pistons, rings and cylinder walls with light engine oil.

3. With bearing caps removed, cover the connecting rod bolts with plastic tubing or other similar device.

4. Install each connecting rod and piston assembly in its respective bore. Install with notch

The piston notch must face toward the front of the engine—gasoline engine

on piston facing front of engine. Use Tool J-26468 to compress the rings. Guide the connecting rod into place on the crankshaft journal. Use a hammer handle and light blows to install the piston into the bore. Hold the ring compressor firmly against the cylinder block until all piston rings have entered the cylinder bore.

5. Remove plastic tubing from connecting rod bolts.

6. Install the bearing caps and torque retaining nuts to specification. Be sure to install new pistons in the same cylinders for which they were fitted, and used pistons in the same cylinder from which they were removed. Each connecting rod and bearing cap should be marked, beginning at the front of the engine. The numbers on the connecting rod and bearing cap must be on the same side when installed in the cylinder bore. If a connecting rod is ever transposed from one block or cylinder to another, new bearings should be fitted and the connecting rod should be numbered to correspond with the new cylinder number.

ROD BEARING INSPECTION AND REPLACEMENT

Connecting rod bearings are of the precision insert type and do not utilize shims for adjustment. If clearances are found to be excessive, a new bearing will be required. Service bearings are available in standard, .026mm U.S. and .050mm U.S. for use with new and used standard crankshafts, and in .250mm U.S. and .500mm U.S. for reconditioned crankshafts.

1. Remove the connecting rod cap and bearing.

2. Inspect the bearing for evidence of wear or damage. (Bearings showing the above should not be reinstalled.)

3. Wipe both upper and lower bearing shells and crankpin clean of oil.

4. Measure the crankpin for out-of-round or taper with a micrometer. If not within specifications replace or recondition the crankshaft. If within specifications and a new bearing is to be installed, measure the maximum diameter of the crankpin to determine new bearing size required.

5. If within specifications measure new or used bearing clearances with Plastigage or its equivalent.

If a bearing is being fitted to an out-of-round crankpin, be sure to fit to the maximum diameter of the crankpin. If the bearing is fitted to the minimum diameter and the crankpin is out-of-round .025mm, interference between the bearing and crankpin will result in rapid bearing failure.

   a. Place a piece of gaging plastic the full width of the crankpin (parallel to the crankshaft).

   b. Install the bearing in the connecting rod and cap.

   c. Install the bearing cap and evenly torque nuts to specifications. Do not turn the crankshaft with the gaging plastic installed.

   d. Remove the bearing cap and using the scale on the gaging plastic envelope, measure the gaging plastic width at the widest point.

6. If the clearance exceeds specifications select a new, correct size, bearing and remeasure the clearance. Be sure to check what size bearing is being removed in order to determine proper replacement size bearing.

If clearance cannot be brought to within specifications, the crankpin will have to be ground undersize. If the crankpin is already at maximum undersize, replace crankshaft.

7. Coat the bearing surface with oil, install the rod cap and torque nuts to specifications.

8. When all connecting rod bearings have been installed, tap each rod lightly (paralled to the crankpin) to make sure they have clearance.

9. Measure all connecting rod side clearances (see specifications), between the connecting rod cap and side of crankpin.

Pistons and Connecting Rods (Diesel Engine)

REMOVAL

1. Remove the engine assembly as outlined earlier in this chapter.

2. Remove the timing belt.

3. Remove the cam cover.

4. Remove the rocker arm assembly.

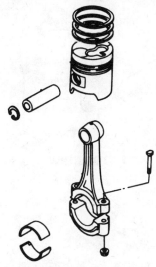

Piston and connecting rod—diesel engine

5. Remove the camshaft.

6. Remove the cylinder head assembly.

7. Remove the oil pan.

8. Remove carbon deposits from upper part of cylinder wall (cylinders to be serviced) with a scraper.

9. Remove connecting-rod cap nuts and remove bearing and cap.

10. Remove the piston and connection-rod by pushing on the edge of connecting rod with a hammer handle or piece of wood.

NOTE: *When removing piston and rod assembly, remove with rod parallel with cylinder bore. Use care to prevent damage to the rod bearing.*

DISASSEMBLY

NOTE: *Refer to the piston disassembly illustration for removal of the piston pin and rings.*

INSPECTION

Pistons

1. Check the pistons for scuffs, cracking or wear. Replace the pistons with new ones if found to be defective.

2. Measure clearance between pistons and cylinder wall as follows:

   a. With an outside micrometer, measure the diameter of the piston at a point below the piston head (grading position) in direction at a right angle to the piston pin. Standard—63.7 mm (2.507 in.)

   b. With a cylinder bore indicator, measure the cylinder bore diameter at the lower section where the amount of wear is smallest. Compare the value obtained with the cylinder bore diameter to determine the

PISTON RINGS

SNAP RINGS

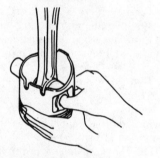

PISTON PIN

Piston disassembly—diesel engine

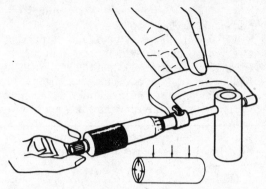

Measuring piston pin outside diameter—diesel engine

Measuring clearance between piston pin and hole—diesel engine

several points around circumference. Clearance between piston pin and piston pin hole.

Pin outside diameter:
- Standard—25.0mm (0.984 in.)
- Limit—24.97mm (0.983 in.)

Piston pin and hole:
- Standard—0.002–0.012mm (0.0001–0.0005 in.)
- Limit—0.05mm (0.0019 in.)

Piston Rings

The piston rings should be replaced with new ones whenever the engine is overhauled or if found to be worn or damaged.

1. Insert the piston rings into the cylinder bore and push them down to the skirt (portion where bore diameter is smallest) using the piston head. This will position piston rings at a right angle to the cylinder wall. Measure the ring gap with a feeler gage. Replace the piston rings with new ones if the measured value is beyond the limit shown in the chart.

2. With a feeler gage, measure the clearance between the piston ring and ring grooves in the piston at several points around the circumference of the piston. Replace the piston rings together with the piston if the measured

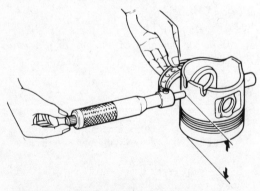

Measuring piston diameter—diesel engine

clearance. If the amount of clearance deviates from 0.005–0.045 (.0002–.0017 in.), replace the pistons with new ones.

Piston Pins

Visually inspect for damage, wear or other abnormal conditions. Measure the diameter at

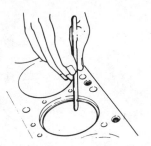

Measuring piston ring gap—diesel engine

Measuring piston ring and ring groove—diesel engine

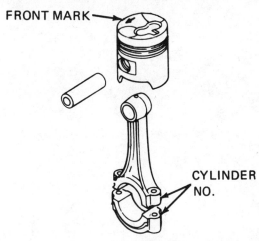

FRONT MARK

CYLINDER NO.

Piston and connecting rod mark—diesel engine

value is greater than 0.15mm (0.0059″) or if abnormal contact is noticeable on the upper or lower face of the piston rings.

NOTE: *Refer to the Piston and Ring Specifications Chart at the beginning of this chapter.*

Connecting Rods

If distortion of connecting rod is suspicious, remove piston from the connecting rod and check for parallelism. Check the connecting rods for distortion and bending by installing on a connecting rod aligner. Correct or replace the connecting rod if the amount of distortion is greater than 0.2mm (0.0078″) or bending is greater than 0.15mm (0.0058″) per 100 mm (3.94″) of length.

Bushing Replacement

Measure the inside diameter of the connecting-rod, small-end bushing and outside diameter of the piston pin clearance between bushing and piston pin .05mm (.0019 in.).

1. Remove and install bushing using remover/installer J-29765 as shown. Align the bushing hole with the connecting rod oil hole.

2. After installing a new bushing, finish the bushing bore with a pin hole grinder.

REASSEMBLY

1. Install the piston on the connecting-rod, so that combustion chamber on piston head is on the same side with the cylinder number mark side (side with bearing stopper) of the connecting-rod big-end. Mark on the connecting-rod should be on the same side of the front mark on the piston.

2. Apply engine oil to the piston pin and install it into the piston pin hole in the piston using finger pressure.

3. Install the snap rings into slots in piston pin hole properly.

4. Install the piston rings in sequence of coil expander, oil ring, 2nd compression ring and 1st compression ring.

5. Install the 1st and 2nd compression rings and oil ring with the "N" mark facing upward. The ends of coil expander should be opposed to the oil ring gap.

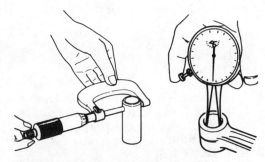

Bushing and pin clearance—diesel engine

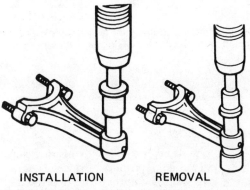

INSTALLATION   REMOVAL

Bushing replacement—diesel engine

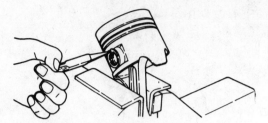

Snap ring installation—diesel engine

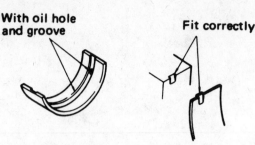

With oil hole and groove

Fit correctly

Rod bearing installation—diesel engine

Piston ring installation—diesel engine

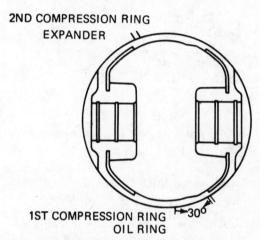

2ND COMPRESSION RING EXPANDER

1ST COMPRESSION RING
OIL RING

30°

Ring gap location—diesel engine

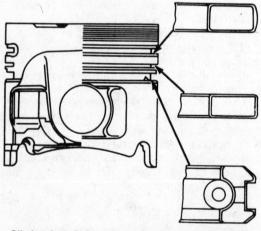

Oil ring installation, the ends of the coil expander should be opposed to the oil ring gap—diesel engine

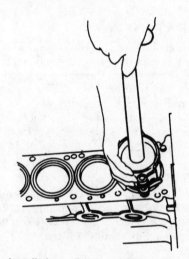

Piston installation—diesel engine

NOTE: *After installation of piston rings, apply engine oil to the circumference of the rings and check that each ring rotates smoothly.*

INSTALLATION

1. Apply clean engine oil to bearing surfaces, outer edge of piston and rings. Be sure rod bearing projected portions are fitted to the recess in the rod and cap.

2. The position ring gaps should be set in piston 180 degrees apart.

3. Using a piston installer, push piston (with its notched mark to front of engine) into the cylinder until the connecting-rod is brought into contact with the crank pin. Use a piece of wood or hammer handle to push piston into bore (Piston Installer J-8037).

4. Install the connecting-rod bearing cap by

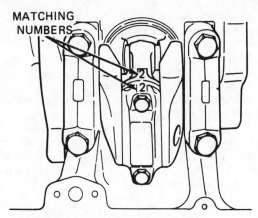

MATCHING NUMBERS

Installation of bearing cap—diesel engine

aligning it with the cylinder number mark on the connecting-rod.

5. Apply engine oil to the threads and seating face of the nuts, then install and tighten the nuts to 88 N·m (65 ft. lbs.).

6. Check that crankshaft turns smoothly.

7. The remainder of the installation is the reverse of removal.

Crankshaft (Gasoline Engine)

REMOVAL

The crankshaft can be removed while the engine is disassembled for overhaul or without complete disassembly as outlined below.

1. With the engine removed from the vehicle. Remove the following:
   a. Drive belts and pulleys.
   b. Timing belt front upper and lower covers.
   c. Timing belt and idler pulley.
   d. Coil
   e. Fuel pump and push rod.
   f. Distributor
   g. Crankcase front cover.
   h. Oil pan
   i. Oil pump and pick up tube.
   j. Spark Plugs

2. Check the connecting rod caps for cylinder number identification. If necessary mark caps with corresponding cylinder number.

3. Remove the connecting rod caps and push the pistons to top of bores.

4. Remove main bearing caps, rear main oil seal and lift crankshaft out of cylinder block.

CLEANING AND INSPECTION

1. Wash crankshaft in solvent and dry with compressed air.

2. Measure dimensions of main bearing journals and crankpins with a micrometer for out-of-round, taper or undersize (see specifications).

3. Check crankshaft for run-out by supporting at the front and rear main bearings journals in "V" blocks and check at the front and rear intermediate journals with a dial indicator (see specifications).

4. Replace or recondition the crankshaft if out of specifications.

Main Bearings (Gasoline Engine)

Main bearings are of the precision insert type and do not utilize shims for adjustment. If clearances are found to be excessive, a new bearing, both upper and lower halves, will be required. Service bearings are available in standard, .026mm, .050mm, .250mm and .500mm undersizes.

Selective fitting of main bearing inserts is necessary in production in order to obtain close tolerances. For this reason you may find one half of a standard insert with one half of a .026mm undersize insert which will decrease the clearance .013mm from using a full standard bearing.

When a production crankshaft cannot be precision fitted by this method, it is then ground .250mm undersize ON ONLY THOSE MAIN JOURNALS THAT CANNOT BE PROPERLY FITTED, ALL JOURNALS WILL NOT NECESSARILY BE GROUND. A .250mm undersize bearing will then be used for precision fitting in the same manner as previously described.

INSPECTION

In general, the lower half of the bearing, except #1 bearing shows a greater wear and the most distress from fatigue. If upon inspection the lower half is suitable for use, it can be assumed that the upper half is also satisfactory. If the lower half shows evidence of wear or damage, both upper and lower halves should be replaced. Never replace one half without replacing the other half.

CHECKING CLEARANCE

To obtain the most accurate results with "Plastigage" (or its equivalent), a wax-like plastic material which will compress evenly between the bearing and journal surfaces without damaging either surface, certain precautions should be observed.

If the engine is out of the vehicle and upside down, the crankshaft will rest on the upper bearings and the total clearance can be measured between the lower bearing and journal. If the engine is to remain in the vehicle, the crankshaft should be supported both front and rear to remove the clearance from the upper bearing. The total clearance can then be mea-

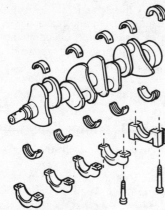

ASSEMBLE MAIN BEARING CAPS WITH "F" TOWARD FRONT OF ENGINE.

Main bearings—gasoline engine

sured between the lower bearing and journal.

To assure the proper seating of the crankshaft, all bearing cap bolts should be at their specified torque. In addition, preparatory to checking fit of bearings, the surface of the crankshaft journal and bearing should be wiped clean of oil.

1. Starting with the rear main bearing, remove bearing cap and wipe oil from journal and bearing cap.

2. Place a piece of gaging plastic the full width of the bearing (parallel to the crankshaft) on the journal. Do not rotate the crankshaft while the gaging plastic is between the bearing and journal.

3. Install the bearing cap and evenly torque the retaining bolts to specifications. Bearing cap MUST be torqued to specifications in order to assure proper reading. Variations in torque affect the compression of the plastic gage.

4. Remove bearing cap. The flattened gaging plastic will be found adhering to either the bearing shell or journal.

5. On the edge of gaging plastic envelope there is a graduated scale which is correlated in thousandths of a millimetre. Without removing the gaging plastic, measure its compressed width (at the widest point) with the graduations on the gaging plastic envelope.

Normally, main bearing journals wear evenly and are not out-of-round. However, if a bearing is being fitted to an out-of-round journal .025mm max., be sure to fit to the maximum diameter of the journal: If the bearing is fitted to the minimum diameter and the journal is out-of-round .025mm, interference between the bearing and journal will result in rapid bearing failure.

If the flattened gaging plastic tapers toward the middle or ends, there is a difference in clearance indicating taper, low spot or other irregularity of the bearing or journal. Be sure to measure the journal with a micrometer if the flattened gaging plastic indicates more than .025mm difference.

6. If the bearing clearance is within specifications, the bearing insert is satisfactory. If the clearance is not within specifications, replace the insert. Always replace both upper and lower insert as a unit. If a new bearing cap is being installed and clearance is less than .025mm, inspect for burrs or nicks, if none are found then install shims as required.

7. A standard .025mm or .050mm undersize bearing may produce the proper clearance. If not, it will be necessary to regrind the crankshaft journal for use with the next undersize bearing. After selecting new bearing, recheck clearance.

8. Proceed to the next bearing. After all bearings have been checked, rotate the crankshaft to see that there is no excessive drag. When checking #1 main bearing, loosen accessory drive belts and timing belt so as to prevent tapered reading with plastic gage.

9. Measure crankshaft end play (see specifications) by forcing the crankshaft to the extreme front position. Measure at the front end of the #5 bearing with a feeler gage.

10. Install a new rear main bearing oil seal.

REPLACEMENT

Main bearings may be replaced with or without removing the crankshaft.

With Crankshaft Removal

1. Remove and inspect the crankshaft.

2. Remove the main bearings from the cylinder block and main bearing caps.

3. Coat bearing surfaces of new, correct size main bearings with oil and install in the cylinder block and main bearing caps.

4. Install crankshaft.

Without Crankshaft Removal

1. With oil pan, oil pump and spark plugs removed, remove cap on main bearing requiring replacement and remove bearing from cap.

2. Install a main bearing removing and installing tool in oil hole in crankshaft journal. If such a tool is not available, a cotter pin may be bent as required to do the job.

3. Rotate the crankshaft clockwise as viewed from the front of engine. This will roll upper bearing out of block.

4. Oil new selected size upper bearing and insert plain (unnotched) end between crankshaft and indented, or notched, side of block. Rotate the bearing into place and remove tool from oil hole in crankshaft journal.

5. Oil new lower bearing and install in bearing cap.

6. Install main bearing cap with arrows pointing toward front of engine.

7. Torque all main bearing caps, EXCEPT THE REAR MAIN CAP, to specification. Torque rear main bearing cap to 14–16 N·m (10–12 lb. ft.) then tap end of crankshaft, first rearward then forward with a lead hammer. This will line up rear main bearing and crankshaft thrust surfaces. Retorque all main bearing caps to specification.

Crankshaft and Main Bearings (Diesel Engine)

REMOVAL

1. Remove the engine as previously outlined in this chapter.

2. Remove the fan and pulley.

3. Remove the upper dust cover.

4. Remove the lower cover.

5. Remove the timing belt cover.

6. Remove the cam cover.

7. Rotate the crankshaft, and install a camshaft holding tool No. J-29761 or equivalent then install an injection pump lock bolt. Refer to Injection Pump removal and installation in Chapter 4.

8. Remove the adjusting spring.

9. Remove the cam gear.

10. Remove the crankshaft hub and gear.

11. Remove the front cover bolts.

12. Rotate the engine on the stand.

13. Remove the oil pan front cover.

14. Remove the oil strainer.

15. Remove the connecting rod caps.

16. Remove the rear main caps.

17. Remove the flywheel or flexplate.

18. Remove the crankshaft.

INSPECTION

1. Check the faces of the crankshaft journals, crank pin and oil seal fitting faces for wear and damage, and oil port restrictions. No attempt should be made to grind finish the faces of the crankshaft journals and crank pins.

2. Support crankshaft on aligner or "V" blocks at #1 and #5 journals and check for runout by turning the crankshaft carefully in one direction with the probe of a dial indicator resting on #3 journal. Take the highest reading. If the amount of runout is greater than .06mm (.0023), correct or replace the crankshaft.

3. Measure the diameters of the crankshaft journals and crankpins at the front and rear (I and II) in directions of A and B, to determine the amount of wear and taper wear.
Standard Journal Diameter:

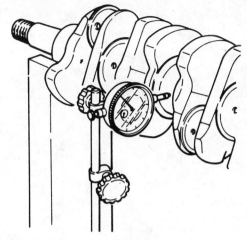

Crankshaft runout—diesel engine

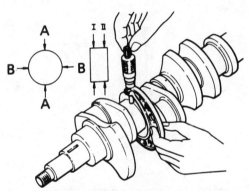

Journal and pin diameter—diesel engine

- 55.92–55.935mm
- (2.201–2.202 in.)
Standard Pin Diameter:
- 48.925–48.94mm
- (1.925–1.926 in.)

Inspect and measure bearing inside diameter as follows:

a. Check the inner face of the bearings for pin holes, separation or scuffing. Replace the entire set of bearing if any of them are found to be defective.

b. Install crankshaft bearings in position on the cylinder blocks. Then install the bearing caps and bolts. Tighten the bearing cap bolts to 100 N·m (75 lb. ft.) and measure the inside diameter with an inside micrometer or a cylinder bore indicator.
Standard Bearing and Journal Clearance:
- 0.039–0.08mm. (.0015–0.0027 in.)

c. Install the connecting rod bearing on the rod big-end with the bearing cap. Install and toruqe the bearing cap bolts to 80 N·m (60 lb. ft.); then measure the inside diameter

Bearing and journal clearance—diesel engine

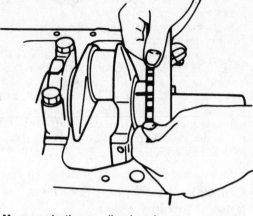

Measure plastigage—diesel engine

Pin and bearing clearance—diesel engine

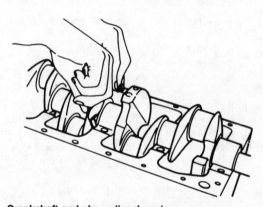

Crankshaft end play—diesel engine

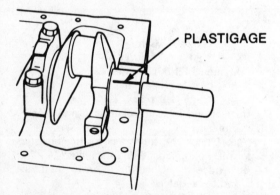

Install plastigage—diesel engine

of the bearing with an inside micrometer or a cylinder bore indicator.

Pin and bearing clearance:
- Standard—0.04–0.07mm (0.0016–0.0027 in.)
- Limit—0.12mm (0.0047 in.)

Measurement of clearance with gaging plastic.

a. Wipe the crankshaft journals and crankpins to remove oil.

b. Install the bearings on the cylinder block and mount the crankshaft in position carefully; then turn the crankshaft about thirty degrees to ensure a good contact between the crankshaft and bearings.

c. Position gaging plastic over the crankshaft journal in direction in line with the axis of the crankshaft, so that it covers the entire width of the bearing.

d. Install the bearing cap and tighten the bearing cap bolts to 95 N·m (70 lb. ft.). Do not turn the crankshaft with gaging plastic installed.

e. Remove the bearing cap and check the width of the gaging plastic against the scale printed on the packet.

f. Follow the same steps to measure the oil clearance between the crankpins and bearings.

Check crankshaft end play as follows:

a. Install the bearings on the cylinder block and position the crankshaft over the bearings.

b. Install the thrust bearing in position on both sides of the #3 journal.

c. Move the crankshaft fully endwise and check the clearance between the crankshaft and thrust bearing using a feeler gage. If the clearance is greater than 0.3mm (0.0117″), replace the thrust bearings with new ones; standard value is 0.06–0.24mm (0.0024–0.0094″).

INSTALLATION

1. Install the bearings properly and apply generous amounts of engine oil to the inner face of the bearings. Position the crankshaft over the bearings carefully, then install the thrust bearing. The bearings should be installed correctly in their respective position. Install the thrust bearing with the oil grooved side turned outward.

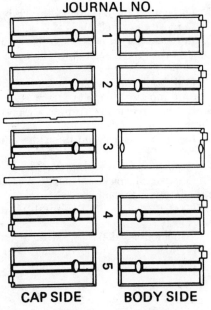

JOURNAL NO.

CAP SIDE   BODY SIDE

Main bearing installation—diesel engine

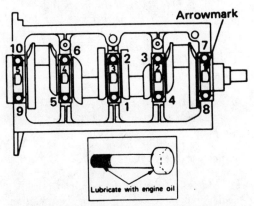

Arrowmark

Lubricate with engine oil

Bearing cap bolt torque sequence—diesel engine

2. Apply a coat of silicone gasket evenly to the joining faces of the No. 5 bearing caps and cylinder body. The No. 1 and No. 5 bearing caps should be installed flush with the face of the cylinder body.

3. Apply engine oil to the threads and seating face of the bolts. Install the bearing caps in sequence of cylinder numbers with the arrow mark pointing to front of engine and semi-tighten the bolts. Then retighten the bolts to 88–99 N·m (65–72 ft. lbs.).

Oil Pan
GASOLINE ENGINE
180 Automatic and Manual Transmission

REMOVAL

NOTE: *A special lifting tool is necessary for this procedure. This tool can be fabricated from channel iron; pattern it after the tool shown in the illustration.*

1. Remove the heater housing assembly from the firewall and rest it on top of the engine.

2. Drain the cooling system.

3. Remove upper radiator support. On A/C equipped vehicles, remove the upper half of the fan shroud.

4. Remove radiator hoses and radiator.

NOTE: *If equipped with automatic transmission, disconnect the cooler lines from the radiator.*

5. If equipped with A/C, remove the condenser to radiator support attaching nuts and remove condenser from support. Lay it on top of the engine.

6. Remove the engine mount retaining nuts and clips.

7. Disconnect the fuel line from the charcoal cannister.

8. Raise the vehicle and drain the engine oil.

9. Remove the exhaust pipe bolts at the manifold.

10. Remove the body to cross member braces.

11. On manual transmission equipped vehicles, remove the rack and pinion-to-front crossmember attaching bolts. Pull the unit down and out of the way.

12. Remove the stabilizer from the body.

13. Install tool J-26436 and raise the engine.

14. Remove the oil pan bolts.

15. With the oil pan lowered down from the block, remove the oil pump suction pipe. On 1976–77 models remove the screen. On newer models, the screen is attached to the pick-up tube.

16. Remove the oil pan through the front of

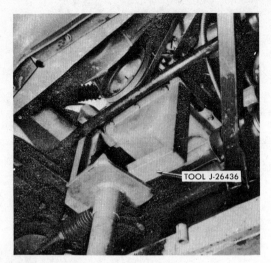
TOOL J-26436

Engine lift tool for oil pan removal

the car. On vehicles equipped with manual transmission, lower the oil pan about 1 inch, rotate the front of the pan to the right and the rear to the left. Tilt the pan 45° and remove it.

INSTALLATION

NOTE: *Most 1978 and later engines have RTV sealer in between the block and the oil pan. These can be identified by a smooth sealing surface on the oil pan rather than having a raised bead. These units MUST be reassembled using RTV sealer. The use of a gasket may allow an oil leak to develop.*

Conversely, if the oil pan has a raised bead, a gasket MUST be used for reinstallation. The use of RTV sealer in this case may cause an oil leak to develop.

Before installing an oil pan using RTV, it is necessary to remove all old RTV which is loose or will interfere with the installation. All old RTV need not be removed. The new sealer may be placed on top of the remaining RTV.

1. Install a new oil pump suction pipe and screen seal in the oil pump.
2. Lay the suction pipe and screen in the oil pan.
3. Clean the mating surfaces of the block and oil pan as necessary. Apply RTV or a gasket to the oil pan.
4. Tilt the pan and install it under the block.
5. Attach the oil pan bolts. Torque to 6 N·m (55 in. lb.). On oil pans using RTV sealer, the bolts must be attached while the sealer is still wet.
6. Replace the rack and pinion-to-front crossmember.
7. Attach the exhaust pipe to the manifold.
8. Lower the engine on to the engine

mounts and remove the lifting tool. Attach the mounting nuts and clips.
9. Install the heater core housing.
10. Connect the fuel line to the charcoal cannister.
11. If equipped with A/C, install the condenser assembly and attach the radiator support.
12. Install the radiator and attach the hoses.
13. If equipped with automatic transmission, connect the cooler lines to the radiator.
14. Install the upper radiator support.
15. On A/C equipped models, install the upper half of the fan shroud.
16. Refill the cooling system.
17. Refill the crankcase with oil.
18. Start the engine and check for leaks.

200 Automatic Transmission

REMOVAL

1. Disconnect the negative battery cable.
2. Remove the air cleaner.
3. Remove the heater housing assembly from the front of the dash and rest on top of the engine.
4. Pull back the motor mount wire restraints and remove the motor mount nuts.
5. Remove the radiator upper support or fan shroud, as necessary.
6. Raise the vehicle and drain the crankcase.
7. Remove the flywheel splash shield.
8. Remove the rack and pinion assembly from the front crossmember.
9. Loosen the converter to rear exhaust pipe clamp bolts.
10. Install tool J-26436 and raise the engine.
11. Remove the oil pan bolts and remove the oil pan.

INSTALLATION

NOTE: *Most 1978 and later engines have RTV sealer in between the block and the oil pan. These can be identified by a smooth sealing surface on the oil pan rather than having a raised bead. These units MUST be reassembled using RTV sealer. The use of a gasket may allow an oil leak to develop.*

Conversely, if the oil pan has a raised bead, a gasket MUST be used for reinstallation. The use of RTV sealer in this case may cause an oil leak to develop.

Before installing an oil pan using RTV, it is necessary to remove all old RTV which is loose or will interfere with the installation. All old RTV need not be removed. The new sealer may be placed on top of the remaining RTV.

1. Place a bead of RTV sealant on the oil pan and while still wet position up against the block. Install the attaching bolts and torque to 55 ft. lbs.

2. Lower the engine onto the mounts and remove tool J-26436.

3. Tighten the converter to rear exhaust pipe clamp bolts to 23 ft. lbs.

4. Install the rack and pinion to the front crossmember. Torque the bolts to 14 ft. lbs.

5. Install the flywheel and lower the vehicle.

6. Install the radiator upper support or fan shroud.

7. Install the engine mount nuts. Torque the nuts to 48 ft. lbs., then position the wire restraints.

8. Install the heater assembly to the front of the dash.

9. Fill the crankcase with oil.

10. Install the air cleaner and the negative battery cable. Start the engine and check for leaks.

DIESEL ENGINE

Removal and Installation

1. Remove the engine as detailed earlier in this section.

2. Support the engine in a stand.

3. Unscrew the nuts and bolts attaching the oil pan to the crankcase and then remove the pan.

4. Clean the mating surfaces of the oil pan and the block. Apply a suitable liquid gasket to the front and rear mating surfaces and then install a new gasket.

5. Install the oil pan retaining bolts and tighten them to 5 ft. lbs.

6. Reinstall the engine.

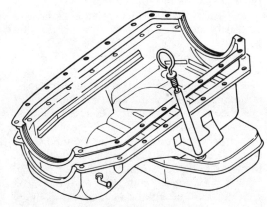

Oil pan assembly—diesel engine

Oil Pump

REMOVAL AND INSTALLATION

Gasoline Engine

1976–77

1. Remove the ignition coil attaching bolts and lay the coil aside.

2. Raise the car and remove the fuel pump, pushrod, and gasket.

3. Lower the car and remove the distributor. On air conditioned cars, remove the compressor mounting bolts and lay it aside. Do not disconnect any refrigerant lines.

4. Raise the car and remove the oil pan.

5. Remove the oil pump pipe and screen assembly clamp and remove the bolts attaching the pipe and screen assembly to the cylinder and case.

6. Remove the pipe and screen assembly from the oil pump.

7. Remove the pick-up tube seal from the oil pump.

8. Remove the oil pump attaching bolts and remove the oil pump.

To install:

9. Install the oil pump. Torque the oil pump bolts to 45–60 in. lbs.

NOTE: *Make certain that the pilot on the oil pump engages the case.*

10. Install the pick-up tube seal in the oil pump.

11. Install the pick-up pipe and screen assembly in the oil pump and install the pickup pipe and screen clamp. Torque the clamp bolt to 70–95 in. lbs. Torque the pick-up tube and screen mounting bolt to 19–25 ft. lbs.

12. Install the oil pan.

13. Lower the car and install the distributor.

14. Raise the car and install the fuel pump with gasket and pushrod.

15. Lower the car and install the ignition coil. Torque the coil bracket attaching bolts to 13–18 ft. lbs.

1978–84

REMOVAL

1. Remove the coil attaching bracket bolts and set the coil aside.

2. Raise the vehicle and remove the fuel pump and push rod.

3. Lower the vehicle and remove the distributor.

4. On A/C equipped vehicles, remove the A/C compressor and set it aside. Do not remove any of the lines from the compressor.

5. Raise the vehicle and remove the oil pan.

6. If equipped with a 200 automatic trans-

mission, remove the oil pump screen and pick up tube assembly.

7. Remove the oil pump.

8. Remove the oil pump cover bolts.

9. Remove the cover and gasket.

10. Remove the pump and gear assembly.

11. Remove the pressure regulator valve and connecting parts.

12. If necessary, remove the pick-up tube from the pump and replace it with a new tube and "O" ring seal. Do not separate the screen from the tube as they are one unit.

Clean the parts of the pump with solvent and allow to dry. Inspect the body of the pump for cracks and inspect the gears of the pump for damage or excessive wear. Also check the inside of the pump for any wear that would permit oil to leak past the ends of the gears. Check the pick-up tube and screen for any damage. If the gears or body of the pump are damaged, replace the entire oil pump assembly.

INSTALLATION

1. Install the pressure regulator valve and connecting parts.

2. Install the pump gear assemblies.

3. Replace the cover and torque the bolts to 9 N·m (85 in. lbs.)

4. Install the oil pump and attaching screws.

5. Install the oil pan.

6. Replace the distributor.

7. Raise the vehicle and install the fuel pump gasket, fuel pump and push rod assembly.

8. Lower the vehicle and install the coil attaching bracket bolts. Torque to 20 N·m (15 ft. lb.)

Diesel Engine

1. Remove the timing belt as previously detailed.

2. Unscrew the four allen bolts attaching the

Removing the four allen head bolts retaining the oil pump—diesel engine

oil pump to the front plate and remove the pump complete with the pulley.

3. Coat the vane with clean engine oil and then install it with the taper side toward the cylinder body.

4. Install a new O-ring, coated with engine oil, into the pump housing.

5. Position the rotor in the vane and then install the pump body together with the pulley. Tighten the Allen bolts to 15 ft. lbs.

6. Install the timing belt as previously detailed.

Rear Main Oil Seal Replacement

Gasoline Engine

1. Remove the engine from the car and place it in a stand.

2. Remove the oil pan.

3. Remove the rear main bearing cap.

4. Clean the bearing cap and case.

5. Check the crankshaft seal for excessive wear, etc.

6. Install a new crankshaft seal. Make sure that it is properly seated against the rear main bearing seal bulkhead.

7. Apply RTV sealer or its equivalent to the bearing cap horizontal split line.

8. With the sealer still wet, install the rear main bearing cap. On 1976–77 models, tighten the cap bolts to 40–52 ft. lbs.

On 1978 and later models, tighten the cap bolts to 10–12 ft. lbs. then tap the crankshaft, first rearward then forward, and tighten the bolts to 50 ft. lbs.

9. Apply RTV sealer or its equivalent in the vertical grooves of the rear main bearing cap.

10. Remove any excess sealer and install the oil pan. Torque the oil pan bolts to 45–60 in. lbs.

11. Install the engine in the car.

Diesel Engine

1. Remove the transmission as detailed later in this section. If equipped with a manual transmission remove the clutch.

2. Unscrew the flywheel retaining bolts in a diagonal pattern and then remove the flywheel.

3. Use a screwdriver and pry off the old oil seal.

4. Coat the lipped portion and the fitting face of the new oil seal with engine oil and install it into the crankshaft bearing. *Make sure that the seal is properly seated.*

5. Coat the threads of the new mounting bolts with Loctite® and install the flywheel. Tighten the bolts to 40 ft. lbs. in a diagonal sequence. *Do not reuse the old bolts, they must be new.*

6. Installation of the remaining components is in the reverse order of removal.

Radiator

REMOVAL AND INSTALLATION

CAUTION: *Do not remove the radiator cap while the engine is still hot as the hot steam may cause personal injury.*

1. Drain the radiator.

2. Disconnect the upper and lower radiator hoses and the coolant recovery reservoir hose.

3. Remove the radiator baffle or shroud. Remove the baffle by removing the four baffle-to-radiator support screws. Remove the shroud by removing the two upper screws and the two middle screws. Remove the upper radiator shroud. Remove the lower shroud from its mounting clips.

4. Disconnect and plug the transmission cooler lines if necessary.

5. Remove the radiator upper mounting panel or brackets and lift the radiator out of the lower brackets.

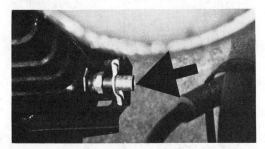

Radiator petcock

Radiator hoses are retained by screw clamps

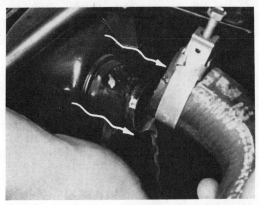

Remove the hoses by twisting and pulling simultaneously

6. To install, reverse the removal procedure.

Water Pump

REMOVAL AND INSTALLATION

Gasoline Engine

1. Disconnect the battery negative cable, and remove engine drive belt(s).

2. Remove the engine fan, spacer (air conditioned models), and the pulley.

CAUTION: *A bent or damaged fan assembly should always be replaced. Do not attempt repairs as fan balance is critical. If unbalanced, the fan could fail and break apart while in use.*

3. Remove the timing belt front cover by removing the two upper bolts, center bolt, and two lower nuts.

4. Drain the coolant from the engine.

5. Remove the lower radiator hose and the heater hose at the water pump.

It's necessary to first remove the idler pulley to remove the water pump

The thermostat housing is retained by two bolts (arrows)

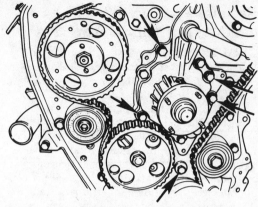

Water pump attaching bolts—diesel engine

6. Turn the crankshaft pulley so that the mark on the pulley is aligned with the "O" mark on the timing scale and that a ⅛ in. drill bit can be inserted through the timing belt upper cover and cam gear.

7. Remove the idler pulley and pull the timing belt off the gear. Don't disturb crankshaft position.

8. Remove the water pump retaining bolts and remove the pump and gasket from the engine.

9. Clean all the old gasket material from the cylinder case.

10. With a new gasket in place on the water pump, position the water pump in place on the cylinder case and install the water pump retaining bolts.

11. Install the timing belt onto the cam gear.

12. Apply sealer to the idler pulley attaching bolt and install the bolt and the idler pulley. Turn the idler pulley counterclockwise on its mounting bolt to remove the slack in the timing belt.

13. Use a tension gauge to adjust timing belt tension. Check belt tension midway between the tensioner and the cam sprocket on the idler pulley side. Correct belt tension is 55 lbs. for 1976, 70 lbs. for 1977 and later. Torque the idler pulley mounting bolt to 13–18 ft. lbs.

14. Remove the ⅛ in. drill bit from the upper timing belt cover and cam gear.

15. Install the lower radiator hose and the heater hose to the water pump.

16. Install the timing belt front cover.

17. Install the water pump pulley, spacer (if equipped), and engine fan.

18. Install the engine drive belt(s).

19. Refill the cooling system.

20. Connect the battery negative cable.

21. Start the engine and check for leaks.

Diesel Engine

1. Disconnect the negative battery cable and drain the cooling system.

2. Remove the fan shroud, fan assembly and the accessory drive belt.

3. Unscrew the retaining bolts and remove the damper pulley.

4. Remove the upper and lower halves of the front cover and then remove the bypass hose at the pump.

5. Unscrew the pump retaining bolts and remove the pump assembly.

6. Installation is in the reverse order of removal.

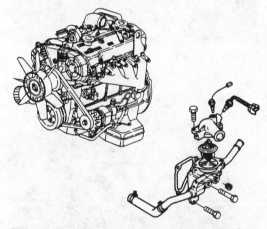

Thermostat housing assembly—diesel engine

Install the new thermostat with the spring down

Thermostat

REMOVAL AND INSTALLATION

1. Drain the radiator.
2. Remove the thermostat housing bolts and remove the housing with upper hose attached, gasket, and thermostat.

3. Install the thermostat. Use a new gasket on the thermostat housing and install the thermostat housing bolts.
4. Install the upper radiator hose at the water outlet.
5. Fill the cooling system.

Emission Controls and Fuel System

GASOLINE ENGINE EMISSION CONTROLS

Positive Crankcase Ventilation

Positive Crankcase Ventilation (PCV) is a system which returns combustible gases which have leaked past the piston rings into the crankcase, back through the intake manifold for reburning. This leakage is the normal result of the necessary working clearance of the piston rings. If these gases were to remain in the crankcase they would react with the oil to form sludge. Since there is also a certain amount of unburned fuel in the gases, dilution of the oil would occur. Both sludge and diluted oil will accelerate the wear of the engine.

Along with gases returning to the intake manifold, the PCV valve also returns a certain amount of additional air. The carburetor used with this system has been calibrated to compensate for the additional air intake.

The system consists of a hose connecting the air cleaner to the cam cover and another hose connecting the PCV valve mounted in a grommet in the cam cover and the intake manifold.

The PCV valve regulates the flow of combustion gases through the system. During engine idle and deceleration when intake manifold vacuum is high, the PCV valve restricts vapor flow to the intake manifold. When the engine is accelerated or is at constant speed, intake manifold vacuum is low and the PCV valve allows crankcase gases to flow into the intake manifold. Should the engine backfire, the plunger inside the valve is forced against its seat preventing the backfire from traveling through the PCV valve and into the engine crankcase.

The PCV valve is checked for proper operation simply by removing it from the grommet in the cam cover and shaking. If the plunger in the valve rattles, the valve is good and can be replaced. At the required mileage intervals, in-

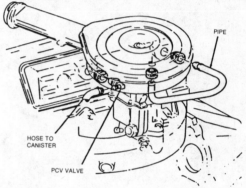

PCV system

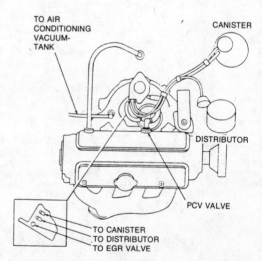

Emission hose routing without air injection (non-California)

stall a new PCV valve and use compressed air to blow out the PCV valve hose to eliminate any restrictions.

PCV valve removal and installation procedures are covered in Chapter One.

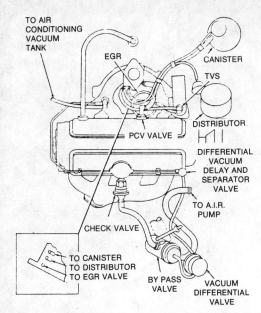

Emission hose routing with air injection (California)

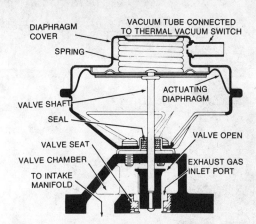

Cross-section of an EGR valve (typical)

Exhaust Gas Recirculation

Exhaust Gas Recirculation (EGR), is used to reduce oxides of nitrogen (NO_x) exhaust emissions. NO_x formation occurs at very high combustion temperatures so that the EGR system reduces combustion temperature slightly by introducing small amounts of inert exhaust gas into the intake manifold. The result is reduced formation of NO_x.

The EGR valve is mounted on the intake manifold and contains a vacuum diaphragm. The unit is operated by intake manifold vacuum and controls the flow of exhaust gases.

A vacuum signal supply port is located in the throttle body of the carburetor above the throttle plate. Vacuum is supplied to the EGR valve (causing recirculation), at part-throttle conditions. EGR does not occur at idle or at wide open throttle.

Some models also use a thermal vacuum switch (TSV), mounted in the outlet water housing to block vacuum to the EGR valve until engine coolant temperature is approximately 100°F.

An engine that idles roughly may be caused by a bad EGR valve. Push on the diaphragm plate to check for freedom of movement. If it sticks, replace the valve. Hook up a vacuum gauge between the signal tube and the vacuum hose. With the engine running and warmed up, increase the engine speed to obtain 5 hg. in. of vacuum. Remove the vacuum hose downward. This should be accompanied by increased engine speed. Replace the vacuum hose and check

to see that the plate moves upward. The engine speed should drop. If the diaphragm is not moving check for vacuum at the EGR hose. If there is none, check for leaking, plugged, or misplaced hoses. If the diaphragm moves but there is no change in rpm, check for blocked EGR manifold passages.

EGR VALVE REMOVAL AND INSTALLATION

1. Disconnect the vacuum line at the EGR valve.
2. Remove the bolt securing the EGR valve and remove the valve from the intake manifold.
3. Use a new gasket and install the EGR valve on the intake manifold. Torque the mounting bolt to 13–18 ft. lbs.
4. Connect the vacuum line to the valve.

THERMAL VACUUM SWITCH CHECK

NOTE: *This test must be performed with the engine at normal operating temperatures, permitting the vacuum signal to reach the EGR valve.*

1. Remove EGR valve vacuum hose at EGR valve and attach the hose to a vacuum gauge.
2. Start the engine and open the throttle partially. Do not race the engine. As the throttle is opened, the vacuum gauge should respond proportionately.
3. If the vacuum gauge responds correctly, remove it and replace the hose to the EGR valve.
4. If the gauge does not react correctly, remove the carburetor to switch hose at the switch and attach the vacuum gauge to it. Repeat Step 2. If the gauge responds to the opening of the throttle, the switch is defective and must be replaced.
5. If the gauge does not respond to the opening throttle, suspect a plugged hose or a defective carburetor.

Location of EGR thermal vacuum switch

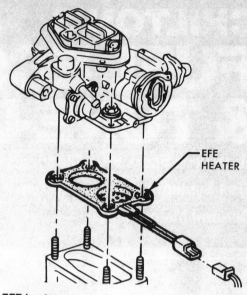

EFE heater

THERMAL VACUUM SWITCH REMOVAL AND INSTALLATION

1. Disconnect the vacuum lines.
2. Remove the switch from the thermostat housing.
3. Use sealer on the threads of the switch, install the switch and torque to 15 ft. lbs.
4. Turn the switch head if necessary to align for hose routing and connect vacuum hoses.

Early Fuel Evaportaion System (EFE)

The electric EFE system utilizes a ceramic heater grid located underneath the primary bore of the carburetor as part of the carburetor insulator gasket. It heads the incoming fuel-air charge for improved vaporization and driveability on cold drive-away.

On 1980 models when the ignition switch is turned on, voltage is applied to a snap action bi-metal switch. If engine coolant temperature is below a calibrated value, a circuit is completed to the heater and current begins to flow. The heater, incorporating a positive temperature coefficient (PTC) semiconductor element, increases in temperature and then self-regulates at a calibrated temperature, except at high engine speeds when the fuel-air flow will reduce the temperature below the regulated value. When coolant temperature reaches the calibrated value, the snap action switch breaks the circuit and shuts off the heater.

On 1981 and later models when the ignition switch is turned "on" and engine coolant temperature is low, voltage is applied to the EFE relay through the ECM. With the EFE relay energized, voltage is applied to the EFE heater. When coolant temperature increases, the ECM de-energizes the relay which shuts "off" EFE heater.

Air Injection Reactor

The Air Injection Reactor (AIR) system reduces carbon monoxide and unburned hydrocarbon emissions by injecting air into the exhaust system at the rear of the exhaust valves. The AIR system is used on California cars only. The system consists of an air pump, air injection tubes (one for each cylinder), a vacuum differential valve, an air by-pass valve, a differential vacuum delay and separator valve, a check valve, and the required hoses to connect the components.

The air pump (with an integral filter), compresses and injects the air through the air manifolds into the exhaust system to the rear of the exhaust valves. The additional air brings about further combustion of hydrocarbons and carbon monoxide in the exhaust manifold. The vacuum differential valve stops air injection to prevent backfiring during engine deceleration by activating the air by-pass valve. The vacuum differential valve is triggered by sharp increases in manifold vacuum. On engine deceleration total air pump output is vented to the atmosphere through a muffler in the air by-pass valve. Also in the air by-pass valve is a pressure relief valve which vents excess air from the air pump at high engine speeds. The by-pass valve also vents air through its muffler at times of low intake manifold vacuum (engine acceleration). This low manifold vacuum venting is con-

CHILTON'S
FUEL ECONOMY
& TUNE-UP TIPS

Tune-up • Spark Plug Diagnosis • Emission Controls

Fuel System • Cooling System • Tires and Wheels

General Maintenance

CHILTON'S FUEL ECONOMY & TUNE-UP TIPS

Fuel economy is important to everyone, no matter what kind of vehicle you drive. The maintenance-minded motorist can save both money and fuel using these tips and the periodic maintenance and tune-up procedures in this Repair and Tune-Up Guide.

There are more than 130,000,000 cars and trucks registered for private use in the United States. Each travels an average of 10-12,000 miles per year, and, and in total they consume close to 70 billion gallons of fuel each year. This represents nearly ⅔ of the oil imported by the United States each year. The Federal government's goal is to reduce consumption 10% by 1985. A variety of methods are either already in use or under serious consideration, and they all affect you driving and the cars you will drive. In addition to "down-sizing", the auto industry is using or investigating the use of electronic fuel delivery, electronic engine controls and alternative engines for use in smaller and lighter vehicles, among other alternatives to meet the federally mandated Corporate Average Fuel Economy (CAFE) of 27.5 mpg by 1985. The government, for its part, is considering rationing, mandatory driving curtailments and tax increases on motor vehicle fuel in an effort to reduce consumption. The government's goal of a 10% reduction could be realized — and further government regulation avoided — if every private vehicle could use just 1 less gallon of fuel per week.

How Much Can You Save?

Tests have proven that almost anyone can make at least a 10% reduction in fuel consumption through regular maintenance and tune-ups. When a major manufacturer of spark plugs sur-

TUNE-UP

1. Check the cylinder compression to be sure the engine will really benefit from a tune-up and that it is capable of producing good fuel economy. A tune-up will be wasted on an engine in poor mechanical condition.

2. Replace spark plugs regularly. New spark plugs alone can increase fuel economy 3%.

3. Be sure the spark plugs are the correct type (heat range) for your vehicle. See the Tune-Up Specifications.

Heat range refers to the spark plug's ability to conduct heat away from the firing end. It must conduct the heat away in an even pattern to avoid becoming a source of pre-ignition, yet it must also operate hot enough to burn off conductive deposits that could cause misfiring.

The heat range is usually indicated by a number on the spark plug, part of the manufacturer's designation for each individual spark plug. The numbers in bold-face indicate the heat range in each manufacturer's identification system.

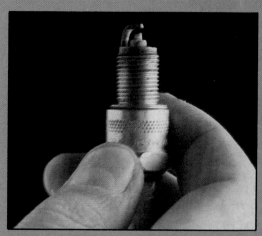

Periodically, check the spark plugs to be sure they are firing efficiently. They are excellent indicators of the internal condition of your engine.

Manufacturer	Typical Designation
AC	R **45** TS
Bosch (old)	WA **145** T30
Bosch (new)	HR **8** Y
Champion	RBL **15** Y
Fram/Autolite	4**15**
Mopar	P-**62** PR
Motorcraft	BRF-**42**
NGK	BP **5** ES-15
Nippondenso	W **16** EP
Prestolite	14GR **5** 2A

On AC, Bosch (new), Champion, Fram/Autolite, Mopar, Motorcraft and Prestolite, a higher number indicates a hotter plug. On Bosch (old), NGK and Nippondenso, a higher number indicates a colder plug.

4. Make sure the spark plugs are properly gapped. See the Tune-Up Specifications in this book.

5. Be sure the spark plugs are firing efficiently. The illustrations on the next 2 pages show you how to "read" the firing end of the spark plug.

6. Check the ignition timing and set it to specifications. Tests show that almost all cars have incorrect ignition timing by more than 2°.

veyed over 6,000 cars nationwide, they found that a tune-up, on cars that needed one, increased fuel economy over 11%. Replacing worn plugs alone, accounted for a 3% increase. The same test also revealed that 8 out of every 10 vehicles will have some maintenance deficiency that will directly affect fuel economy, emissions or performance. Most of this mileage-robbing neglect could be prevented with regular maintenance.

Modern engines require that all of the functioning systems operate properly for maximum efficiency. A malfunction anywhere wastes fuel. You can keep your vehicle running as efficiently and economically as possible, by being aware of your vehicle's operating and performance characteristics. If your vehicle suddenly develops performance or fuel economy problems it could be due to one or more of the following:

PROBLEM	POSSIBLE CAUSE
Engine Idles Rough	Ignition timing, idle mixture, vacuum leak or something amiss in the emission control system.
Hesitates on Acceleration	Dirty carburetor or fuel filter, improper accelerator pump setting, ignition timing or fouled spark plugs.
Starts Hard or Fails to Start	Worn spark plugs, improperly set automatic choke, ice (or water) in fuel system.
Stalls Frequently	Automatic choke improperly adjusted and possible dirty air filter or fuel filter.
Performs Sluggishly	Worn spark plugs, dirty fuel or air filter, ignition timing or automatic choke out of adjustment.

Check spark plug wires on conventional point type ignition for cracks by bending them in a loop around your finger.

Be sure that spark plug wires leading to adjacent cylinders do not run too close together. (Photo courtesy Champion Spark Plug Co.)

7. If your vehicle does not have electronic ignition, check the points, rotor and cap as specified.

8. Check the spark plug wires (used with conventional point-type ignitions) for cracks and burned or broken insulation by bending them in a loop around your finger. Cracked wires decrease fuel efficiency by failing to deliver full voltage to the spark plugs. One misfiring spark plug can cost you as much as 2 mpg.

9. Check the routing of the plug wires. Misfiring can be the result of spark plug leads to adjacent cylinders running parallel to each other and too close together. One wire tends to

pick up voltage from the other causing it to fire "out of time".

10. Check all electrical and ignition circuits for voltage drop and resistance.

11. Check the distributor mechanical and/or vacuum advance mechanisms for proper functioning. The vacuum advance can be checked by twisting the distributor plate in the opposite direction of rotation. It should spring back when released.

12. Check and adjust the valve clearance on engines with mechanical lifters. The clearance should be slightly loose rather than too tight.

SPARK PLUG DIAGNOSIS

Normal

APPEARANCE: This plug is typical of one operating normally. The insulator nose varies from a light tan to grayish color with slight electrode wear. The presence of slight deposits is normal on used plugs and will have no adverse effect on engine performance. The spark plug heat range is correct for the engine and the engine is running normally.

CAUSE: Properly running engine.

RECOMMENDATION: Before reinstalling this plug, the electrodes should be cleaned and filed square. Set the gap to specifications. If the plug has been in service for more than 10-12,000 miles, the entire set should probably be replaced with a fresh set of the same heat range.

Oil Deposits

APPEARANCE: The firing end of the plug is covered with a wet, oily coating.

CAUSE: The problem is poor oil control. On high mileage engines, oil is leaking past the rings or valve guides into the combustion chamber. A common cause is also a plugged PCV valve, and a ruptured fuel pump diaphragm can also cause this condition. Oil fouled plugs such as these are often found in new or recently overhauled engines, before normal oil control is achieved, and can be cleaned and reinstalled.

RECOMMENDATION: A hotter spark plug may temporarily relieve the problem, but the engine is probably in need of work.

Incorrect Heat Range

APPEARANCE: The effects of high temperature on a spark plug are indicated by clean white, often blistered insulator. This can also be accompanied by excessive wear of the electrode, and the absence of deposits.

CAUSE: Check for the correct spark plug heat range. A plug which is too hot for the engine can result in overheating. A car operated mostly at high speeds can require a colder plug. Also check ignition timing, cooling system level, fuel mixture and leaking intake manifold.

RECOMMENDATION: If all ignition and engine adjustments are known to be correct, and no other malfunction exists, install spark plugs one heat range colder.

Carbon Deposits

APPEARANCE: Carbon fouling is easily identified by the presence of dry, soft, black, sooty deposits.

CAUSE: Changing the heat range can often lead to carbon fouling, as can prolonged slow, stop-and-start driving. If the heat range is correct, carbon fouling can be attributed to a rich fuel mixture, sticking choke, clogged air cleaner, worn breaker points, retarded timing or low compression. If only one or two plugs are carbon fouled, check for corroded or cracked wires on the affected plugs. Also look for cracks in the distributor cap between the towers of affected cylinders.

RECOMMENDATION: After the problem is corrected, these plugs can be cleaned and reinstalled if not worn severely.

MMT Fouled

APPEARANCE: Spark plugs fouled by MMT (Methycyclopentadienyl Maganese Tricarbonyl) have reddish, rusty appearance on the insulator and side electrode.

CAUSE: MMT is an anti-knock additive in gasoline used to replace lead. During the combustion process, the MMT leaves a reddish deposit on the insulator and side electrode.

RECOMMENDATION: No engine malfunction is indicated and the deposits will not affect plug performance any more than lead deposits (see Ash Deposits). MMT fouled plugs can be cleaned, regapped and reinstalled.

High Speed Glazing

APPEARANCE: Glazing appears as shiny coating on the plug, either yellow or tan in color.

CAUSE: During hard, fast acceleration, plug temperatures rise suddenly. Deposits from normal combustion have no chance to fluff-off; instead, they melt on the insulator forming an electrically conductive coating which causes misfiring.

RECOMMENDATION: Glazed plugs are not easily cleaned. They should be replaced with a fresh set of plugs of the correct heat range. If the condition recurs, using plugs with a heat range one step colder may cure the problem.

Ash (Lead) Deposits

APPEARANCE: Ash deposits are characterized by light brown or white colored deposits crusted on the side or center electrodes. In some cases it may give the plug a rusty appearance.

CAUSE: Ash deposits are normally derived from oil or fuel additives burned during normal combustion. Normally they are harmless, though excessive amounts can cause misfiring. If deposits are excessive in short mileage, the valve guides may be worn.

RECOMMENDATION: Ash-fouled plugs can be cleaned, gapped and reinstalled.

Detonation

APPEARANCE: Detonation is usually characterized by a broken plug insulator.

CAUSE: A portion of the fuel charge will begin to burn spontaneously, from the increased heat following ignition. The explosion that results applies extreme pressure to engine components, frequently damaging spark plugs and pistons.

Detonation can result by over-advanced ignition timing, inferior gasoline (low octane) lean air/fuel mixture, poor carburetion, engine lugging or an increase in compression ratio due to combustion chamber deposits or engine modification.

RECOMMENDATION: Replace the plugs after correcting the problem.

Photos Courtesy Champion Spark Plug Co.

EMISSION CONTROLS

13. Be aware of the general condition of the emission control system. It contributes to reduced pollution and should be serviced regularly to maintain efficient engine operation.

14. Check all vacuum lines for dried, cracked or brittle conditions. Something as simple as a leaking vacuum hose can cause poor performance and loss of economy.

15. Avoid tampering with the emission control system. Attempting to improve fuel econ-

FUEL SYSTEM

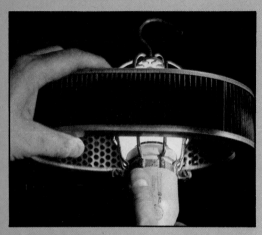

Check the air filter with a light behind it. If you can see light through the filter it can be reused.

Extremely clogged filters should be discarded and replaced with a new one.

18. Replace the air filter regularly. A dirty air filter richens the air/fuel mixture and can increase fuel consumption as much as 10%. Tests show that 1/3 of all vehicles have air filters in need of replacement.

19. Replace the fuel filter at least as often as recommended.

20. Set the idle speed and carburetor mixture to specifications.

21. Check the automatic choke. A sticking or malfunctioning choke wastes gas.

22. During the summer months, adjust the automatic choke for a leaner mixture which will produce faster engine warm-ups.

COOLING SYSTEM

29. Be sure all accessory drive belts are in good condition. Check for cracks or wear.

30. Adjust all accessory drive belts to proper tension.

31. Check all hoses for swollen areas, worn spots, or loose clamps.

32. Check coolant level in the radiator or expansion tank.

33. Be sure the thermostat is operating properly. A stuck thermostat delays engine warm-up and a cold engine uses nearly twice as much fuel as a warm engine.

34. Drain and replace the engine coolant at least as often as recommended. Rust and scale

TIRES & WHEELS

38. Check the tire pressure often with a pencil type gauge. Tests by a major tire manufacturer show that 90% of all vehicles have at least 1 tire improperly inflated. Better mileage can be achieved by over-inflating tires, but never exceed the maximum inflation pressure on the side of the tire.

39. If possible, install radial tires. Radial tires deliver as much as 1/2 mpg more than bias belted tires.

40. Avoid installing super-wide tires. They only create extra rolling resistance and decrease fuel mileage. Stick to the manufacturer's recommendations.

41. Have the wheels properly balanced.

omy by tampering with emission controls is more likely to worsen fuel economy than improve it. Emission control changes on modern engines are not readily reversible.

16. Clean (or replace) the EGR valve and lines as recommended.

17. Be sure that all vacuum lines and hoses are reconnected properly after working under the hood. An unconnected or misrouted vacuum line can wreak havoc with engine performance.

23. Check for fuel leaks at the carburetor, fuel pump, fuel lines and fuel tank. Be sure all lines and connections are tight.

24. Periodically check the tightness of the carburetor and intake manifold attaching nuts and bolts. These are a common place for vacuum leaks to occur.

25. Clean the carburetor periodically and lubricate the linkage.

26. The condition of the tailpipe can be an excellent indicator of proper engine combustion. After a long drive at highway speeds, the inside of the tailpipe should be a light grey in color. Black or soot on the insides indicates an overly rich mixture.

27. Check the fuel pump pressure. The fuel pump may be supplying more fuel than the engine needs.

28. Use the proper grade of gasoline for your engine. Don't try to compensate for knocking or "pinging" by advancing the ignition timing. This practice will only increase plug temperature and the chances of detonation or pre-ignition with relatively little performance gain.

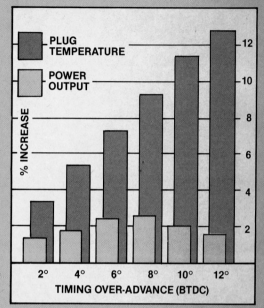

Increasing ignition timing past the specified setting results in a drastic increase in spark plug temperature with increased chance of detonation or preignition. Performance increase is considerably less. (Photo courtesy Champion Spark Plug Co.)

that form in the engine should be flushed out to allow the engine to operate at peak efficiency.

35. Clean the radiator of debris that can decrease cooling efficiency.

36. Install a flex-type or electric cooling fan, if you don't have a clutch type fan. Flex fans use curved plastic blades to push more air at low speeds when more cooling is needed; at high speeds the blades flatten out for less resistance. Electric fans only run when the engine temperature reaches a predetermined level.

37. Check the radiator cap for a worn or cracked gasket. If the cap does not seal properly, the cooling system will not function properly.

42. Be sure the front end is correctly aligned. A misaligned front end actually has wheels going in differed directions. The increased drag can reduce fuel economy by .3 mpg.

43. Correctly adjust the wheel bearings. Wheel bearings that are adjusted too tight increase rolling resistance.

Check tire pressures regularly with a reliable pocket type gauge. Be sure to check the pressure on a cold tire.

GENERAL MAINTENANCE

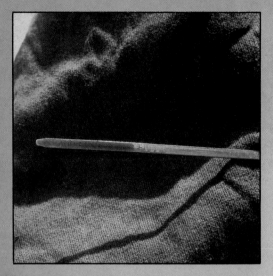

Check the fluid levels (particularly engine oil) on a regular basis. Be sure to check the oil for grit, water or other contamination.

A vacuum gauge is another excellent indicator of internal engine condition and can also be installed in the dash as a mileage indicator.

44. Periodically check the fluid levels in the engine, power steering pump, master cylinder, automatic transmission and drive axle.

45. Change the oil at the recommended interval and change the filter at every oil change. Dirty oil is thick and causes extra friction between moving parts, cutting efficiency and increasing wear. A worn engine requires more frequent tune-ups and gets progressively worse fuel economy. In general, use the lightest viscosity oil for the driving conditions you will encounter.

46. Use the recommended viscosity fluids in the transmission and axle.

47. Be sure the battery is fully charged for fast starts. A slow starting engine wastes fuel.

48. Be sure battery terminals are clean and tight.

49. Check the battery electrolyte level and add distilled water if necessary.

50. Check the exhaust system for crushed pipes, blockages and leaks.

51. Adjust the brakes. Dragging brakes or brakes that are not releasing create increased drag on the engine.

52. Install a vacuum gauge or miles-per-gallon gauge. These gauges visually indicate engine vacuum in the intake manifold. High vacuum = good mileage and low vacuum = poorer mileage. The gauge can also be an excellent indicator of internal engine conditions.

53. Be sure the clutch is properly adjusted. A slipping clutch wastes fuel.

54. Check and periodically lubricate the heat control valve in the exhaust manifold. A sticking or inoperative valve prevents engine warm-up and wastes gas.

55. Keep accurate records to check fuel economy over a period of time. A sudden drop in fuel economy may signal a need for tune-up or other maintenance.

trolled by the differential vacuum delay and separator valve which blocks this venting during very short periods of 20 seconds or less to prevent possible overheating of the catalytic converter. The check valve prevents exhaust gases from entering the air pump.

When properly installed and maintained the AIR system will effectively reduce contaminating exhausts. However, if any AIR component or any engine component that operates in conjunction with the AIR system malfunctions, the pollutant level will be increased. Whenever the AIR system seems to be malfunctioning, the engine tune-up should be checked, particularly the PCV system, carburetor, and other systems which directly affect the fuel-air ratio.

AIR PUMP REMOVAL AND INSTALLATION

CAUTION: *Do not pry on the pump housing or clamp the pump in a vise; the housing is soft and may become distorted.*

1. Disconnect the air output hose at the pump.

2. Hold the pump pulley from rotating and loosen the pulley bolts. Remove the drive belt and pump pulley.

3. Remove the air pump mounting bolts and remove the air pump.

3. Install the air pump by reversing the removal procedure.

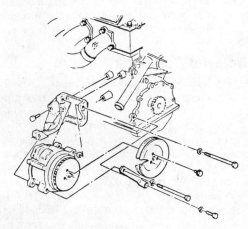

Air pump mounting details

Air Management System—Pulse Air System—PAIR

The PAIR system is used only on California cars. It consists of a pulse air valve which has four check valves. The firing of the engine creates a pulsating flow of exhaust gases which are either positive or negative, depending whether the exhaust valve is seated or not.

If the pressure is positive the check valve is forced closed and no exhaust gas will be able to

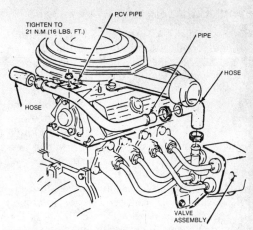

Pulse Air System—PAIR

flow past the valve and into the fresh air supply.

If there is negative pressure, a vacuum, in the exhaust system, the check valve will open and allow fresh air to be drawn in and mixed with the exhaust gases. During high engine rpm the check valve will remain closed.

If one or more of the check valves has failed the engine may surge or perform poorly. A short hissing noise may also indicate a defective pulse air valve. Inspect the valve.

When exhaust gases are allowed to pass through the pulse air valve, excessive heat will be transferred to the valve body. This will be indicated by burned off paint or deteriorated rubber hoses. Replace the air valve as necessary.

To inspect the pulse air valve create a vacuum at the hose end of the valve to 5kPa (15 in. Hg.). The vacuum is permitted to drop to 17 kPa (5 in. Hg.) in two seconds. If the vacuum drops in less than two seconds, replace the valve.

PULSE AIR VALVE REMOVAL AND INSTALLATION

1. Remove the air cleaner and disconnect the rubber hose from the pulse air valve.

2. Disconnect the support bracket and remove the attaching bolts.

3. Remove the pulse air valve.

4. Install the new pulse air valve and tighten the attaching bolts to 14–18 N·m (10–13 ft. lbs.)

5. Connect the support bracket.

6. Connect the rubber hose to the pulse air valve and install the air cleaner.

NOTE: *In some cases the support bracket is not present in the vehicle. If so, simply omit this step.*

Evaporative Emission Control

The Evaporative Control System (ECS) limits gasoline vapor escape into the atmosphere. A domed fuel tank and pressure-vacuum filler cap is used with a plastic, charcoal-filled storage canister.

Fuel vapors travel from the fuel tank vent pipe (located above fuel level in the dome of the fuel tank), by way of steel tubing and fuel-resistant rubber hose to the plastic vapor storage canister in the engine compartment. Fuel vapors are routed into the PCV system for burning when ported carburetor vacuum operates a valve in the canister. As fuel is pumped from the tank, a relief valve in the tank cap opens to allow air to enter the fuel tank.

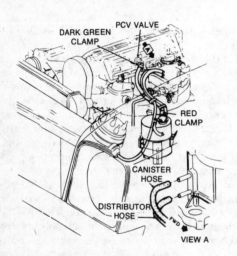

Evaporative emission control system

CHARCOAL CANISTER REMOVAL AND INSTALLATION

1. Carefully note the installed position of the hose connected to the canister, then disconnect the hoses.
2. Loosen the mounting clamps and remove the canister. To replace the canister filter, remove the filter from the bottom of the canister with your fingers.

Check to ensure that the hose connection openings are clear and check the purge valve by applying vacuum to it. If OK, it will hold vacuum. Check the condition of the hoses and replace as necessary. When replacing ECS hoses, use only fuel-resistant hose marked "EVAP."

If the purge valve is defective, disconnect the lines at the valve and snap off the valve cap. Turn the cap slowly as the diaphragm is under spring tension. Remove the diaphragm, spring retainer, and spring. Check all orifices and replace parts as necessary. Install the spring,

spring retainer, diaphragm, and cap. Connect the lines to the valve.

3. Install a new filter in the bottom of the charcoal canister.
4. Install the canister and tighten its mounting clamp bolts.
5. Connect the hoses to the top of the canister in their original positions.

Controlled Combustion System

The Controlled Combustion System (CCS) increases combustion efficiency by means of leaner carburetor mixtures and revised distributor calibration. Also, a thermostatically-controlled damper in the air cleaner snorkel maintains warm air intake to the carburetor to optimize fuel vaporization.

An air intake duct routes air from the radiator support to the air cleaner snorkel, then to the air cleaner. Air temperature is automatically controlled by a thermostatic damper inside the air cleaner snorkel. The damper selects warm air from the exhaust manifold heat stove when air temperature is below 50°F. When air temperature is above 110°F, the damper selects outside air from the air intake duct.

When replacing the air cleaner, remove the air cleaner from the air intake snorkel and the carburetor and throw it away. Check the carburetor air horn gasket and replace it if damaged or cracked, and install a new air cleaner.

Catalytic Converter

All models are equipped with an underfloor catalytic converter. The converter contains pellets coated with the catalyst material containing platinum and palladium. The converter reduces hydrocarbon and carbon monoxide emissions by transforming them into carbon dioxide and water through a chemical reaction which takes place at great heat.

Unleaded fuel only must be used with converter equipped cars because lead in leaded fuel is not consumed in the combustion process and will enter the converter and coat the pellets, eventually rendering the catalytic converter useless for emission control. To ensure the use of unleaded fuel only, all models have a small diameter fuel inlet filler which will accept only the smaller unleaded fuel nozzle.

Computer Controlled Catalytic Converter (C-4) System

The GM designed Computer Controlled Catalytic Converter System (C-4 System), was introduced in 1979 and used on California Chevettes in 1980. The C-4 System primarily maintains the ideal air/fuel ratio at which the catalytic converter is most effective. Some versions of the system also control ignition timing of the distributor.

Major components of the system include an Electronic Control Module (ECM), an oxygen sensor, and electronically controlled variable-mixture carburetor, and a three-way oxidation-reduction catalytic converter.

The oxygen sensor generates a voltage which varies with exhaust gas oxygen content. Lean mixtures (more oxygen) reduce voltage; rich mixtures (less oxygen) increase voltage. Voltage output is sent to the ECM.

An engine temperature sensor installed in the engine coolant outlet monitors coolant temperatures. Vacuum control switches and throttle position sensors also monitor engine conditions and supply signals to the ECM.

The Electronic Control Module (ECM) monitors the voltage input of the oxygen sensor along with information from other input signals. It processes these signals and generates a control signal sent to the carburetor. The control signal cycles between ON (lean command) and OFF (rich command). The amount of ON and OFF time is a function of the input voltage sent to the ECM by the oxygen sensor. The ECM has a calibration unit called a PROM (Programable Read Only Memory) which contains the specific instructions for a given engine application. In other words, the PROM unit is specifically programmed or "tailor made" for the system in which it is installed. The PROM assembly is a replaceable component which plugs into a socket on the ECM and requires a special tool for removal and installation.

To maintain good idle and driveability under all conditions, other input signals are used to modify the ECM output signal. Besides the sensors and switches already mentioned, these input signals include the manifold absolute pressure (MAP) or vacuum sensors and the barometric pressure (BARO) sensor. The MAP or vacuum sensors sense changes in manifold vacuum, while the BARO sensor sense changes in barometric pressure. One important function of the BARO sensor is the maintenance of good engine performance at various altitudes.

Computer Command Control (CCC) System

The CCC system is used on all 1981 and later carbureted engines.

The CCC has many components in common with the C-4 system (although they should probably not be interchanged between systems). These include the Electronic Control Module (ECM), which is capable of monitoring and adjusting more sensors and components than the ECM used on the C-4 System, an oxygen sensor, an electronically controlled variable-mixture carburetor, a three way catalytic converter, throttle position and coolant sensors, a barometric pressure (BARO) sensor, a manifold absolute pressure (MAP) sensor, a "check engine" light for the instrument cluster.

Components used almost exclusively by the CCC System include the Air Injection Reaction (AIR) Management System, charcoal canister purge solenoid, EGR valve control, vehicle speed sensor (located in the instrument cluster), transmission torque converter clutch solenoid (automatic transmission models only), idle speed control, and early fuel evaporative (EFE) system.

See the operation descriptions under C-4 System for those components (except the ECM) the CCC System shares with the C-4 System.

The CCC System ECM, in addition to monitoring sensors and sending a control signal to the carburetor, also control the following components or sub-systems: charcoal canister purge, AIR Management System, idle speed control, automatic transmission converter lockup, distributor ignition timing, EGR valve control, EFE control, and the air conditioner compressor clutch operation. The CCC ECM is equipped with a PROM assembly similiar to the one used in the C-4 ECM. See above for description.

The AIR Management System is an emission control which provides additional oxygen either to the catalyst or the cylinder head ports (in some cases exhaust manifold). An AIR Management System, composed of an air switching valve and/or an air control valve, controls the air pump flow and is itself controlled by the ECM. A complete description of the AIR system is given elsewhere in this unit repair section. The major difference between the CCC AIR System and the systems used on other cars is that the flow of air from the air pump is controlled electrically by the ECM, rather than by vacuum signal.

The charcoal canister purge control is an electrically operated solenoid valve controlled by the ECM. When energized, the purge control solenoid blocks vacuum from reaching the canister purge valve. When the ECM de-energizes the purge control solenoid, vacuum is allowed to reach the canister and operate the purge valve. This releases the fuel vapors collected in the canister into the induction system.

The EGR valve control solenoid is activated by the ECM in similar fashion to the canister purge solenoid. When the engine is cold, the

ECM energizes the solenoid, which blocks the vacuum signal to the EGR valve. When the engine is warm, the ECM de-energizes the solenoid and the vacuum signal is allowed to reach and activate the EGR valve.

The Early Fuel Evaporative (EFE) System is used on some engines to provide rapid heat to the engine induction system to promote smooth start-up and operation. There are two types of systems: vacuum servo and electrically heated. They use different means to achieve the same end, which is to pre-heat the incoming air/fuel mixture. They are controlled by the ECM.

The Transmission Converter Clutch (TCC) lock is controlled by the ECM through an electrical solenoid in the automatic transmission. When the vehicle speed sensor in the instrument panel signals the ECM that the vehicle has reached the correct speed, the ECM energizes the solenoid which allows the torque converter to mechanically couple the engine to the transmission. When the brake pedal is pushed or during deceleration, passing, etc., the ECM returns the transmission to fluid drive.

The idle speed control adjusts the idle speed to load conditions, and will lower the idle speed under no-load or low-load conditions to conserve gasoline.

C-4 AND CCC SYSTEM—BASIC TROUBLESHOOTING

NOTE: *The following explains how to activate the Trouble Code signal light in the instrument cluster and gives an explanation of what each code means. This is not a full C-4 or CCC System troubleshooting and isolation procedure.*

Before suspecting the C-4 or CCC System or any of its components as faulty, check the ignition system including distributor, timing, spark plugs and wires. Check the engine compression, air cleaner, and emission control components not controlled by the ECM. Also check the intake manifold, vacuum hoses and hose connectors for leaks and the carburetor bolts for tightness.

The following symptoms could indicate a possible problem with the C-4 or CCC System.

1. Detonation
2. Stalls or rough idle—cold
3. Stalls or rough idle—hot
4. Missing
5. Hesitation
6. Surges
7. Poor gasoline mileage
8. Sluggish or spongy performance
9. Hard startings—cold
10. Hard starting—hot

11. Objectionable exhaust odors
12. Cuts out

As a bulb and system check, the "Check Engine" light will come on when the ignition switch is turned to the ON position but the engine is not started.

The "Check Engine" light will also produce the trouble code or codes by a series of flashes which translate as follows. When the diagnostic test lead (C-4) or terminal (CCC) under the dash is grounded, with the ignition in the ON position and the engine not running, the "Check Engine" light will flash once, pause, then flash twice in rapid succession. This is a code 12, which indicates that the diagnostic system is working. After a longer pause, the code 12 will repeat itself two more times. The cycle will then repeat itself until the engine is started or the ignition is turned off.

When the engine is started the "Check Engine" light will remain on for a few seconds, then turn off. If the "Check Engine" light remains on, the self-diagnostic system has detected a problem. If the test lead (C-4) or test terminal (CCC) is then grounded, the trouble code will flash three times. If more than one problem is found, each trouble code will flash three times. Trouble codes will flash in numerical order (lowest code number to highest). The trouble codes series will repeat as long as the test lead or terminal is grounded.

A trouble code indicates a problem with a given circuit. For example, trouble code 14 indicates a problem in the cooling sensor circuit. This includes the coolant sensor, its electrical harness, and the Electronic Control Module (ECM).

Since the self-diagnostic system cannot diagnose every possible fault in the system, the absence of a troublecode does not mean the system is trouble-free. To determine problems within the system which do not activate a trouble code, a system performance check must be made. This job should be left to a qualified technician.

In the case of an intermittant fault in the system, the "Check Engine" light will go out when the fault goes away, but the trouble code will remain in the memory of the ECM. Therefore, if a trouble code can be obtained even though the "Check Engine" light is not on, the trouble code must be evaluated. It must be determined if the fault is intermittant or if the engine must be at certain operating conditions (under load, etc.) before the "Check Engine" light will come on. Some trouble codes will not be recorded in the ECM until the engine has been operated at part throttle for about 5 to 18 minutes.

On the C-4 System, the ECM erases all

trouble codes every time the ignition is turned off. In the case of intermittent faults, a long term memory is desirable. This can be produced by connecting the orange connector/lead from terminal "S" of the ECM directly to the battery (or to a "hot" fuse panel terminal). This terminal must be disconnected after diagnosis is complete or it will drain the battery.

On the CCC System, a trouble code will be stored until terminal "R" of the ECM has been disconnected from the battery for 10 seconds.

An easy way to erase the computer memory on the CCC System is to disconnect the battery terminals from the battery. If this method is used, don't forget to reset clocks and electronic preprogramable radios. Another method is to remove the fuse marked ECM in the fuse panel. Not all models have such a fuse.

ACTIVATING THE TROUBLE CODE

On the C-4 System, activate the trouble code by grounding the trouble code test lead under the instrument panel (usually a white and black wire or a wire with a green connector). Run a jumper wire from the lead to ground.

On the CCC System locate the test terminal under the instrument panel. Ground the test lead. On many systems, the test lead is situated side by side with a ground terminal. In addition, on some models, the partition between the test terminal and the ground terminal has a cut out section so that a spade terminal can be used to connect the two terminals.

NOTE: *Ground the test lead or terminal according to the instructions given in "Basic Troubleshooting," above.*

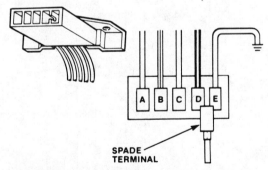

CCC system test terminal ground location found under the instrument panel

DIESEL ENGINE EMISSION CONTROLS

Positive Crankcase Ventilation (PCV) is the only emission control system that the diesel engine requires. Although the Diesel PCV system differs in appearance and construction, it still performs the same function; to reroute combustion blow-by from the crankcase to the intake manifold for reburning.

This system is of a closed type, consisting of: a baffle plate inside the cam cover for separating oil particles from blow-by gas, a PCV valve on the cam cover that is opened at a specified differential pressure between the cam cover and intake manifold for controlling pressure in the cam cover, and a hose connecting the PCV valve and inlet pipe.

PCV valve removal and installation procedures are covered in Chapter One.

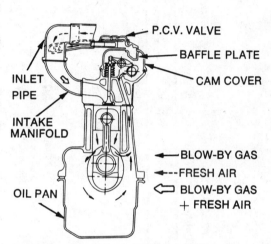

Crankcase ventilation system—diesel engine

GASOLINE ENGINE FUEL SYSTEM

All 1976–78 Chevettes use a Rochester 1ME carburetor. The unit incorporates an automatic choke with an electronically heated choke coil. The choke coil is heated in a housing which is mounted on a bracket connected to the fuel bowl.

The internal fuel filter is made of pleated paper and is located in the fuel bowl behind the fuel inlet nut. The throttle body of the 1ME is made of aluminum for better heat dispersement.

The carburetor identification number is stamed on the float bowl, right next to the fuel inlet nut. When replacing the fuel bowl, be sure to transfer the identification number to the new float bowl.

The 1979–82 Chevettes are equipped with a 2-bbl Holley carburetor. This provides a slight increase in horsepower and at the same time, improves the fuel economy.

Explanation of Trouble Codes GM C—4 and CCC Systems

Ground test lead or terminal AFTER engine is running.

Trouble Code	Applicable System	Notes	Possible Problem Area
12	C-4, CCC		No tachometer or reference signal to computer (ECM). This code will only be present while a fault exists, and will not be stored if the problem is intermittent.
13	C-4, CCC		Oxygen sensor circuit. The engine must run for about five minutes at part throttle (and under road load—CCC equipped cars) before this code will show.
13 & 14 (at same time)	C-4		See code 43.
13 & 43 (at same time)	C-4		See code 43.
14	C-4, CCC		Shorted coolant sensor circuit. The engine has to run 2 minutes before this code will show.
15	C-4, CCC		Open coolant sensor circuit. The engine has to operate for about five minutes at part throttle before this code will show.
21	C-4		Shorted wide open throttle switch and/or open closed-throttle switch circuit (when used).
23	C-4, CCC		Throttle position sensor circuit. The engine must be run up to 10 seconds (25 seconds—CCC System) below 800 rpm before this code will show.
23	C-4, CCC		Open or grounded carburetor mixture control (M/C) solenoid circuit.
24	CCC		Vehicle speed sensor (VSS) circuit. The car must operate up to five minutes at road speed before this code will show.
32	C-4, CCC		Barometric pressure sensor (BARO) circuit output low.
32 & 55 (at same time)	C-4		Grounded +8V terminal or V(REF) terminal for barometric pressure sensor (BARO), or faulty ECM computer.
34	C-4		Manifold absolute pressure (MAP) sensor output high (after ten seconds and below 800 rpm).

Code	System	Note	Description
34	CCC		Manifold absolute pressure (MAP) sensor circuit or vacuum sensor circuit. The engine must run up to five minutes below 800 RPM before this code will set.
35	CCC		Idle speed control (ISC) switch circuit shorted (over ½ throttle for over two seconds).
41	CCC		No distributor reference pulses to the ECM at specified engine vacuum. This code will store in memory.
42	CCC		Electronic spark timing (EST) bypass circuit grounded.
43	C-4		Throttle position sensor adjustment (on some models, engine must run at part throttle up to ten seconds before this code will set).
44	C-4, CCC		Lean oxygen sensor indication. The engine must run up to five minutes in closed loop (oxygen sensor adjusting carburetor mixture), at part throttle and under road load (drive car) before this code will set.
44 & 55 (at same time)	C-4, CCC		Faulty oxygen sensor circuit.
45	C-4, CCC	Restricted air cleaner can cause code 45	Rich oxygen sensor system indication. The engine must run up to five minutes in closed loop (oxygen sensor adjusting carburetor mixture), at part throttle under road load before this code will set.
51	C-4, CCC		Faulty calibration unit (PROM) or improper PROM installation in electronic control module (ECM). It takes up to thirty seconds for this code to set.
52 & 53	C-4		"Check Engine" light off: Intermittent ECM computer problem. "Check Engine" light on: Faulty ECM computer (replace.)
52	C-4, CCC		Faulty ECM computer.
53	CCC		Faulty ECM computer.
54	C-4, CCC		Faulty mixture control solenoid circuit and/or faulty ECM computer.
55	C-4		Faulty oxygen sensor, open manifold absolute pressure sensor. Faulty throttle position sensor or ECM computer.
55	CCC		Grounded +8 volt supply (terminal 19 of ECM computer connector), grounded 5 volt reference (terminal 21 of ECM computer connector), faulty oxygen sensor circuit or faulty ECM computer.

Fuel Pump

REMOVAL AND INSTALLATION

NOTE: *Air conditioned cars require removal of the rear compressor bracket to gain working room.*

1. Working from under the car, remove the ignition coil.

2. On some later models it may be necessary to remove the air cleaner assembly and the distributor cap.

3. Disconnect the fuel inlet and outlet lines at the pump and plug the inlet line.

4. Remove the two pump mounting bolts and lockwashers and remove the fuel pump and gasket.

5. Install the fuel pump with a new gasket coated with sealer. Tighten the two mounting bolts.

6. Connect the fuel inlet and outlet lines at the pump. Install the ignition coil.

7. Start the engine and check for leaks.

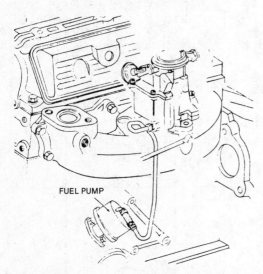

Fuel pump location

Carburetor

REMOVAL AND INSTALLATION

1. Remove the air cleaner.

2. Disconnect the fuel line. Disconnect all vacuum lines, but note where they attach.

3. Disconnect the electrical connector at the choke.

4. Disconnect the accelerator linkage.

5. Disconnect the solenoid electrical connector.

6. On cars with an automatic transmission, disconnect the detent cable.

7. Remove the carburetor retaining nuts and remove the carburetor/solenoid assembly.

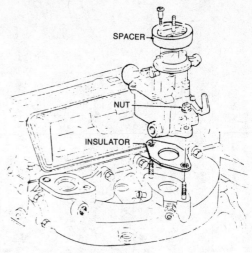

Carburetor mounting details

8. On 1980 and later models remove the electric EFE insulator gasket.

9. Installation is the reverse of removal. Start the engine and check for leaks.

FLOAT LEVEL ADJUSTMENT

1. Remove the top of the carburetor.

2. Hold the float retaining pin in place and push down on the float arm at the outer end against the top of the float needle valve.

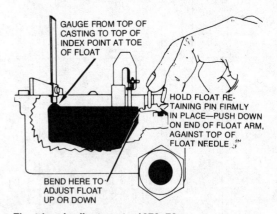

Float level adjustment—1976–78

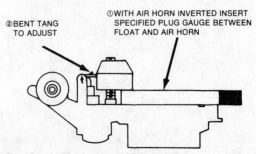

Float level adjustment—1979 and later

3. Measure the distance from the bumb on the top of the float at the end to the bowl gasket surface, without the gasket.

4. To adjust, bend the float arm at the point where it joins the float.

METERING ROD ADJUSTMENT

Through 1978

1. Remove the top of the carburetor.

2. Back out the idle stop solenoid and rotate the fast idle cam so that the fast idle screw does not contact the cam.

3. With the throttle valve completely closed, make sure that the power piston is all the way up.

4. Insert the specified size gauge between the bowl gasket surface with no gasket and the lower surface of the metering rod holder, next to the metering rod.

5. To adjust, carefully bend the metering rod holder.

Fast idle adjusting screw—1976–78

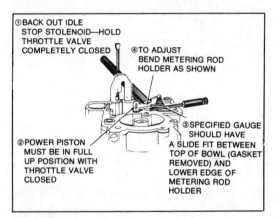

Metering rod adjustment

FAST IDLE SPEED ADJUSTMENT

1. The engine should be at normal temperature with the air cleaner in place. Disconnect and plug the EGR valve vacuum line.

2. Make sure that the curb idle speed is as specified.

3. Place the fast idle screw on the highest cam step with the engine running.

4. Adjust the fast idle speed screw to the correct fast idle speed.

FAST IDLE CAM ADJUSTMENT

1976–78

1. Hold the fast idle speed screw on the second cam step against the shoulder of the high step.

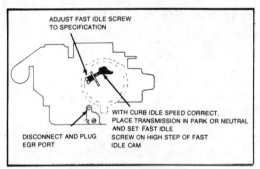

Fast idle adjusting screw—1979–80

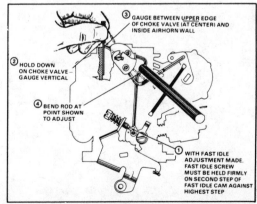

Fast idle cam adjustment—1976–78

2. Hold the choke valve closed with a finger.

3. Insert the specified gauge between the center upper edge of the choke valve and the airhorn wall.

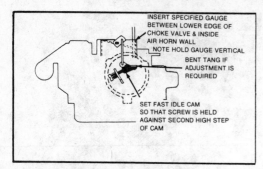

Fast idle cam adjustment—1979 and later

4. Bend the linkage rod at the upper angle to adjust.

1979–82

1. Set the fast idle cam so that the screw is held against the second high step of the cam.
2. Insert the specified gauge between the lower edge of the choke valve and the inside air horn wall.
3. Bend the tang to adjust.

VACUUM BREAK ADJUSTMENT

1976–78

1. Place the fast idle speed screw on the highest cam step.
2. Tape over the bleed hole in the diaphragm unit. Apply suction by mouth to seat the diaphragm.
3. Push down on the choke valve with a finger.
4. Insert the gauge between the upper edge of the choke valve and the airhorn wall.
5. Bend the link to adjust.

1979

1. Position fast idle cam by opening throttle ⅓ open, manually closing choke plate, then closing throttle. Check to see that fast idle screw rests on top step.
2. Note position of choke index. Remove the three screws and ring retaining the choke assembly. Unplug wire from choke housing and remove entire choke assembly as a unit (bimetal assembly, grounding ring, nylon eye, and plastic housing).

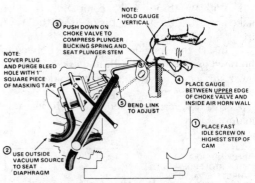

Vacuum break adjustment—1976–78

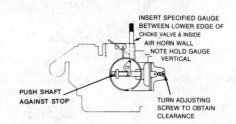

Vacuum break adjustment—1979

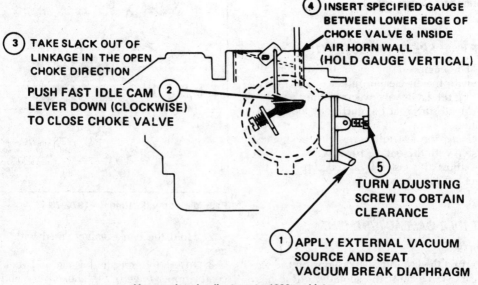

Vacuum break adjustment—1980 and later

3. With a screwdriver or suitable tool, push diaphragm shaft against stop.

4. Take slack out of linkage by holding the choke housing shaft tang (the tang that mates with the bimetal eye) in the direction of the choke plate closing.

5. Insert a specified gauge between lower edge of choke and air horn wall (with no weight on the choke plates).

6. Turn adjusting screw in or out with an Allen wrench to obtain specified clearance.

7. After adjustment, reassemble in the following sequence: plastic core housing, grounding ring, nylon eye, bimetal assembly, retaining ring, 3 attaching screws. Rotate the bimetal cover making sure choke valves operate in both directions without interference of binding. Return index on bimetal cover to original position and tighten screws to 7 in. lbs. Plug wire back onto choke housing.

1980–84

1. Apply an external vacuum source and seat the vacuum break diaphragm.

2. Push the fast idle cam lever down (clockwise) to close the choke valve.

3. Take the slack out of the linkage in the open choke direction.

4. Insert the specified gauge between the lower edge of the choke valve and the inside air horn wall. Hold the gauge vertical.

5. Turn the adjusting screw to obtain the clearance.

CHOKE UNLOADER ADJUSTMENT

1976–78

1. Hold the throttle valve wide open.
2. Hold down the choke valve with a finger

and insert the specified gauge between the upper edge of the choke valve and the airhorn wall.

3. Bend the linkage tang to adjust.

1979–84

1. Position the throttle lever to wide-open.
2. Insert the specified gauge between the lower edge of the choke valve and the inside air horn wall. Hold the gauge vertical.

3. Bend the tang at the existing radius to adjust.

CHOKE COIL LEVER ADJUSTMENT

1976–78

1. Place the fast idle speed screw on the highest cam step.

2. Hold the choke valve closed.

3. Insert a 0.120 in. gauge through the hole in the arm on the choke housing and into the hole in the casting.

4. Bend the link to adjust.

ELECTRIC CHOKE ADJUSTMENT

1976–78

1. Place the fast idle cam hollower on the high step.

2. Loosen the three retaining screws and rotate the cover counterclockwise until the choke valve just closes.

3. Align the index mark on the cover with the specified housing mark.

4. Tighten the three screws.

1979

1. Loosen the retaining screws.
2. With the choke coil lever located inside

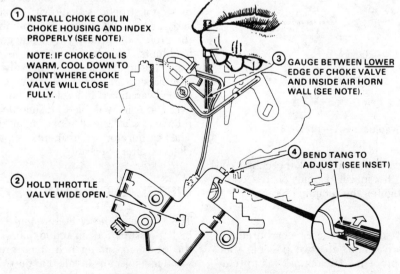

① INSTALL CHOKE COIL IN CHOKE HOUSING AND INDEX PROPERLY (SEE NOTE).

NOTE: IF CHOKE COIL IS WARM, COOL DOWN TO POINT WHERE CHOKE VALVE WILL CLOSE FULLY.

③ GAUGE BETWEEN LOWER EDGE OF CHOKE VALVE AND INSIDE AIR HORN WALL (SEE NOTE).

④ BEND TANG TO ADJUST (SEE INSET)

② HOLD THROTTLE VALVE WIDE OPEN.

Choke unloader adjustment—1976–78

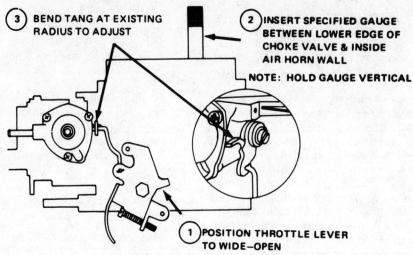

③ BEND TANG AT EXISTING RADIUS TO ADJUST

② INSERT SPECIFIED GAUGE BETWEEN LOWER EDGE OF CHOKE VALVE & INSIDE AIR HORN WALL

NOTE: HOLD GAUGE VERTICAL

① POSITION THROTTLE LEVER TO WIDE–OPEN

Choke unloader adjustment—1979 and later

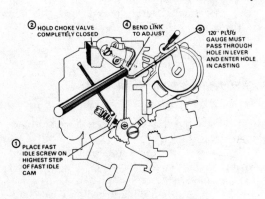

② HOLD CHOKE VALVE COMPLETELY CLOSED

④ BEND LINK TO ADJUST

③ 120" PLUG GAUGE MUST PASS THROUGH HOLE IN LEVER AND ENTER HOLE IN CASTING

① PLACE FAST IDLE SCREW ON HIGHEST STEP OF FAST IDLE CAM

Choke coil cover adjustment—1976–78

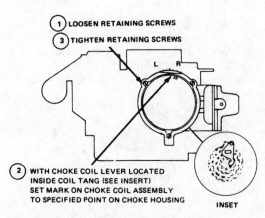

① LOOSEN RETAINING SCREWS

③ TIGHTEN RETAINING SCREWS

② WITH CHOKE COIL LEVER LOCATED INSIDE COIL TANG (SEE INSERT) SET MARK ON CHOKE COIL ASSEMBLY TO SPECIFIED POINT ON CHOKE HOUSING

INSET

Electric choke adjustment—1979

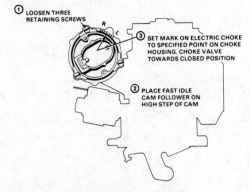

① LOOSEN THREE RETAINING SCREWS

③ SET MARK ON ELECTRIC CHOKE TO SPECIFIED POINT ON CHOKE HOUSING. CHOKE VALVE TOWARDS CLOSED POSITION

② PLACE FAST IDLE CAM FOLLOWER ON HIGH STEP OF CAM

Electric choke adjustment—1976–78

the coil tang set the mark on the choke coil assembly to the specified point on the choke housing. Retighten the retaining screws.

OVERHAUL

Whenever wear or dirt causes a carburetor to perform poorly, there are two possible solutions to the problem. The simplest is to trade in the old unit for a rebuilt one. The other, cheaper alternative is to purchase a carburetor overhaul kit and rebuild the original unit. Some of the better overhaul kits contain complete step by step instructions along with exploded views and gauges. Other kits, probably intended for the professional, have only a few general overhaul hints. The second type can be moderately confusing to the novice, especially since a kit may have extra parts so that one kit can cover several variations of the same carburetor. In any event, it is inadvisable to dismantle any carburetor without at least replacing all the gaskets. The carburetor adjustments should all be checked after overhaul.

DIESEL ENGINE FUEL SYSTEM

The Chevette diesel fuel system consists of a high pressure fuel injection pump driven by the camshaft timing belt, four pressure activated fuel injectors installed in the cylinder head and connected by fuel lines to the pump, a fuel

Carburetor Specifications

Year	Carburetor Identifi-cation Number ①	Float Level (in.)	Metering Rod (in.)	Fast Idle Speed (rpm)	Fast Idle Cam (in.)	Vacuum Break (in.)	Choke Unloader (in.)	Choke Setting (notches)
1976–77	17056030	5/32	0.072	2000 ②	0.065	0.070	0.165	3 Rich
	17056036							
	17056031							
	17056037							
	17056032	5/32	0.073	2000 ③	0.045	0.070	0.200	3 Rich
	17056034							
	17056033							
	17056035							
	17056330	5/32	0.072	2000	0.065	0.070	0.165	3 Rich
	1705631							
	17056332	5/32	0.073	2000	0.045	0.070	0.200	3 Rich
	17056333							
	17056334							
	17056335	5/32	0.073	2000	0.045	0.120	0.200	3 Rich
1978	17058031	5/32	0.080	2400	0.105	0.150	0.500	2 Rich
	17058032	5/32	0.080	2400	0.080	0.130	0.500	3 Rich
	17058034							
	17058036							
	17058038							
	17058033	5/32	0.080	2400	0.080	0.130	0.500	2 Rich
	17058037							
	17058042	5/32	0.080	2400	0.080	0.130 ④	0.500	2 Rich
	17058044							
	17058332							
	17058334							
	17058035	5/32	0.080	2300	0.080	0.130	0.500	3 Rich
	17058045	5/32	0.080	2300 ⑤	0.080	0.130 ④	0.500	2 Rich
	17058035							
1979	466361	0.50	NA	2500	0.110	0.245	0.350	2 Rich
	466363							
	466369							
	466371							
	466362	0.50	NA	2500	0.110	0.250	0.350	2 Rich
	466364							
	466370							
	466372							
	466365	0.50	NA	2500	0.130	0.300	0.350	1 Rich
	466366							
	466367							

Carburetor Specifications (cont.)

Year	Carburetor Identification Number ①	Float Level (in.)	Metering Rod (in.)	Fast Idle Speed (rpm)	Fast Idle Cam (in.)	Vacuum Break (in.)	Choke Unloader (in.)	Choke Setting (notches)
1979	466368							
	466373							
	466374							
	466375	0.50	NA	2500	0.130	0.300	0.350	1 Rich
	466376							
1980	14004461	0.50	NA	2500	0.110	0.120	0.350	Fixed
	14004462	0.50	NA	2500	0.110	0.120	0.350	Fixed
	14004463	0.50	NA	2500	0.110	0.120	0.350	Fixed
	14004464	0.50	NA	2500	0.110	0.120	0.350	Fixed
	14004465	0.50	NA	2500	0.110	0.120	0.350	Fixed
	14004466	0.50	NA	2500	0.110	0.120	0.350	Fixed
	14004467	0.50	NA	2500	0.110	0.120	0.350	Fixed
	14004468	0.50	NA	2500	0.110	0.120	0.350	Fixed
	14004469	0.50	NA	2500	0.130	0.300	0.350	Fixed
	14004470	0.50	NA	2500	0.130	0.300	0.350	Fixed
	14004471	0.50	NA	2600	0.130	0.275	0.350	Fixed
	14004472	0.50	NA	2600	0.130	0.275	0.350	Fixed
1981	All	0.50	NA	2500	0.130	0.300	0.350	Fixed
1982	All	0.50	NA	⑥	0.080	0.080	0.270	Fixed
1983	14048827	0.50	NA	⑥	0.080	0.080	0.270	Fixed
	14048828	0.50	NA	⑥	0.080	0.080	0.300	Fixed
	14048829	0.50	NA	⑥	0.080	0.080	0.270	Fixed

① Stamped on float bowl, next to fuel inlet nut
② 2200 rpm for the first two numbers
③ 2200 rpm for the last two numbers
④ .160 above 30,000 miles
⑤ Non-adjustable by design
⑥ See underhood decal
NA—Not applicable

filter with built in water separator, drain and hand primer, a fuel tank and connecting fuel feed and return lines. The injection pump is equipped with an electrically operated fuel cut-off solenoid which halts fuel flow (and the engine) whenever the ignition key is turned to the "Off" position.

Idle Speed

ADJUSTMENT

1. Set the parking brake and block the wheels.
2. Place the transmission in Neutral. Connect a tachometer as per the manufacturer's instructions.
3. Start the engine and allow it to reach normal operating temperature.
4. Loosen the lock nut on the idle speed adjusting screw and turn the screw to obtain the correct idle speed (see underhood specifications sticker).
5. Tighten the lock nut, turn the engine off and disconnect the tachometer.

Fast Idle Speed

ADJUSTMENT

1. Set the parking brake and block the wheels.
2. Place the transmission in neutral.
3. Connect a tachometer.
4. Start the engine and allow it to run until it reaches normal operating temperature.
5. Apply vacuum to the fast idle actuator.
6. Loosen the lock nut on the fast idle adjusting screw and adjust the knurled nut to obtain the fast idle speed specified on the emission label. After adjusting, retighten the lock nut.

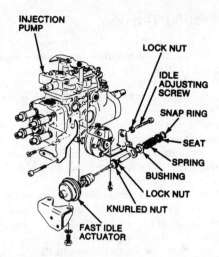

Exploded view of diesel injection pump linkage showing the idle adjusting screw and the fast idle adjuster (knurled nut)

Injection Pump

REMOVAL AND INSTALLATION

NOTE: *This procedure will require the use of two special tools: a gear puller (J-22888), and a fixing plate (J-29761). It is a long and complicated procedure and must be performed in conjunction with the following "injection timing" procedure. We do not suggest that the average amateur mechanic perform these procedures.*

1. Disconnect the negative battery cable.
2. Drain the cooling system. Remove the fan shroud, radiator and coolant recovery tank.
3. Disconnect the bypass hose leading from the front cover and then remove the upper half of the front cover.

NOTE: *Fan removal may facilitate better access to certain front cover retaining bolts.*

4. Loosen the timing belt tension pulley and plate bolts. Slide the tensioner over.
5. Unscrew the two retaining bolts and remove tension spring from behind the front plate, by the injection pump.
6. Remove the injection pump gear retaining nut and then remove the gear with a gear puller.
7. Tag and disconnect any wires, hoses or cables leading from the pump. Disconnect and plug the fuel feed lines.
8. Remove the fuel filter. Disconnect the injector lines at the pump and at the injector nozzles and remove the lines.
9. Unscrew the four retaining bolts and remove the pump rear bracket.
10. Unscrew the nuts attaching the pump flange to the front plate and then remove the pump complete with the fast idle device and return spring. To install:

11. Place the pump in position and tighten the flange bolts. Position the rear bracket and tighten the bracket-to-pump bolts. There should be no clearance between the rear bracket and pump bracket.
12. Reconnect all wires, hoses and cable.
13. Slide the pump gear onto its shaft, making sure that it is aligned with the key groove. Turn the gear until the notch mark aligns with the index mark on the front plate. Thread a lock bolt (8mm x 1.25) through the gear and into the front plate and then tighten the retaining nut to 45 ft. lbs.
14. Remove the cylinder head cover. Position the No. 1 piston at TDC of the compression stroke and install the fixing plate into the slot in the rear of the camshaft to prevent it from rotating.
15. Unscrew the cam gear retaining bolt and, using a puller, remove the gear. Reinstall the gear loosely so that it can be turned smoothly by hand.
16. Grasp the timing belt on each side near the lower half of the front cover; move it back and forth until the cogs on the belt engage with those on the lower gears. Slide the belt over the pump gear and then over the cam gear (you may need to turn the cam gear slightly to facilitate proper engagement of the cogs).
17. Make sure that any slack in the belt is concentrated around the tension pulley and NOT around or between the two upper gears. Depress the tension pulley with your finger and then install the tension spring.
18. Partially tighten the tension pulley bolts; first the upper, then the lower. Tighten the cam gear retaining bolt to 45 ft. lbs.
19. Remove the pump gear lock bolt. Remove the fixing plate from the end of the camshaft.

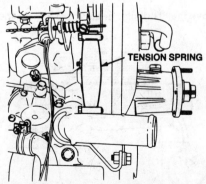

Tension spring, located behind the front plate beside the injection pump on diesel engine

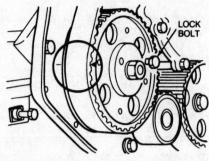

Use a lockbolt to ensure that the index marks on the injection pump gear and the front plate stay in alignment—diesel engine

20. Check that the No. 1 piston is still at TDC. Check that the marks on the front plate and the pump gear are still aligned. Check that the fixing plate still fits properly into the rear of the camshaft.

NOTE: *If these three steps do not check out correctly, repeat the entire procedure, DO NOT attempt to compensate by moving the camshaft, pump gear or crankshaft.*

21. Loosen the tension pulley and plate bolts. Make sure the belt slack is concentrated around the pulley and then tighten the bolts in the same manner as before. Belt tension should be checked at a point between the cam gear and the pump gear.

22. Installation of the remaining components is in the reverse order of removal.

23. Check the injection timing.

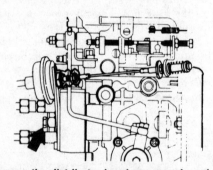

Remove the distributor head screw and washer

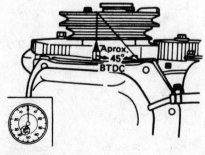

Zeroing the dial indicator

Injection Timing

1. Check that the No. 1 piston is at TDC of the compression stroke. Make sure that the timing belt is properly tensioned and the timing marks are aligned.

2. Remove the cylinder head cover and check that the fixing plate used in the previous section will still fit smoothly into the slot at the rear of the camshaft.

3. Remove the injection lines as detailed earlier and then remove the distributor head screw and washer.

4. Position a Static Timing Gauge (J-29763) and a dial indicator in the distributor head hole. Set the lift approximately 0.04 in. (1 mm) from the end of the plunger.

5. Turn the crankshaft until the No. 1 piston is 45–60 degrees BTDC and then zero the dial indicator.

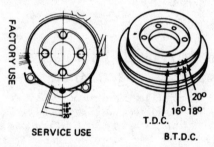

Staic timing notches on the damper pulley

NOTE: *The damper pulley is notched with eleven lines; four in one position, seven in another. The group of four are to be used for static timing.*

6. Turn the crankshaft until the 18° notch on the damper pulley is aligned with the timing pointer.

7. The dial indicator should read 0.02 in. (0.05mm). If it does not, hold the crankshaft in the 18° position, loosen the two nuts on the injection pump flange and move the pump until the proper reading is achieved. Swivel the pump up to retard the timing and down to advance the timing. When adjustment is correct, retighten the pump flange nuts.

8. Remove the dial indicator and install the distributor head screw and washer.

9. Install the cylinder head cover, injection lines and fuel filter.

10. Reconnect all necessary wires and hoses. Installation of the remaining components is in the reverse order of removal.

Fuel Injector Nozzle

REMOVAL AND INSTALLATION

NOTE: *The primary function of an injection nozzle is to distribute fuel in the combustion chamber. Do not, under any circumstances, crank the engine while an injection line or injector is disconnected.*

1. Disconnect the negative battery cable.
2. Remove the fresh air duct and disconnect the PCV hose.
3. Disconnect the injection line at the injec-

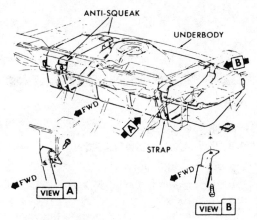

ANTI-SQUEAK

UNDERBODY

B

FWD

A

FWD

STRAP

FWD

VIEW A

FWD

VIEW B

Fuel tank mounting

tor nozzle and then loosen it at the injection pump. Carefully move it out of the way.

4. Remove the fuel return line.
5. Unscrew and remove the injector.
6. Installation is in the reverse order of removal.

Fuel Tank

REMOVAL AND INSTALLATION

All Models

1. Disconnect the battery.
2. Drain the fuel tank.
3. Raise the rear of the car and support it safely on jackstands.
4. Disconnect the meter wire at the rear harness connector and the ground strap at the fuel tank reinforcement.
5. Disconnect the fuel filler neck hose and the vent hose.
6. Disconnect the fuel feed line and the vapor line at the hose connections.
7. Remove the fuel tank strap rear support bolts and lower and remove the fuel tank.
8. To install the tank, reverse the above steps.

Chassis Electrical

HEATER

Blower

REMOVAL AND INSTALLATION

1. Disconnect the negative battery cable.
2. Disconnect the electrical lead from the blower motor.
3. Scribe a mark to reference the blower motor flange-to-case position.
4. Remove the blower motor-to-case attaching screws and remove the blower motor and wheel as an assembly. Pry the flange gently if the sealer acts as an adhesive.
5. Remove the blower wheel retaining nut and separate the motor and wheel.
6. Reverse Steps 1–5 to install. Be sure to align the scribe marks made during removal.

NOTE: *Assemble the blower wheel to the motor with the open end of the wheel away from the motor. If necessary, replace the sealer at the motor flange.*

The heater blower is located on the passenger side of the firewall

Heater Core

REMOVAL AND INSTALLATION

Without Air Conditioning

1. Disconnect the negative battery cable.
2. Drain the radiator.
3. Disconnect the heater hoses at the heater core tube connections. Use care when detaching the hoses as the core tube attachments can easily be damaged if too much force is used on them. If the hoses will not come off, cut the hose just forward of the core tube connection. Remove the remaining piece by splitting it lengthwise. When the hoses are removed, install plugs in the core tubes to prevent coolant spilling out when the core is removed.

NOTE: *The larger diameter hose goes to the water pump; the smaller diameter hose goes to the thermostat housing.*

4. Remove the screws around the perimeter of the heater core cover on the engine side of the dash panel.
5. Pull the heater core cover from its mounting in the dash panel.
6. Remove the core from the distributor assembly.
7. Reverse the removal procedure to install. Be sure that the core-to-case sealer is intact before replacing the core; use new sealer if necessary. When installation is complete, check for coolant leaks.

With Air Conditioning

1. Disconnect the negative battery cable.
2. Disconnect the heater hoses at the core with a drain pan under the car. Plug the hoses to prevent spillage.
3. Remove the A/C hose bracket.
4. Remove the heater core case cover and remove the core from the case.
5. Reverse to install.

RADIO

REMOVAL AND INSTALLATION

1. Disconnect the negative battery cable.
2. Remove the nut from the mounting stud on the bottom of the radio.
3. Remove all control knobs and/or spacers from the right and left radio control shafts.
NOTE: *The volume control knob and tuning control knob will fit on either shaft but are not interchangeable. The tone control knob and balance control knob are interchangeable.*
4. Remove the four screws from the center trim plate and pull the trim plate and the radio forward slightly.
5. Disconnect the antenna lead from the rear of the radio.
6. Disconnect the speaker and electrical connectors from the radio harness.
7. Disconnect the electrical connectors from the rear window defogger and cigarette lighter.
8. Use a deep well socket to remove the retaining nuts from both control shafts and remove the radio.
9. To install, reverse the removal procedure.

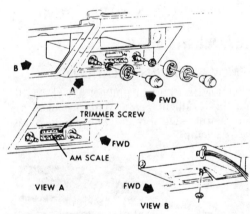

Radio mounting

WINDSHIELD WIPERS

Motor

REMOVAL AND INSTALLATION

1. Working inside the car, reach up under the instrument panel above the steering column and loosen, but do not remove, the transmission drive link-to-motor crank arm attaching nuts.
2. Disconnect the transmission drive link from the motor crank arm.

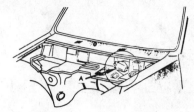
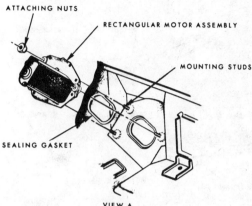

Wiper motor mounting

3. Raise the hood and disconnect the motor wiring.
4. Remove the three motor attaching bolts.
5. Remove the motor while guiding the crank arm through the hole.
6. To install, align the sealing gasket to the base of the motor and reverse the rest of the removal procedure. Tighten the motor attaching bolts to 30–45 in. lbs. Tighten the transmission drive link-to-motor crank arm attaching nuts to 25–35 in. lbs.
NOTE: *If the wiper motor-to-dash panel sealing gasket is damaged during removal, it should be replaced with a new gasket to prevent possible water leaks.*

Wiper Blade

REMOVAL AND INSTALLATION

1. To replace the wiper blade, lift up on the spring release tab on the wiper arm connector.
2. Work the blade assembly off.
3. Snap the new blade assembly into place.
NOTE: *To only replace the rubber insert, press down and away from the wiper blade to free it. Insert the rubber wiper. Bend the insert upward slightly to engage the retaining clips.*

INSTRUMENT CLUSTER

REMOVAL AND INSTALLATION

The instrument cluster must be removed to replace light bulbs, gauges, and printed circuit.

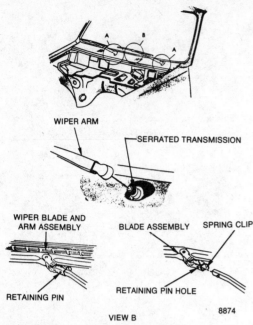

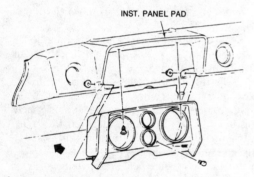

VIEW B 8874

Wiper blade removal and installation

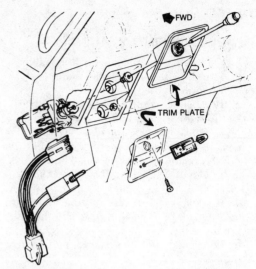

Headlight switch mounting

4. Remove the three screws and remove the headlight switch trim plate.

5. Use a large-bladed screwdriver to remove the light switch ferrule nut from the front of the instrument panel.

6. Disconnect the multi-contact connector from the bottom of the headlight switch. (A small screwdriver will aid removal).

7. Installation is the reverse of removal.

HEADLIGHTS

REMOVAL AND INSTALLATION

1. Remove the four phillips screws that retain the headlight bezel. With a hooked tool pull the retaining spring to one side to release the headlamp.

Instrument cluster mounting

1. Disconnect the negative battery cable.
2. Remove the clock stem knob.
3. Remove the four screws and remove the instrument cluster bezel and lens.
4. Remove the two nuts securing the instrument cluster to the instrument panel and pull the cluster slightly forward.
5. Disconnect the electrical connector and speedometer cable from the cluster and remove it.
6. Installation is the reverse of removal.

Headlight Switch
REMOVAL AND INSTALLATION

1. Disconnect the negative battery cable.
2. Pull the headlight switch control knob to the "On" position.
3. Reach up under the instrument panel and depress the switch shaft retainer button while pulling on the switch control shaft knob.

Arrows point out the headlight bezel retaining screw

These are the headlight aiming screws, don't touch them when removing the headlight

Unsnap the connector from the headlight

2. Rotate the right head lamp clockwise to release it from the aiming pins. Rotate the left headlamp counterclockwise to release it.

3. Pull out the headlight and detach the electrical connector.

4. Remove the retaining ring.

5. Install the new headlight in the reverse order of removal.

Front Parking Lights, Turn Signals and Side Marker Lights

REMOVAL AND INSTALLATION

The bulb socket for these lights is reached from under the front bumper or under the front wheel well.

1. Turn the bulb socket counterclockwise 90° and lift it out.

2. Pull the bulb out of the socket and replace it with a new bulb. Test the operation of the bulb.

3. Replace the bulb socket in the housing and turn it clockwise 90° to lock it in place.

Rear Parking Lights and Turn Signals

REMOVAL AND INSTALLATION

1. On the inside of the car, remove the block-out panel.

2. Remove the bulb from the socket and replace as necessary.

3. To install, reverse the procedure.

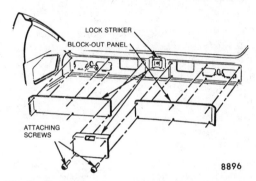

Block-out panel

Rear Side Marker Lamp

1. Remove the lens attaching screws and lens.

2. Remove the bulb from the socket and replace it with a new bulb.

3. Install the lens with the attaching screws.

FUSES AND FLASHERS

The fuse panel is located under the instrument panel on the left-hand side. The headlight circuit is protected by a circuit breaker in the light switch. An electrical overload will cause the

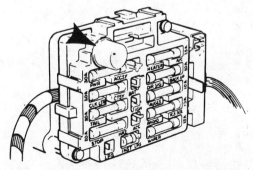

1976–80 fuse box—flasher is indicated by arrow

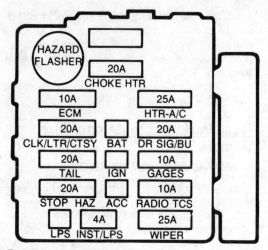

Fuse panel—1981 and later

Radio and Idle Stop Solenoid	10 Amp.
Directional Signal and Backup Lamps	20 Amp.
Tail, License, Sidemarker and Parking Lamps	20 Amp.
Clock, Lighter, Key Warning Buzzer, Courtesy, Dome and Glove Box Lamps	20 Amp.
Windshield Wiper	25 Amp.
Gauges and Warning Lamps	10 Amp.
Instrument Lamps	4 Amp.
Stop and Hazard Warning Lamps	20 Amp.
Heater and Air Conditioning	25 Amp.
Choke Heater (1980–84)	20 Amp.
Electronic Control Module (1981–84)	10 Amp.

lights to go on and off, or in some cases to stay off. If this condition develops, check the wiring circuits immediately.

An Air Conditioning high blower speed fuse, 30 amp, is located in an in-line fuse holder running from the junction block to the Air Conditioning relay.

Fusible Link

In addition to circuit breakers and fuses, the wiring harness incorporates fusible links to protect the wiring. Links are used rather than a fuse in wiring circuits that are not normally fused, such as the ignition circuit. Fusible links are color coded red in the charging and load circuits to match color coding of the circuit they protect. Each link is four gauge sizes smaller than the cable it is designed to protect and are marked on the insulation with wire gauge size because the heavy insulation makes the link appear a heavier gauge than it actually is.

Engine compartment wiring harnesses incorporate several fusible links. The same size wire with special hypalon insulation must be used when replacing a fusible link.

The links are:
1. A molded splice at the starter solenoid "Bat" terminal, 14 gauge red wire. Servicing requires splicing in a new link.
2. A 16 gauge red fusible link is located at junction block to protect all unfused wiring of 12 gauge or larger. The link is terminated at the bulkhead connector.
3. The generator warning light and field circuitry (16 gauge wire) is protected by a fusible link (20 gauge red wire) used in the "battery feed to voltage regulator #3 terminal" wire. The link is installed as a molded splice in the circuit at the junction block. Service by splicing in a new 20 gauge wire.

4. The ammeter circuit is protected by two red 20 gauge wire fusible links installed as molded splices in the circuit at the junction block and battery to starter circuit. Service by splicing in new gauge wires.

REPLACEMENT

1. Disconnect the battery ground cable.
2. Disconnect the fusible link from the junction block or starter solenoid.
3. Cut the harness directly behind the connector to remove the damaged fusible link.
4. Strip the harness wire approximately ½ in.
5. Connect the new fusible link to the harness wire using a crimp on connector. Soder the connection using rosin core solder.
6. Tape all exposed wires with plastic electrical tape.
7. Connect the fusible link to the junction block or starter solenoid and reconnect the battery ground cable.

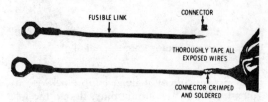

Fusible link replacement

WIRING DIAGRAMS

Wiring diagrams have been left out of this book. As cars have become more complex, and available with longer and longer option lists, wiring diagrams have grown in size and complexity. It has become virtually impossible to provide a readable reproduction in a reasonable number of pages. Information on ordering wiring diagrams from the vehicle manufacturer can be found in the owners manual.

CLUTCH

Chevette and Pontiac 1000 manual transmission models use a cable-operated, diaphragm spring-type clutch. The clutch cable is attached to the clutch pedal at its upper end and is threaded at its lower end where it attaches to the clutch fork. The clutch release fork pivots on a ball stud located opposite the clutch cable attaching point. The pressure plate, clutch disc, and throwout bearing are of conventional design.

When the clutch pedal is depressed, the clutch release fork pivots on the ball stud and pushes the throwout bearing forward. The throwout bearing presses against the inner ends of the pressure plate diaphragm spring fingers to release pressure on the clutch disc, disengaging the clutch. The return spring preloads the clutch release mechanism to remove any looseness. Clutch pedal free-play will increase with release mechanism wear and will decrease with clutch disc wear.

Clutch Disc and Pressure Plate
REMOVAL AND INSTALLATION
Gasoline Engine

1. Raise the car.
2. Remove the transmission.
3. Remove the throwout bearing from the clutch fork by sliding the fork off the ball stud against spring tension. If the ball stud is to be replaced, remove the locknut and stud from the bellhousing.
4. If the balance marks on the pressure plate and the flywheel are not easily seen, remark them with paint or centerpunch.
5. Alternately loosen the pressure plate-to-flywheel attaching bolts one turn at a time until spring tension is released.
6. Support the pressure plate and cover assembly, then remove the bolts and the clutch assembly.

CAUTION: *Do not disassemble the clutch cover and pressure plate for repair. If defective, replace the assembly.*

7. Align the balance marks on the clutch assembly and the flywheel. Place the clutch disc on the pressure plate with the long end of the splined hub facing forward and the damper springs inside the pressure plate. Insert a used or dummy shaft through the cover and clutch disc.
8. Position the assembly against the flywheel and insert the dummy shaft into the pilot bearing in the crankshaft.
9. Align the balance marks and install the pressure plate-to-flywheel bolts finger-tight.

CAUTION: *Tighten all bolts evenly and gradually until tight to avoid possible clutch distortion. Torque the bolts to 18 ft. lbs. and remove the dummy shaft.*

10. Pack the groove on the inside of the throwout bearing with graphite grease. Coat the fork groove and ball stud depression with the lubricant.
11. Install the throwout bearing and release fork assembly in the bellhousing with the fork spring hooked under the ball stud and the fork spring fingers inside the bearing groove.
12. Position the transmission and clutch housing and install the clutch housing attaching bolts and lockwashers. Torque the bolts to 25 ft. lbs. (33 Nm).
13. Complete the transmission installation.

CAUTION: *Check position of the engine in the front mounts and realign as necessary.*

NOTE: *A special gauge (part no. J-28449 or its equivalent) is necessary to adjust the ball position.*

14. Perform "Initial Ball Stud Adjustment" and "Clutch Cable Attachment and Adjustment." Adjust clutch pedal free-play if necessary.
15. Lower the car and check operation of the clutch and transmission.

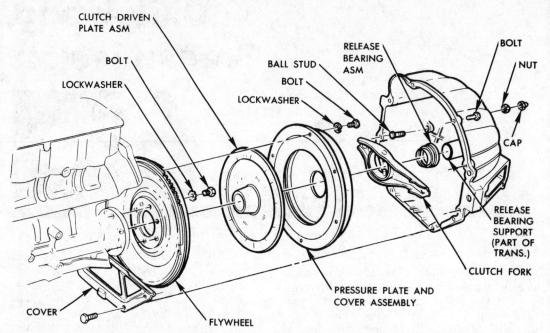

Four speed transmission clutch assembly—typical

Diesel Engine

1. Remove the transmission as described later in this chapter.

2. Mark the clutch assembly to flywheel so that it can be installed in the original position.

3. Install aligning Tool J-24547 or an appropriate dummy shaft through the pressure plate and disc.

4. Remove the release bearing to fork retaining springs and remove the release bearing with the support.

5. Remove the shift fork from the transmission ball stud.

6. Installation is the reverse of removal. Install the clutch assembly in the original posi-

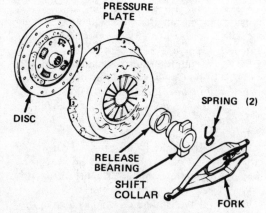

Clutch assembly—diesel engine

tion while aligning with Tool J-24547 or equivalent. Tighten the bolts evenly to 14 ft. lbs.

INITIAL BALL STUD ADJUSTMENT
4-speed

1. Install throwout bearing assembly, release fork, and ball stud to the transmission.

2. Install and secure the transmission to the engine.

3. Cycle the clutch once.

4. Place the special gauge (Part No. J-28449) so that the flat end is against the front face of the clutch housing and the hooked end is located at the bottom depression in the clutch fork.

5. Turn the ball stud inward by hand until the throwout bearing makes contact with the clutch spring.

6. Install the locknut and tighten it to 25 ft. lbs. (33 Nm), being careful not to change the ball stud adjustment.

7. Remove the gauge by pulling outward at the housing end.

CLUTCH CABLE ATTACHMENT AND ADJUSTMENT
1976–77

These adjustments are made before the return spring is installed and with the clutch cable attached to the clutch pedal at its upper end.

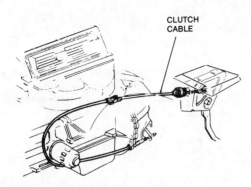

Clutch cable positioning

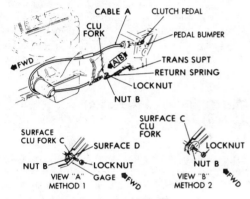

Clutch cable adjustment 1976–77

1. Place the clutch cable through the hole in the clutch fork.

2. Pull the clutch cable until the clutch pedal is firmly against the pedal bumper and hold it in position.

3. Push the release fork forward until the throwout bearing contacts the clutch spring fingers and hold it in position.

4. Thread the nut or the cable until it bottoms out against the spherical surface of the release fork.

5. Depress the clutch pedal to the floor a minimum of four times to establish cable position at clearance points.

6. To obtain the correct clutch pedal lash, use either Step 7 or Step 8.

7. See View "A" of the accompanying illustration.

    a. Place a 0.171 in. (4.35 mm) thick gauge or shim stock against surface "D" of nut "B."

    b. Thread the locknut on the cable "A" until the locknut contacts the gauge.

The clutch fork locknut is a 10 mm nut

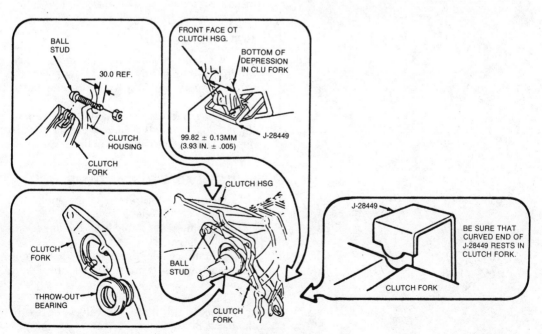

Ball stud adjustment

c. Remove the gauge and back off nut "B" until it contacts the locknut.

d. Tighten the locknut to 4 ft. lbs.

8. See View "B" of the accompanying illustration.

a. Turn nut "B" 4.35 turns counterclockwise.

b. Thread the locknut on the cable "A" until the locknut contacts nut "B."

c. Tighten the locknut to 4 ft. lbs.

9. Attach the return spring.

10. This procedure should yield 0.812 ± 0.25 in. (20.6 ± 6 mm) lash at the clutch pedal.

1978 and Later

The following adjustments are to be made with the cable and loose parts assembled to the front of the dash and the cable attached to the clutch pedal.

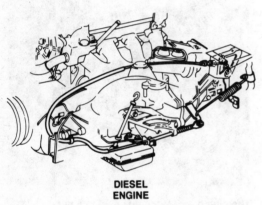

DIESEL ENGINE

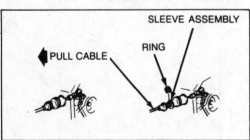

PULL CABLE   RING   SLEEVE ASSEMBLY

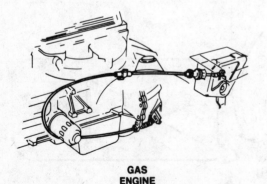

GAS ENGINE

Clutch cable adjustment—1978 and later

1. Place the cable through the hole in the clutch fork and properly seat it.

2. Install the return spring.

3. From the engine compartment, pull the cable away from the dash until the clutch pedal is firmly seated against the pedal bumper.

4. Holding the pedal in position, install the circlip in the first fully visible groove in the cable from the sleeve. Release the cable.

5. Depress the clutch cable at least four times to make sure that all the elements are properly seated.

6. This procedure should produce a lash of $0.83 \pm .25$ in. (21 ± 6mm) at the clutch pedal.

NOTE: *If the above procedure produces excessive pedal lash, remove the circlip from the cable and move it into the dash by one ring. If the lash is unsufficient remove the circlip and move it away from the dash one ring.*

CLUTCH PEDAL FREE-PLAY ADJUSTMENT

1976–77

Adjustment for normal wear is made by turning the release fork ball stud counterclockwise to give 0.812 ± 0.25 in. (20.6 ± 6mm) lash at the clutch pedal.

1. Loosen the locknut on the ball stud end located to the right of the transmission on the clutch housing.

2. Adjust the ball stud to obtain the correct free-play (lash) as mentioned previously.

3. Tighten the locknut to 25 ft. lbs., being careful not to change the adjustment.

4. Check for proper clutch operation.

1978 and Later

1. If there is insufficient play in the pedal, remove the circlip from the cable and allow the cable to move into the dash by one notch. Reinstall the circlip.

2. If there is excessive pedal lash, remove the circlip and pull the cable out of the dash by one notch and reinstall the circlip ring.

CLUTCH CABLE REPLACEMENT

1. Disconnect the return spring and clutch cable at the clutch release fork.

2. Disconnect the cable from the upper end of the clutch pedal.

3. Pull the cable through the body reinforcement and disconnect it from the fender retainer.

4. Push the new cable through the body reinforcement and attach the cable end to the clutch pedal.

5. Route the cable down to the clutch re-

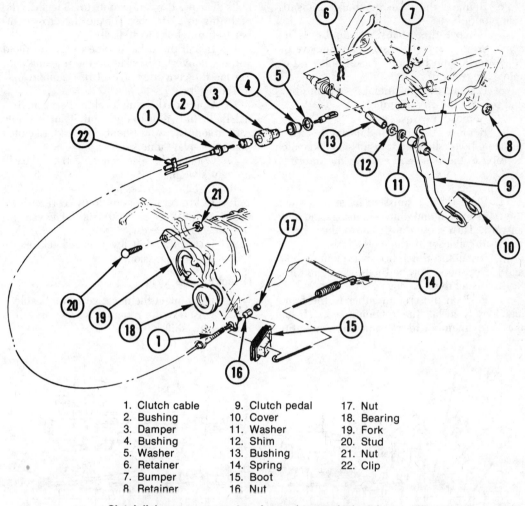

1. Clutch cable	9. Clutch pedal	17. Nut
2. Bushing	10. Cover	18. Bearing
3. Damper	11. Washer	19. Fork
4. Bushing	12. Shim	20. Stud
5. Washer	13. Bushing	21. Nut
6. Retainer	14. Spring	22. Clip
7. Bumper	15. Boot	
8. Retainer	16. Nut	

Clutch linkage components—4-speed transmission shown

lease fork. Install the cable end in the release fork and install the nuts.

6. Perform "Initial Ball Stud Adjustment" and "Clutch Cable Attachment and Adjustment." Also, adjust clutch pedal free-play if necessary.

MANUAL TRANSMISSION

The Chevette and Pontiac 1000 use either a four or five speed fully synchronized transmission. Gear shifting is accomplished by an internal shifter shaft. No adjustment of the mechanism is possible.

REMOVAL AND INSTALLATION

Gasoline Engine

1. Remove the shift lever as outlined in this chapter.
2. Raise the car on a hoise and drain the lubricant from the transmission.

3. Remove the driveshaft as described in the next chapter.
4. Disconnect the speedometer cable and back-up light switch.
5. Disconnect the return spring and clutch cable at the clutch release fork.

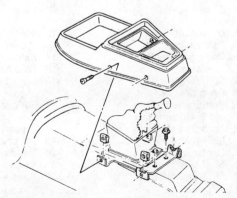

Console removal

6. Remove the crossmember-to-transmission mount bolts.

7. Remove the exhaust manifold nuts and converter-to-tailpipe bolts and nuts. Remove the converter-to-transmission bracket bolts and remove the converter.

8. Remove the crossmember-to-frame bolts and remove the crossmember.

9. Remove the dust cover.

10. Remove the clutch housing-to-engine retaining bolts, slide the transmission and clutch housing to the rear, and remove the transmission.

To install:

11. Place the transmission in gear, position the transmission and clutch housing, and slide forward. Turn the output shaft to align the input shaft splines with the clutch hub.

12. Install the clutch housing retaining bolts and lockwashers. Torque the bolts to 25 ft. lbs.

13. Install the dust cover.

14. Position the crossmember to the frame and loosely install the retaining bolts. Install the crossmember-to-transmission mounting bolts. Torque the center nuts to 33 ft. lbs.; the end nuts to 21 ft. lbs. Torque the crossmember-to-frame bolts to 40 ft. lbs.

15. Install the exhaust pipe to the manifold and the converter bracket on the transmission. Torque the converter bracket rear support nuts to 150 in. lbs.

16. Connect the clutch cable. Perform "Initial Ball Stud Adjustment" and "Clutch Cable Attachment and Adjustment." Also, adjust clutch pedal free-play, if necessary.

17. Connect the speedometer cable and back-up light switch.

18. Install the driveshaft.

19. Fill the transmission to the correct level with SAE 80W or SAE 80W-90 GL-5 gear lubricant. Lower the car.

20. Install the shift lever and check operation of the transmission.

Diesel Engine

1. Disconnect the negative battery cable.

2. Unscrew the retaining screws and then remove the shift lever console.

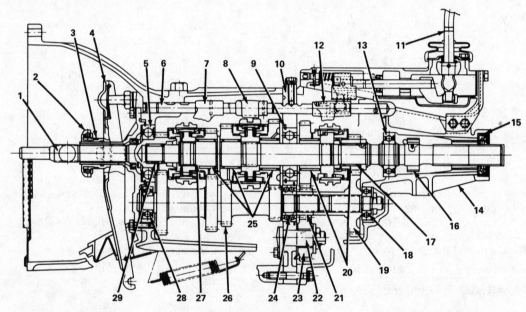

1. Drive gear	13. Mainshaft rear bearing	23. Reverse idler gear
2. Release bearing	14. Extension housing	24. Counter gear bearing
3. Drive gear bearing retainer	15. Rear seal	25. Needle bearing
4. Shift fork	16. Speedometer drive gear	26. Counter gear
5. Drive gear bearing	17. 5th gear assy	27. Mainshaft
6. Shifter shaft	18. Counter gear rear bearing	28. Counter gear front bearing
7. 3rd & 4th shift fork	19. 5th counter gear	29. Needle gearing
8. 1st & 2nd shift fork	20. Needle bearing	
9. Mainshaft bearing	21. Reverse counter gear	
10. Center support	22. Reverse idler shaft	
11. Shift lever		
12. 5th & reverse shift fork		

Cross section of the 5-speed manual transmission (diesel)

1. Drive gear
2. Bearing retainer
3. Pilot bearings
4. Case
5. Bellhousing
6. 3-4 Synchronizer assembly
7. 3-4 Shifter fork
8. Third speed gear
9. Detent bushing
10. Second speed gear
11. 1-2 Shifter fork
12. 1-2 Synchronizer assembly
13. First speed gear
14. Shifter shaft
15. Extension
16. Speedometer drive gear and clip
17. Mainshaft
18. Rear oil seal
19. Retainer oil seal
20. Snap ring—
     bearing to gear
21. Drive gear bearing
22. Snap ring—
     bearing to case
23. Countergear roller bearings
24. Countergear assembly
25. Counter reverse gear
26. Reverse idler gear
27. Reverse gear
28. Snap ring—
     bearing to extension
29. Rear bearing

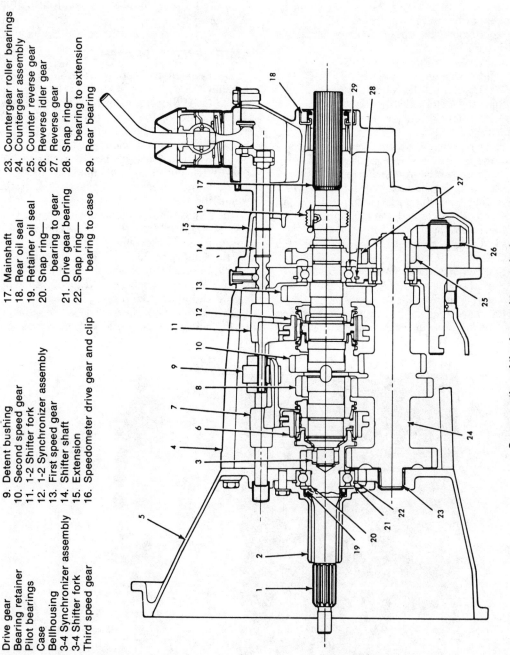

Cross section of the 4-speed transmission

3. Remove the mounting screws and remove the shift lever assembly.

4. Unscrew and remove the upper starter mounting bolts.

5. Raise the front of the car and drain the lubricant from the transmission.

6. Remove the drive shaft as detailed in Chapter 7.

7. Disconnect the speeometer and the back-up light switch wires.

8. Disconnect the return spring and clutch cable at the clutch release fork.

9. Remove the starter lower bolt and support the starter.

10. Unscrew the retaining bolts and disconnect the exhaust pipe from the manifold.

11. Remove the flywheel inspection cover.

12. Unscrew the rear transmission support mounting bolt. Support the transmission underneath the case and then remove the rear support from the frame.

13. Lower the transmission approximately four (4) in.

14. Remove the transmission housing-to-engine block bolts. Pull the transmission straight back and away from the engine.

15. Installation of the remaining components is in the reverse order of removal. Please note the following:

a. Be sure to lubricate the drive gear shaft with a light coat of grease before installing the transmission.

b. After installation, fill the transmission to the level of the filler hole with 5W-30SF engine oil.

SHIFT LEVER REPLACEMENT

1. Remove the floor console and/or boot retainer.

2. Raise the shift lever boot to gain access to the locknut on the lever. Loosen the locknut and unscrew the upper portion of the shift lever with the knob attached.

3. Remove the foam insulator to gain access to the control assembly bolts.

4. Remove the three bolts on the extension and remove the control assembly.

5. Use caution when removing the clip on the control housing as the internal components are under spring pressure.

6. Remove the locknut, boot retainer, and seat from the threaded end of the shift lever.

7. Remove the spring and guide from the forked end of the shift lever.

8. To assemble the shift lever, install the spring and guide on the forked end of the lever.

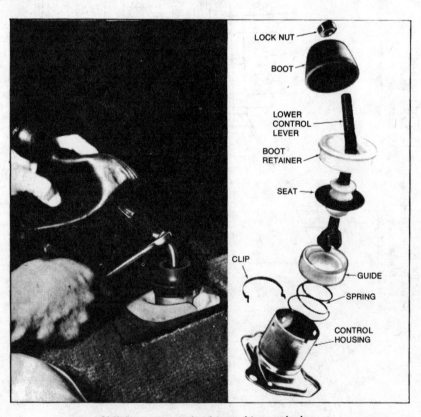

Shift lever removal—4-speed transmission

9. Install the seat, boot retainer, and the locknut over the threaded end of the lever.

10. Assemble the components in the control housing and install the clip on the control housing.

11. Install the control assembly on the extension making sure that the fork at the lower end of the lever engages the shifter shaft lever arm pin. Torque the shift lever retaining bolts to 35 in. lbs.

12. Install the foam insulator, boot, retainer, and/or floor console.

13. Slide the boot below the threaded portion of the shift lever and install the upper shift lever. Tighten the locknut.

AUTOMATIC TRANSMISSION

Chevettes and Pontiac 1000s equipped with automatic transmission use either the Turbo Hydra-Matic 200 or 180 automatic transmission. Both units are fully automatic and provide three forward speeds and reverse.

NEUTRAL SAFETY SWITCH REPLACEMENT

1. Remove the floor console cover.

2. Disconnect the electrical connectors on the back-up, seat belt warning, and neutral starter contacts on the switch.

3. Place the shift lever in Neutral.

4. Remove the two switch attaching screws and remove the switch.

5. Make sure that the shift lever is in the

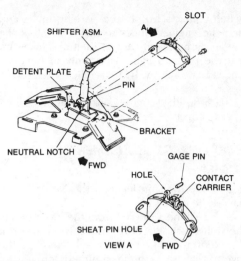

Neutral switch replacement

Neutral position before installing the switch assembly.

6. Place the neutral start switch assembly in position on the shift lever making sure that the pin on the lever is in the slot of the switch.

NOTE: *When installing the same switch, align the contact support slot with the service adjustment hole in the switch and insert a 3/32 in. drill bit to hold the switch in Neutral. Remove the drill bit after the switch is fastened to the shift lever mounting bracket.*

7. Install the two switch attaching screws.

8. Move the shift lever out of Neutral to shear the plastic pin.

9. Connect the electrical connectors to the

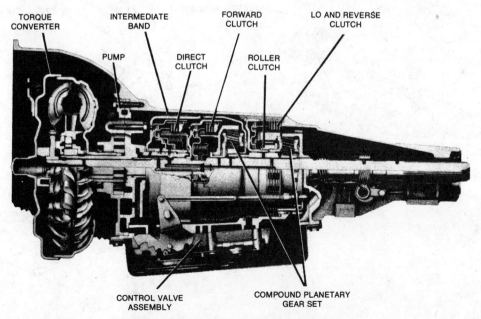

Cutaway of the Turbo Hydra-Matic transmission

switch contacts. Apply the parking brake and start the engine. Check to make sure that the engine starts only in Park or Neutral. Make sure that the back-up lights work only in Reverse. Check that the seat belt warning system operates.

10. Stop the engine and install the floor console cover.

SHIFT LINKAGE ADJUSTMENT

1976–81

1. Place the shift lever in the Neutral position of the detent plate.

2. Disconnect the rod from the lower end of the shift lever. Place the transmission lever in the Neutral position. Do this by moving the lever clockwise to the maximum detent (Park), then moving the lever counterclockwise two (2) detent positions (Neutral).

3. Adjust the rod until the hole in the rod aligns with the pin on the lower end of the shift lever. Install the rod on the pin and secure it by adding the washer and spring clip.

NOTE: *Any inaccuracies in the adjustment may result in a premature failure of the transmission due to operation without the controls in full detent. Such operation results in a loss of fluid pressure and in turn, only a partial engagement of the affected clutches. A partial engagement of the clutches with sufficient pressure to cause apparently normal operation of the vehicle will result in*

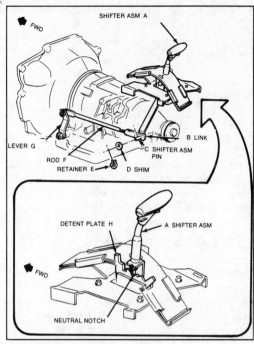

Shift linkage adjustment—1976–81

the failure of clutches or various other internal parts after only a few miles of operation.

1982 and Later

1. Position the Shifter Assembly (A) in the "NEUTRAL" notch of Detent Plate (H).

2. With Link (B) loosely assembled to Rod

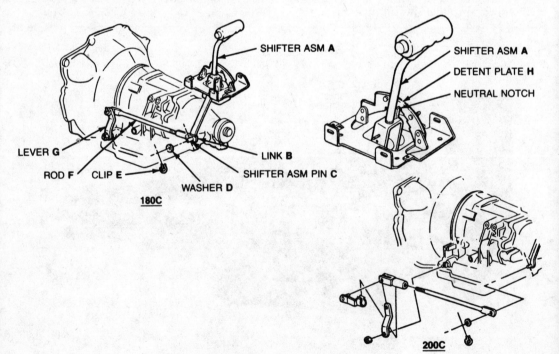

Shift linkage adjustment—1982 and later

(F) and Rod (F) attached to Lever (G), put Lever (G) into the "NEUTRAL" position. Obtain "NEUTRAL" position by moving Lever (G) clockwise to maximum detent position ("PARK"), then counter-clockwise two detents to "NEUTRAL." Maintaining Lever (G) in the "NEUTRAL" position, adjust Link (B) until the hole in Link (B) aligns with the Shifter Asm Pin (C); install Link (B) onto the Pin (C).

3. Add the washer (D) and insert the clip (E).

DOWNSHIFT CABLE ADJUSTMENT

Gasoline Engine 1976–81

The transmission has a cable between the carburetor linkage and the transmission which provides transmission downshifting.

1. Remove the air cleaner.
2. Disengage the snap lock by pushing up on the bottom. Release the lock and cable.
3. Disconnect the snap lock assembly from the bracket by compressing the locking tabs.
4. Disconnect the cable from the carburetor.
5. Remove the clamp around the oil filler tube. Remove the screw and the washer that secure the cable to the transmission and disconnect the cable.
6. Install a new seal on the cable and lubricate it with transmission fluid.
7. Connect the transmission end of the cable and attach it to the transmission with the screw and washer.
8. Feed the cable in front of the oil filler tube and attach it to the tube with the clamp.

9. Feed the cable through the mounting bracket and snap lock assembly and attach it to the carburetor lever.
10. With the cable attached to both the transmission and the carburetor lever, move the carburetor lever to the wide open throttle position. Push the snap lock flush and return carburetor lever to normal position.
11. Install the air cleaner.

Gasoline Engine—1982 and Later

1. After installation of the cable to the transmission, engine bracket, and throttle lever, check to assure that the cable slider is in the zero or fully re-adjusted position. (if not refer to the readjustment procedure which follows.)
2. Rotate the throttle lever to the "Full Travel Stop" position.

RE-ADJUSTMENT

NOTE: In case readjustment is necessary because of inadvertent adjustment before or during assembly, or for repair, perform the following:

1. Depress and hold the metal re-adjust tab.
2. Move the slider back through the fitting in direction away from the throttle lever until the slider stops against the fitting.
3. Release the metal re-adjust tab.
4. Repeat Step 2 of the preceding adjustment procedure.

Diesel Engine

1. After installation into the transmission, install the cable fitting into the engine bracket.
NOTE: The slider must not ratchet through

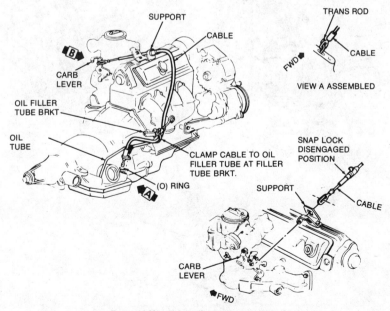

Downshift cable adjustment—1976–81

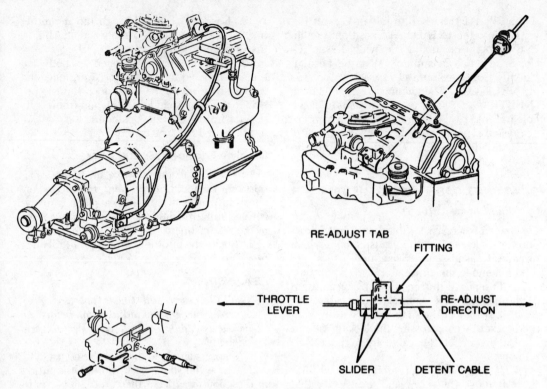

RE-ADJUST TAB

FITTING

THROTTLE
LEVER

RE-ADJUST
DIRECTION

SLIDER

DETENT CABLE

Downshift cable adjustment—1982 and later gasoline engine

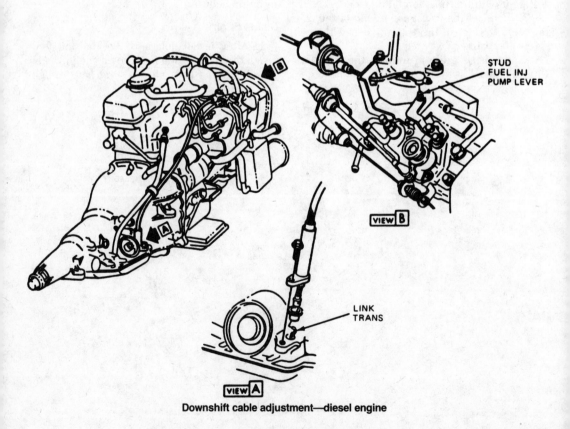

STUD
FUEL INJ
PUMP LEVER

VIEW B

LINK
TRANS

VIEW A

Downshift cable adjustment—diesel engine

the fitting before or during assembly into the bracket. If this condition exist use the readjustment procedure which follows.

2. Install the cable terminal to the fuel injection pump lever.

3. Open the injection pump lever to the "Full Throttle Stop" position to automatically adjust the slider on the cable to the correct setting.

NOTE: The lock tab must not be depressed during this operation.

4. Release the injection pump lever.

RE-ADJUSTMENT

NOTE: In case re-adjustment is necessary because of inadvertent adjustment during assembly, or for repair, perform the following:

1. Depress and hold the metal lock tab.

2. Move the slider back through the fitting in the direction away from the throttle lever until the slider stops against the fitting.

3. Release the metal lock tab.

4. Repeat steps 2, 3 and 4 of the preceding adjustment procedure.

PAN REMOVAL AND INSTALLATION, FLUID AND FILTER CHANGE

Transmission fluid should be drained while at normal operating temperature.

CAUTION: *Transmission fluid temperature can exceed 350°F.*

1. Raise the car and support the transmission with a suitable jack at the transmission vibration damper.

2. Place a receptacle of at least three quarts capacity under the transmission oil pan. Remove the oil pan attaching bolts from the front and side of the pan.

3. Loosen the rear pan attaching bolts approximately four turns.

4. Drain the fluid by carefully prying the oil pan loose with a screwdriver.

5. After the fluid has drained, remove the reamining oil pan attaching bolts. Remove the oil pan and gasket. Throw the old gasket away.

6. Drain the remaining fluid from the pan. Thoroughly clean the pan with solvent and dry with compressed air.

7. Remove the two screen-to-valve body bolts and remove the screen and gasket. Discard the gasket.

8. Thoroughly clean the screen in solvent and dry with compressed air.

9. Install the new gasket on the screen and install the bolts. On 1976–77 models, torque the bolts to 6–10 ft. lbs. On 1978–80 models, torque the bolts to 13–15 ft. lbs.

10. Install a new gasket on the oil pan and install the oil pan. Tighten the bolts to 10–13 ft. lbs. on 1976–77 models, 7–10 ft. lbs. on 1978 models and 12 ft. lbs. on 1979 and later.

11. Lower the car and add about 6 pints of Dexron® II automatic transmission fluid through the filler tube. If the transmission has been overhauled add about 4.9 quarts of fluid.

12. With the transmission in Park, apply the parking brake, start the engine and let it idle (not fast idle). Do not race the engine.

13. Move the gear selector lever slowly through all positions, return the lever to Park, and check the transmission fluid level.

14. Add fluid as necessary to raise the level between the dimples on the dipstick. Be careful not to overfill the transmission; approximately one pint of fluid will raise the level to the correct amount.

Drive Train

7

DRIVELINE

Driveshaft and U-joints

A one-piece driveshaft is mounted to the companion flange with a conventional universal joint at the rear. The driveshaft is connected to the transmission output shaft with a splined slip yoke. The slip yoke contains a thrust spring which seats against the end of the transmission output shaft. The thrust spring MUST be installed for proper operation.

The universal joints are of the long-life design and do not require periodic inspection or lubrication. When the joints are disassembled, repack the bearings and lubricate the reservoirs at the end of the trunnions with chassis grease and replace the dust seals.

DRIVESHAFT REMOVAL AND INSTALLATION

1. Raise the car. Scribe matchmarks on the driveshaft and the companion flange and disconnect the rear universal joint by removing the trunnion bearing straps.
2. Move the driveshaft to the rear under the axle to remove the slip yoke from the transmission. Watch for oil leakage from the transmission output shaft housing.
3. Install the driveshaft in the reverse order

of removal. Tighten the trunnion strap bolts to 16 ft. lbs.

UNIVERSAL JOINT REMOVAL AND INSTALLATION

1. Remove the driveshaft.
2. For reassembly purposes, scribe a line on the transmission end of the driveshaft and on the slip yoke. Remove the snap-rings from the trunnion yoke.
3. Support the trunnion yoke on a piece of 1¼ in. ID pipe on an arbor press or bench vise. Use a suitable socket or rod to press on the trunnion until the bearing cup is almost out. Grasp the cup in the vise and work the cup out of the yoke. Press the trunnion in the opposite direction to remove the other cup.
4. Clean and inspect the dust seals, bearing rollers, and trunnions. Lubricate the bearings. Make sure that the lubricant reservoir at the end of each trunnion is completely filled with lubricant. A squeeze bottle is recommended to fill the reservoirs from the bottom to prevent air pockets.
5. When installing a U-joint rebuilding kit, place the dust seals on the trunnions with the

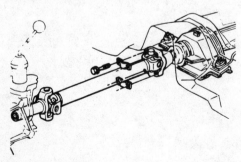

Driveshaft mounting

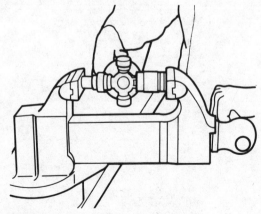

Removing the U-joint from the driveshaft

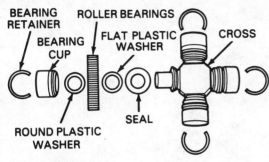

BEARING RETAINER

ROLLER BEARINGS

BEARING CUP

FLAT PLASTIC WASHER

CROSS

ROUND PLASTIC WASHER

SEAL

U-joint rebuilding kit

cavities of the seals toward the end of the trunnions. Use caution when pressing the seals onto the trunnions to prevent seal distortion and to assure proper seal seating.

NOTE: *Install the transmission yoke on the front of the driveshaft as marked in Step 2. If this is not done, driveline vibration may result.*

6. To assemble, position the trunnion into the yoke. Partially install one bearing cup into the yoke and start the trunnion into the bearing cup. Partially install the other cup, align the trunnion into the cup, and press the cups into the yoke.

7. Install the snap-rings.

8. Install the driveshaft.

REAR AXLE

Axle Shaft, Bearing, and Seal
REMOVAL AND INSTALLATION

1. Raise the car. Remove the wheel and tire assembly and the brake drum.

2. Clean the area around the differential carrier cover.

3. Remove the differential carrier cover to drain the rear axle lubricant.

4. Use a metric allen wrench to unscrew the differential pinion shaft lockscrew and remove the differential pinion shaft. It may be necessary to shorten the allen wrench to do this.

5. Push the flanged end of the axle shaft toward the center of the car and remove the "C" lock from the bottom end of the shaft.

6. Remove the axle shaft from the housing making sure not to damage the oil seal.

7. If replacing the seal only, remove the oil seal by using the button end of the axle shaft. Insert the button end of the shaft behind the steel case of the oil seal and carefully pry the seal out of the bore.

8. To remove bearings, insert a bearing and seal remover into the bore so that the tool head grasps behind the bearing. Slide the washer against the seal or bearing and turn the nut against the washer. Attach a slide hammer and remove the bearing.

9. Lubricate a new bearing with hypoid lubricant and install it into the housing with a bearing installer tool. Make sure that the tool contacts the end of the axle tube to make sure that the bearing is at the proper depth.

10. Lubricate the cavity between the seal lips with a high melting point wheel bearing grease. Place a new oil seal on the seal installation tool and position the seal in the axle housing bore. Tap the seal into the bore flush with the end of the housing.

11. To install the axle shaft, slide the axle shaft into place making sure that the splines on the end of the shaft do not damage the oil seal

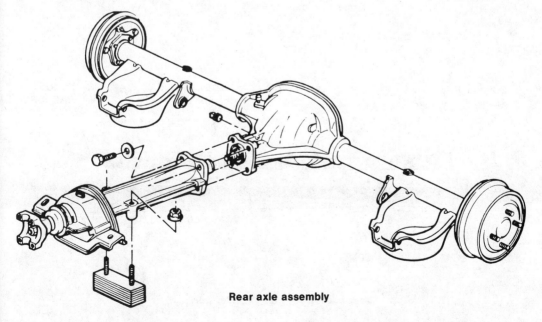

Rear axle assembly

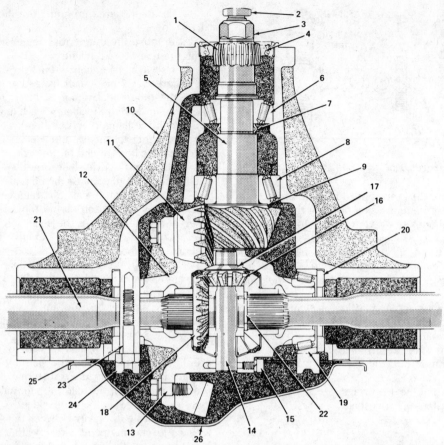

1. Drive coupling	7. Preload spacer	14. Pinion shaft	21. Axle shaft
2. Thrust washer	8. Pinion rear bearing	15. Lock screw	22. Axle shaft 'C' lock
3. Lock nut	9. Pinion depth shim	16. Pinion gear	23. Bearing cap bolt
4. Oil seal	10. Differential carrier	17. Thrust washer	24. Bearing cap
5. Drive pinion	11. Ring gear	18. Side gear	25. Differential cover gasket
6. Pinion front bearing	12. Differential case	19. Differential bearing	26. Differential cover
	13. Ring gear bolt	20. Shim/spacer	

Cross-section of the differential

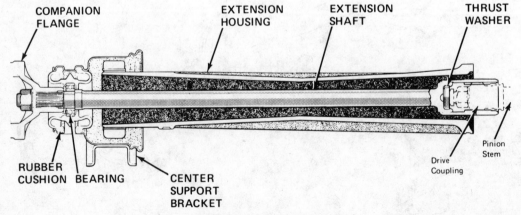

Cross-section of rear axle extension

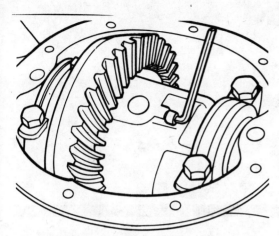

Remove the lock screw with a metric allen wrench. It may be necessary to shorten the wrench

and that they engage the splines of the differential side gear. Install the "C" lock on the button end of the axle shaft and push the shaft outward so that the shaft lock seats in the counterbore of the differential side gear.

12. Position the differential pinion shaft through the case and pinions, aligning the hole in the shaft with the lockscrew hole. Install the lockscrew.

13. Clean the gasket mounting surfaces on the differential carrier and the carrier cover. Install the carrier cover using a new gasket and tighten the cover bolts in a crosswise pattern to 22 ft. lbs.

14. Fill the rear axle with lubricant to the bottom of the filler hole.

15. Install the brake drum and the wheel and tire assembly.

16. Lower the car.

Suspension and Steering

8

FRONT SUSPENSION

The Chevette and Pontiac 1000 front suspension is of conventional long and short control arm design with coil springs. The control arms attach with bolts and bushings at the inner pivot points and to the steering knuckle/front wheel spindle assembly at the outer pivot points. Lower ball joints are the wear indicator type. A front stabilizer bar is used.

Shock Absorber

REMOVAL AND INSTALLATION

1. Hold the shock absorber upper stem and remove the nut, upper retainer, and rubber grommet.
2. Raise the car.
3. Remove the bolt from the lower end of the shock absorber and remove the shock absorber.

To install:

4. With the lower retainer and rubber grommet in position, extend the shock absorber stem and install the stem through the wheelhouse opening.

5. Install and torque the lower bolt to 35–50 ft. lbs.
6. Lower the car.
7. Install the upper rubber grommet, retainer, and nut to the shock absorber stem.
8. Hold the shock absorber upper stem and torque the nut to 60–120 in. lbs.

NOTE: *The required torque is produced by running the nut to the unthreaded part of the stud.*

Lower Ball Joint

REMOVAL AND INSTALLATION

1. Raise the car.
2. Remove the tire and wheel.
3. Support the lower control arm with a hydraulic floor jack.
4. Loosen, but do not remove the lower ball stud nut.
5. Install a ball joint removal tool with the cup end over the upper ball stud nut.
6. Turn the threaded end of the ball joint removal tool until the ball stud is free of the steering knuckle.

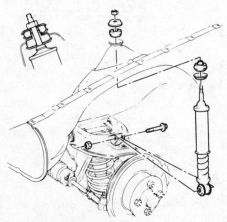

Front shock absorber mounting

The upper nut is 14 mm. Hold the shock absorber stem (arrow) while loosening the nut

The lower bolt and nut will require two 17 mm wrenches

7. Remove the ball joint removal tool and remove the nut from the ball stud.

8. Remove the ball joint.

NOTE: *Inspect the tapered hole in the steering knuckle. Clean the area. If any out-of-roundness, deformation, or damage is found, the steering knuckle MUST be replaced.*

9. To install the lower ball joint, mate the ball stud through the lower control arm and into the steering knuckle.

NOTE: *The ball joint studs use a special nut which must be discarded whenever loosened and removed. On assembly, use a standard nut to draw the ball joint into position on the knuckle, then remove the standard nut and install a new special nut for final installation.*

10. Install and torque the ball stud nut to 41–54 ft. lbs.

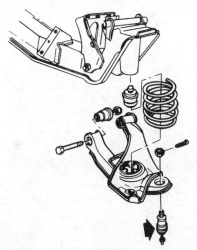

Exploded view of control arm assembly. The arrow points out the ball joints

11. Install the tire and wheel.

12. Lower the car.

Lower Control Arm and Coil Spring

REMOVAL AND INSTALLATION

1. Raise the car.

2. Remove the wheel and tire.

3. Disconnect the stabilizer bar from the lower control arm and disconnect the tie-rod from the steering knuckle.

4. Support the lower control arm with a jack.

5. Remove the nut from the lower ball joint, then use a ball joint removal tool to press out the lower ball joint.

6. Swing the knuckle and hub aside and attach them securely with wire.

7. Loosen the lower control arm pivot bolts.

8. As a safety precaution, install a chain through the coil spring.

9. Slowly lower the jack.

10. When the spring is extended as far as possible, use a pry bar to carefully lift the spring over the lower control arm seat. Remove the spring.

11. Remove the pivot bolts and remove the lower control arm.

To install:

12. Install the lower control arm and pivot bolts to the underbody brackets. Torque the lower control arm pivot bolts to 40 ft. lbs.

13. Position the spring correctly and install it in the upper pocket. Use tape to hold the insulatator onto the spring.

14. Install the lower end of the spring onto the lower control arm. An assistant may be necessary to compress the spring far enough to slide it over the raised area of the lower control arm seat.

15. Use a jack to raise the lower control arm and compress the coil spring.

NOTE: *The ball joint studs use a special nut which must be discarded whenever loosened and removed. On assembly, use a standard nut to draw the ball joint into position on the knuckle, then remove the standard nut and install a new special nut for final installation.*

16. Install the ball joint through the lower control arm and into the steering knuckle. Install the nut on the ball stud nut and torque to 41–54 ft. lbs.

17. Connect the stabilizer bar to the lower control arm and torque its attaching bolt to 15 ft. lbs. Connect the tie-rod to the steering knuckle. Install the wheel and tire.

18. Lower the car.

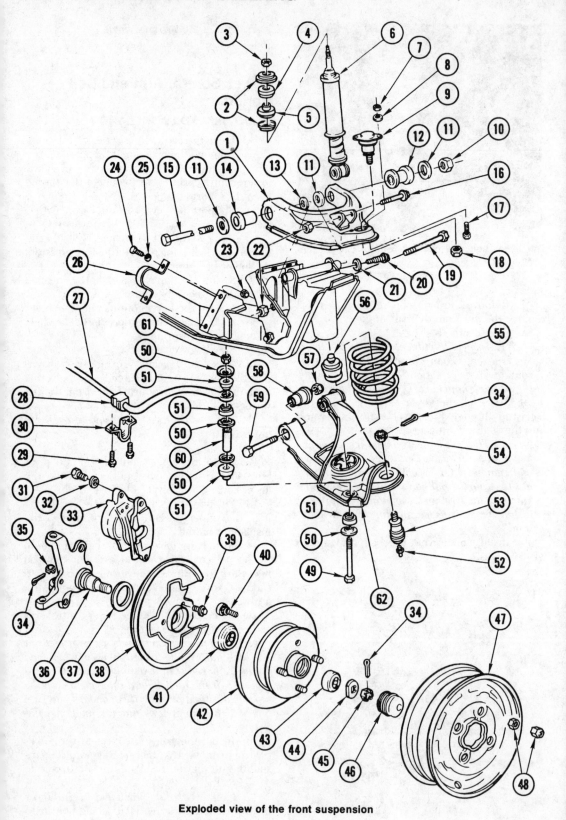

Exploded view of the front suspension

Upper Ball Joint
REMOVAL AND INSTALLATION

1. Raise the car and support it safely on jackstands.

2. Remove the tire and wheel.

3. Support the lower control arm with a floor jack.

4. Loosen, but do not remove the upper ball stud nut.

5. Install a ball joint removal tool with the cup end over the lower ball stud nut.

6. Turn the threaded end of the ball joint removal tool until the upper ball stud is free of the steering knuckle.

7. Remove the ball joint removal tool and remove the nut from the ball stud.

8. Remove the two nuts and bolts attaching the ball joint to the upper control arm and remove the ball joint.

NOTE: *Inspect the tapered hole in the steering knuckle. Clean the area. If any out-of-roundness, deformation, or damage is found, the steering knuckle MUST be replaced.*

9. To install the upper ball joint, install the nuts and bolts attaching the ball joint to the upper control arm. Torque the nuts to 20 ft. lbs. Then mate the upper control arm ball stud to the steering knuckle.

NOTE: *The ball joint studs use a special nut which must be discarded whenever loosened and removed. On assembly, use a standard nut to draw the ball joint into position on the knuckle, then remove the standard nut and install a new special nut for final installation.*

10. Install and torque the ball stud nut to 29–36 ft. lbs.

11. Install the tire and wheel.

12. Lower the car.

Upper Control Arm
REMOVAL AND INSTALLATION

1. Raise the car.

2. Remove the tire and wheel.

3. Support the lower control arm with a floor jack.

4. Remove the upper ball joint from the steering knuckle as previously described.

5. Remove the upper control arm pivot bolts and remove the upper control arm.

6. To install the upper control arm, install the upper control arm with its pivot bolts.

NOTE: *The inner pivot bolt must be installed with the bolt head toward the front.*

7. Install the pivot bolt nut.

8. Position the upper control arm in a horizontal plane and torque the nut to 43–50 ft. lbs.

NOTE: *The ball joint studs use a sepcial nut which must be discarded whenever loosened and removed. On assembly, use a standard to draw the ball joint into position on the knuckle, then remove the standard nut and install a new special nut for final installation.*

9. Install the ball joint to the upper control arm and to the steering knuckle as previously described. Torque the ball joint-to-upper control arm attaching bolts to 20 ft. lbs. Torque the ball stud nut to 29–36 ft. lbs.

10. Install the tire and wheel.

11. Lower the car.

Stabilizer Bar
REMOVAL AND INSTALLATION

1. Raise the car.

2. Remove the stabilizer bar nuts and bolts from the lower control arms.

1. Steering arm	22. Nut	43. Bearing
2. Retainer	23. Nut	44. Washer
3. Nut	24. Bolt	45. Nut
4. Grommet	25. Washer	46. Nut
5. Grommet	26. Bracket	47. Wheel
6. Absorber	27. Stabilizer shaft	48. Nut
7. Nut	28. Bushing	49. Bolt
8. Washer	29. Screw	50. Retainer
9. Ball joint	30. Bracket	51. Grommet
10. Nut	31. Washer	52. Fitting
11. Washer	32. Bolt	53. Ball joint
12. Bushing	33. Caliper	54. Nut
13. Washer	34. Cotter pin	55. Spring
14. Bushing	35. Nut	56. Bumper
15. Bolt	36. Knuckle	57. Nut
16. Bolt	37. Washer	58. Bushing
17. Bolt	38. Shield	59. Bolt
18. Nut	39. Screw and washer	60. Spacer
19. Bolt	40. Bolt	61. Nut
20. Bolt	41. Bearing	62. Arm
21. Washer	42. Hub and bearing	

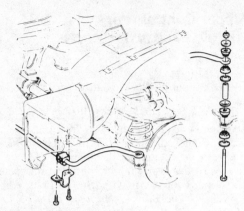

Front stabilizer bar mounting

3. Remove the stabilizer bar brackets and remove the stabilizer bar.

To install:

4. Hold the stabilizer bar in place and install the body bushings and brackets. Torque the bracket bolts to 14 ft. lbs.

5. Install the retainers, grommets, and spacer to the lower control arms and install the attaching nuts.

6. Lower the car.

7. Torque the attaching nuts to 15 ft. lbs.

NOTE: *The correct torque is produced by running the nuts to the unthreaded portions of the link bolts.*

Front End Alignment

CAMBER ADJUSTMENT

Camber angle can be increased by approximately 1° by removing the upper ball joint, rotating it one-half turn, and reinstalling it with the flat of the upper flange on the inboard side of the control arm.

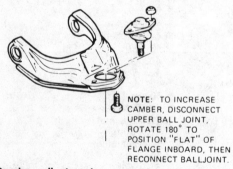

NOTE: TO INCREASE CAMBER, DISCONNECT UPPER BALL JOINT, ROTATE 180° TO POSITION "FLAT" OF FLANGE INBOARD, THEN RECONNECT BALLJOINT.

Camber adjustment

CASTER ADJUSTMENT

Caster angle can be changed with a realignment of the washers located between the legs of the upper control arm. To adjust the caster

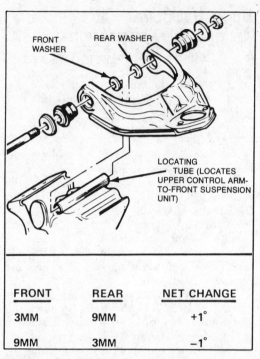

FRONT	REAR	NET CHANGE
3MM	9MM	+1°
9MM	3MM	−1°

Caster adjustment

angle, an adjustment kit consisting of one 3 mm and one 9 mm washer must be used. Install as shown in the illustration.

NOTE: *You must always use two washers that total 12 mm, with one washer at each end of the floating tube.*

TOE-IN ADJUSTMENT

Toe-in is controlled by the position of the tie-rods. To adjust the toe, loosen the nuts at the steering knuckle end of the tie-rod, and the rubber cover at the other end, then rotate the rod as needed to adjust toe-in. Tighten the cover and the locknuts.

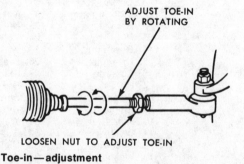

ADJUST TOE-IN BY ROTATING

LOOSEN NUT TO ADJUST TOE-IN

Toe-in—adjustment

REAR SUSPENSION

Chevette and Pontiac 1000 models use a solid rear axle and coil springs. The axle is attached to the body by two tubular lower control arms,

Wheel Alignment Specifications

Year	Model	Caster		Camber		Toe-in (in.)	Steering Axis Inclination (deg)
		Range (deg)	Pref Setting (deg)	Range (deg)	Pref Setting (deg)		
1976–84	All	3½P to 5½P	4½P	¼N to ½P	¼P	1/16	7½

N Negative
P Positive

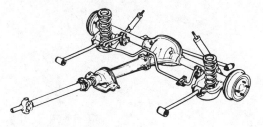

Rear suspension

a straight track rod, two shock absorbers, and a bracket at the front end of the rear axle extension.

The lower control arms maintain fore and aft relationship of the axle to the chassis. The coil springs are located between the brackets on the axle tube and spring seats in the frame. They are held in place by the weight of the car and, during rebound, by the shock absorbers which limit axle movement. The shock absorbers are angle-mounted on brackets behind the axle housing and the rear spring seats in the frame. A rear stabilizer bar is used.

When using a hoist contacting the rear axle be sure that the stabilizer links and the track rod are not damaged.

Shock Absorber
REMOVAL AND INSTALLATION

1. Raise the car.
2. Support the rear axle.
3. Remove the shock absorber upper attaching nut and lower attaching bolt and nut, and remove the shock absorber.
To install:
4. Install the retainer and the rubber grommet onto the shock absorber.
5. Place the shock absorber into its installed position and install and tighten the upper retaining nut to 7 ft. lbs.
6. Install the lower shock absorber nut and bolt and torque to 33 ft. lbs.
7. Remove the rear axle supports and lower the car.

Springs
REMOVAL AND INSTALLATION

1. Raise the car.
2. Support the rear axle with a hydraulic jack.
3. Disconnect both shock absorbers from their lower brackets.
4. Disconnect the rear axle extension center support bracket from the underbody. Use caution when disconnecting the extension and safely support if when disconnected.
5. Lower the rear axle and remove the springs and spring insulators.
NOTE: *One or both springs can be removed now.*
CAUTION: *Do not stretch the rear brake hoses when lowering the rear axle.*
6. To install, place the insulators on top and on the bottom of the springs and position the springs between the their upper and lower seats.
7. Raise the rear axle. Connect the rear axle extension center support bracket to the underbody. Torque the bolts to 37 ft. lbs.
8. Connect the shock absorbers to their lower brackets. Torque the nuts to 33 ft. lbs.
9. Remove the hydraulic jack from the axle.
10. Lower the car.

Stabilizer Bar
REMOVAL AND INSTALLATION

1. Raise the car.
2. Remove the bolts attaching the stabilizer bar to its brackets and links. Remove the stabilizer bar.
3. To install, place the stabilizer bar in position and install the attaching bolts and nuts in the brackets and links. Torque both the bracket and link bolts to 15 ft. lbs.
4. Lower the car.

Lower Control Arm and Track Rod
REMOVAL AND INSTALLATION

CAUTION: *If both control arms are to be replaced, remove and replace one control arm*

4. Nut
5. Bumper
6. Grommet
7. Bumper
8. Retainer
9. Nut
10. Bolt
11. Grommet
12. Shock absorber
13. Nut
14. Retainer
15. Grommet
16. Nut
17. Stem and cap
18. Nut
19. Bushing
20. Arm
21. Bolt

22. Nut
23. Bolt
24. Support
25. Bushing
26. Sleeve
27. Link
28. Nut
29. Shaft
30. Bushing
31. Bracket
32. Screw
33. Bolt
34. Rod
35. Insulator
36. Rear Spring
37. Insulator
38. Nut
39. Retainer

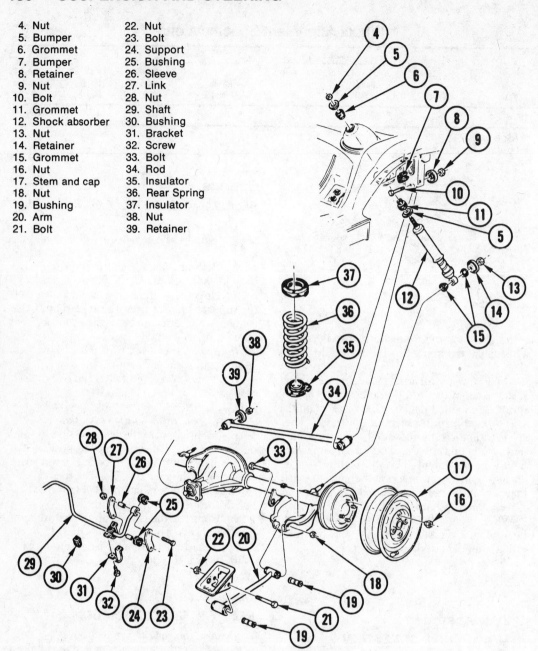

Exploded view of the rear suspension

at a time to prevent the axle from rolling or slipping sideways.

1. Raise the car.
2. Support the rear axle.
3. Disconnect the stabilizer bar.
4. Remove the control arm front and rear attaching bolts and remove the control arm.
5. Remove the track rod attaching bolts and remove the track rod.
6. Press the rubber bushings out of the control arm and track rod with the proper tools. Inspect the private ends of the control arm and

track rod for distortion, burrs, etc., and press new bushings into place.

7. To install, place the lower control arm into position and install and torque the front and rear attaching bolts to 49 ft. lbs.
8. Place the track rod in position and torque both the axle housing nut and body bracket bolt and nut to 49 ft. lbs.

NOTE: *The car must be at curb height when tightening pivot bolts.*

9. Connect the stabilizer bar. Torque all stabilizer bar attaching bolts to 15 ft. lbs.

Rear shock absorber upper mount. Hold the shock absorber stem (arrow) while loosening the 14 mm locknut

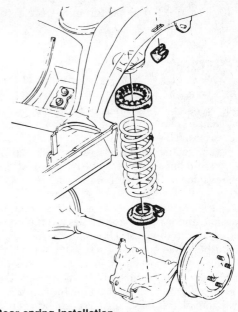

Rear spring installation

One nut retains the bottom shock absorber mount

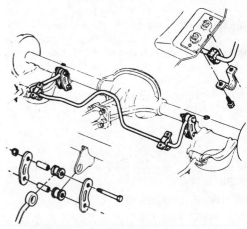

Rear stabilizer mounting

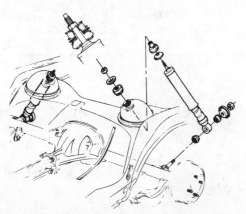

Rear shock absorber mounting detail

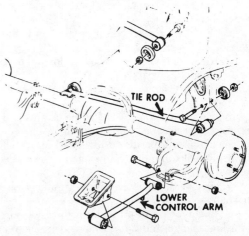

Lower control arm and track rod mounting

10. Remove the support from the axle.
11. Lower the car.

STEERING

All Chevette and Pontiac 1000 models use rack and pinion steering which encloses the steering gear and linkage in one unit. Power steering was available in 1981.

Rotary motion of the steering wheel is converted into linear motion to turn the wheels by the meshing of the helical pinion with the teeth of the rack. The pinion and a major portion of the rack are encased in a die cast aluminum housing. Inner tie-rod assemblies are threaded and staked to the rack. The inner tie-rods contain a belleville spring-loaded ball joint which permits both rocking and rotating tie-rod movement. The outer tie-rods thread onto the inners and are held in position by jam nuts. Two convoluted boots are secured by clamps to the housing and inner tie-rods to prevent the entrance of dirt. The rack and pinion assembly is secured to the front suspension crossmember with two clamps and bushings.

The energy-absorbing steering column has a "smart" switch which operates the turn signals (up and down movement), the headlight dimmer switch (front and back movement), the windshield wipers (rotation), and the windshield washers (by pushing the lever into the column).

Rack and Pinion Steering Assembly

REMOVAL AND INSTALLATION

NOTE: *On models with power steering it is necessary to disconnect and connect the two hydraulic lines.*

1. Raise the car and support it safely on jackstands.
2. Remove the retaining bolts and the shield.
3. Remove both tie-rods cotter pins and nuts and remove the tie-rods.
4. Remove the flexible coupling pinch-bolt-to-shaft.
5. Remove the four bolts at the clamps and remove the rack and pinion steering assembly.
6. To install, position the assembly, install four new bolts into the clamps, and tighten the bolts to 14 ft. lbs.
7. Install the flexible coupling pinch-bolt-to-shaft.
8. Install the tie-rods into the steering knuckles. Install the tie-rod nuts. If the cotter pin holes do not align, tighten the nut until the

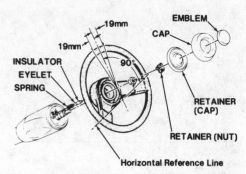

Steering wheel removal

cotter pin can be inserted, and install the cotter pins.
9. Install the bolts and the shield.
10. Lower the car.

Power Steering Pump

REMOVAL AND INSTALLATION

1. Remove the upper adjusting bolt.
2. Remove the lower brace bolt-to-pump bracket.
3. Remove the LH crossmember brace-to-body.
4. Remove the pressure line and the reservoir line at the pump.
5. Remove the rear pump adjusting bracket.
6. Remove the front pivot bolt at the pump.
7. Remove the bolt that attaches the front bracket to the engine and remove the pump and bracket.

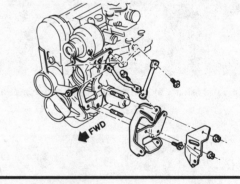

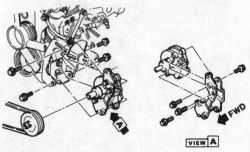

Power steering pump mounting

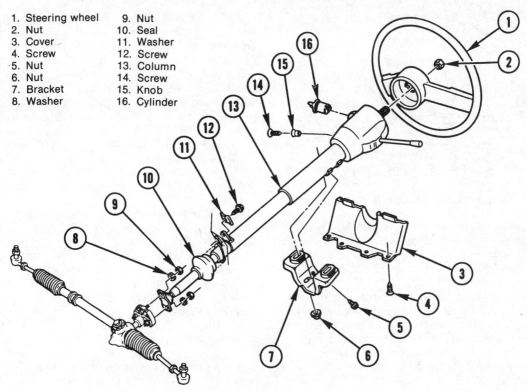

1. Steering wheel
2. Nut
3. Cover
4. Screw
5. Nut
6. Nut
7. Bracket
8. Washer
9. Nut
10. Seal
11. Washer
12. Screw
13. Column
14. Screw
15. Knob
16. Cylinder

Exploded view of the manual rack and pinion steering system

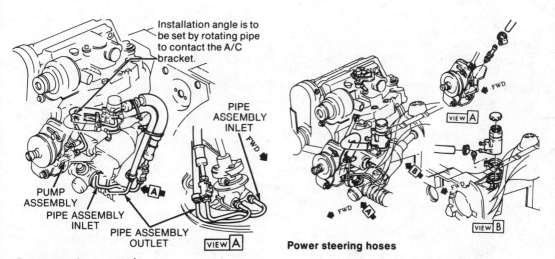

Installation angle is to be set by rotating pipe to contact the A/C bracket.

PIPE ASSEMBLY INLET

FWD

PUMP ASSEMBLY
PIPE ASSEMBLY INLET
PIPE ASSEMBLY OUTLET
VIEW A

Power steering reservoir

Power steering hoses

8. Installation is the reverse of removal. Adjust the belt, fill the reservoir and bleed the system as follows: With the pressure line disconnected at the pump outlet add fluid to the reservoir until fluid begins leaving the pump at the pressure fitting. Attach the pressure line at the pump and fill the reservoir to the proper level.

Steering Wheel
REMOVAL AND INSTALLATION

1. Disconnect the negative battery cable.
2. On models through 1978, remove the two steering wheel shroud screws at the underside of the steering wheel and remove the shroud. On 1979 and later models, pull up on the horn

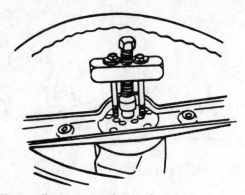

Use a puller to remove the steering wheel

cap to remove it. Remove the horn ring-to-steering wheel attaching screws and remove the ring.

3. Remove the wheel nut retainer and the wheel nut.

CAUTION: *Do not overexpand the retainer.*

4. Using a steering wheel puller, thread the puller anchor screws into the threaded holes in the steering wheel. With the center bolt of the puller butting against the steering shaft, turn the center bolt clockwise to remove the steering wheel.

NOTE: *The puller centering adapter need not be used.*

5. To install, place the turn signal lever in the neutral position and install the steering wheel. Torque the steering wheel nut to 30 ft. lbs. and install the nut retainer. Use caution not to overexpand the nut retainer.

6. Connect the negative battery cable.

Turn Signal Switch

REMOVAL AND INSTALLATION

1. Remove the steering wheel as previously described.

2. Position a screwdriver blade into one of the three cover slots. Pry up and out (at least two slots) to free the cover.

This lockplate compressor is necessary for turn signal switch removal

3. Place the U-shaped lockplate compressing tool on the end of the steering shaft and compress the lockplate. The full load of the spring should not be relieved because the ring will rotate and make removal difficult. Pry the round wire snap-ring out of the shaft groove and discard it. Remove the lockplate compressing tool and lift the lockplate off the end of the shaft.

CAUTION: *If the steering column is being disassembled out of the car, with the snap-ring removed, the shaft could slide out of the lower end of the mast jacket and be damaged.*

4. Slide the turn signal cancelling cam, upper bearing preload spring, and thrust washer off the end of the shaft.

5. Remove the multi-function lever by rotating it clockwise to its top (off position), then pull the lever straight out to disengage it.

6. Push the hazard warning knob in and unscrew the knob.

7. Remove the two screws, pivot arm, and spacer.

8. Wrap the upper part of the connector with tape to prevent snagging the wires during switch removal.

9. Remove the three switch mounting screws and pull the switch straight up, guiding the wiring harness through the column housing.

CAUTION: *On installation it is extremely important that only the specified screws, bolts, and nuts be used. The use of overlength screws could prevent the steering column from compressing under impact.*

10. Position the switch into the husing.

11. Install the three switch mounting screws. Replace the spacer and pivot arm. Be sure that the spacer protrudes through the hole in the arm and that the arm finger encloses the turn signal switch frame. Tighten the truss head screw (secures the spacer to the signal switch) to 20 in. lbs. and the flat head screw to 35 in. lbs.

12. Install the hazard warning knob.

13. Make sure that the turn signal switch is in the neutral position and that the hazard warning knob is out. Slide the thrust washer, upper bearing preload spring, and the cancelling cam into the upper end of the shaft.

14. Place the lockplate and a NEW snap-ring onto the end of the shaft. Using the lockplate compressing tool, compress the lockplate as far as possible. Slide the new snapring into the shaft groove and remove the lockplate compressing tool.

CAUTION: *On assembly, always use a new snap-ring.*

15. Install the multi-function lever, guiding

the wire harness through the column housing. Align the lever pin with the switch slot. Push on the end of the lever until it is seated securely.

16. Install the steering wheel as previously described.

Wiper/Washer Switch
REMOVAL AND INSTALLATION

The wiper/washer switch is located on the left-side of the column under the turn signal switch.

1. Remove the steering wheel and turn signal switch as previously described. The ignition switch is mounted on top of the mast jacket near the front of the dash.

2. Remove the upper attaching screw on the ignition and dimmer switch; this releases the dimmer switch and actuator rod assembly.

NOTE: *Do not move the ignition switch. If this happens, refer to the switch adjustment procedure in "Ignition Switch and Dimmer Switch Removal and Installation."*

3. The wiper/washer switch and pivot assembly now can be removed from the column housing.

4. To install, place the wiper/washer switch and pivot assembly into the housing and guide the connector down through the bowl and shroud assembly.

5. Install the turn signal switch as previously described.

6. Fit the pinched end of the dimmer switch actuator rod into the dimmer switch. Feed the other end of the rod through the hole in the shroud into the hole in the wiper/washer switch and pivot assembly drive, but do not tighten the attaching screw. Depress the dimmer switch slightly to insert a ³⁄₃₂ in. drill bit to lock the switch to the body. Push the switch up to remove the lash between both the ignition and dimmer switches and the actuator rod. Install the wiper/washer switch mounting screw and tighten it to 35 in. lbs. Remove the drill and check dimmer switch operation with the actuating lever.

Ignition Key Buzzer Switch
REMOVAL AND INSTALLATION

1. Remove the steering wheel and turn signal switch as previously described.

2. Make a right angle bend in a short piece of small wire about ¼ in. from one end. The wire should be inserted in the exposed loop of the wedge spring, then a straight pull on the wire will remove both the spring and the switch.

CAUTION: *Do not attempt to remove the switch separately as the clip may fall into the column. If this happens, the clip must be found before assembly.*

NOTE: *The lock cylinder must be in the "Run" position if it is in the housing. Also, if the lock cylinder is in place, the buzzer switch actuating button on the lock cylinder must be depressed before the buzzer switch can be installed.*

3. Install the buzzer switch with the contacts toward the upper end of the steering column and with the formed end of the spring clip around the lower end of the switch. Push the switch and spring assembly into the hole with the internal switch contacts toward the lock cylinder bore.

4. Install the turn signal switch and the steering wheel as previously described.

Lock Cylinder
REMOVAL AND INSTALLATION

The lock cylinder is located on the right-side of the steering column and should be removed only in the "Run" position. Removal in any other position will damage the key buzzer switch. The lock cylinder cannot be disassembled; if replacement is required, a new cylinder coded to the old key must be installed.

1. Remove the steering wheel and turn signal switch as previously described.

2. Do not remove the buzzer switch or damage to the lock cylinder will result.

3. On models through 1978, insert a small screwdriver or similar tool into the turn signal housing slot to the upper right of the steering shaft. Keep the tool to the upper right of the steering shaft. Keep the tool to the right-side of the slot and depress the retainer at the bottom to release the lock cylinder. Remove the lock cylinder.

On 1979 and later models, place the lock cylinder in the RUN position. Remove the securing screw and remove the cylinder.

4. To install the lock cylinder, hold the cylinder sleeve in the left hand and rotate knob (key in) clockwise to stop. (This retracts the actuator.) Insert the cylinder into the housing bore with the key on the cylinder sleeve aligned with the keyway in the housing. Push the cylinder in until it bottoms. On models through 1978, rotate the knob counterclockwise while maintaining a light pressure inward until the drive section of the cylinder mates with the sector. Push the cylinder in fully until the retainer pops into the housing groove. On 1979 and later models, install the retaining screw.

5. Install the turn signal switch and the steering wheel as previously described.

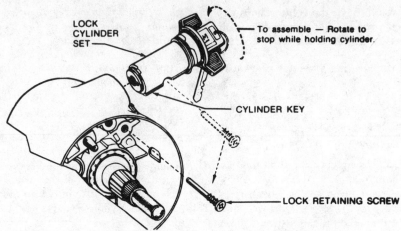

LOCK CYLINDER SET

To assemble — Rotate to stop while holding cylinder.

CYLINDER KEY

LOCK RETAINING SCREW

Lock cylinder removal and installation—1979 and later

Lock cylinder removal—through 1978

Ignition Switch and Dimmer Switch

REMOVAL AND INSTALLATION

The ignition switch is mounted on top of the mast jacket near the front of the dash. The switch is located inside the channel section of the brake pedal support and is compeltely inaccessible without first lowering the steering column.

1. Disconnect the negative battery cable.

2. Remove the steering wheel as previously described.

3. Move the driver's seat as far back as possible.

4. Remove the floor pan bracket screw.

5. Remove the two column bracket-to-instrument panel nuts and lower the column far enough to disconnect the ignition switch wiring harness.

CAUTION: *Be sure that the steering column is properly supported before proceeding.*

6. The switch should be in the "Lock" position before removal. If the lock cylinder has already been removed, the actuating rod to the switch should be pulled up until there is a definite stop, then moved down one detent which is the "Lock" position.

7. Remove the two mounting screws and remove the ignition and dimmer switch.

8. Refer to the installation procedure previously described in "Lock Cylinder Removal and Installation."

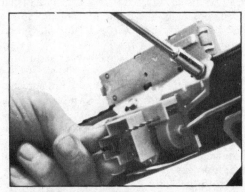

Installing the dimmer switch

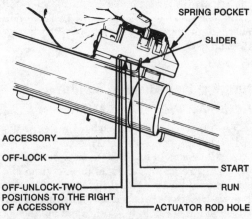

SPRING POCKET

SLIDER

ACCESSORY

OFF-LOCK

START

RUN

OFF-UNLOCK-TWO-POSITIONS TO THE RIGHT OF ACCESSORY

ACTUATOR ROD HOLE

Positioning the ignition switch for installation

9. Turn the cylinder clockwise to stop and then counterclockwise to stop ("Off-Unlock" position).

10. Place the ignition switch in the "Off-Unlock" position by positioning the switch as shown in the accompanying illustration. Move the slider two positions to the right from "Accessory" to the "Off-Unlock" position.

11. Fit the actuator rod into the slider hole and install the switch on the column. Be sure to use only the correct screws. Tighten only one bottom screw to 35 in. lbs. Be careful not to move the switch out of its detent.

12. Perform the dimmer switch adjustment procedure previously outlined in "Wiper/Washer Switch Removal and Installation."

13. Connect the ignition switch wiring harness.

14. Loosely install the column bracket-to-instrument panel nuts to within 1 mm ± ½mm of being tight.

15. Install the floor pan bracket screw and tighten it to 25 ft. lbs.

16. Tighten the column bracket-to-instrument panel nuts to 20 ft. lbs.

17. Install the steering wheel as previously outlined.

18. Connect the battery negative cable.

Brakes

9

UNDERSTANDING THE BRAKES

Front disc brakes are standard equipment on all models. Power brakes are available as an option. The disc is 9.68 in. in diameter and ½ in. thick and is a one-piece casting with the hub. Single-piston sliding calipers are used.

The rear brakes are of conventional leading-trailing shoe design. Brake drum diameter is 7.87 in. Automatic adjusters are used in the rear brakes which provide adjustment when needed whenever the brakes are applied.

The master cylinder is a two-piece design: a cast housing containing the primary and secondary pistons and a stamped steel reservoir. The reservoir is attached to the cast housing with two retainers and sealed with two O-rings. The reservoir is not divided, however a dual braking system is used. The front (secondary) piston operates the rear brakes, while the rear (primary) piston operates the front brakes.

The front and rear brake lines are routed through a distributor and switch assembly located on the left-hand engine compartment side panel. The switch is a pressure differential type which lights the brake warning light on the instrument panel if either the front or rear hydraulic system fails. The switch is nonadjustable and nonserviceable; it must be replaced if defective.

Brake Adjustment

All Chevettes and Pontiac 1000s are equipped with front disc brakes which require no adjustment. Rear brake adjustment takes place every time the brakes are applied through the use of an automatic brake adjuster. Only an initial adjustment is necessary when the brakes have been installed. This is done by depressing the brake pedal a few times until the pedal becomes firm. Check the fluid level in the master cylinder frequently during the adjustment procedure.

HYDRAULIC SYSTEM

Master Cylinder

REMOVAL AND INSTALLATION

CAUTION: *Never allow brake fluid to spill on painted surfaces.*

1. Disconnect the master cylinder pushrod from the brake pedal.
2. Remove the pushrod boot.
3. Remove the air cleaner.
4. Thoroughly clean all dirt from the master cylinder and the brake lines. Disconnect the brake lines from the master cylinder and plug them to prevent the entry of dirt.
5. Remove the master cylinder securing nuts and remove the master cylinder.
6. Install the master cylinder with its spacer. Tighten the securing nuts to 150 in. lbs.
7. Connect the brake lines to their proper ports. Tighten the nuts to 150 in. lbs.
8. Place the pushrod boot over the end of the pushrod. Secure the pushrod to the brake pedal with the pin and clip.
9. Fill the master cylinder and bleed the entire hydraulic system. After bleeding, fill the

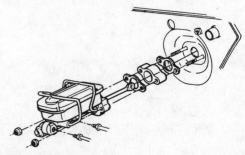

Master cylinder mounting

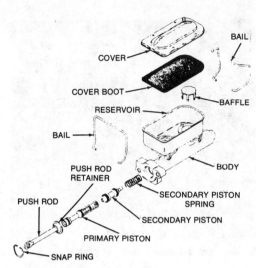

COVER

BAIL

COVER BOOT

BAFFLE

RESERVOIR

BAIL

PUSH ROD
RETAINER

BODY

SECONDARY PISTON
SPRING

PUSH ROD

SECONDARY PISTON

PRIMARY PISTON

SNAP RING

Exploded view of the master cylinder

master cylinder to within ¼ in. from the top of the reservoir. Check for leaks.

10. Install the air cleaner.

11. Check brake operation before moving the car.

OVERHAUL

If the master cylinder leaks externally, or if the pedal sinks while being held down, the master cylinder is worn. There are three ways to correct this situation:

 a. Buy a new master cylinder;

 b. Trade in the worn unit for a rebuilt unit;

 c. Rebuild the old master cylinder with a rebuilding kit.

Your choice depends on the time and finances available.

To rebuild the master cylinder:

1. Remove the old master cylinder from the car as previously outlined.

2. Remove the cover and drain all fluid from the reservoir. Pump the fluid from the cylinder bore by depressing the pushrod.

3. Position the master cylinder in a vise. Use soft wood or rags to protect the cylinder from the vise jaws.

4. Remove the snap-ring.

5. Remove the pushrod and retainer as a unit.

6. Remove the primary piston.

NOTE: *A new primary piston is included in the rebuilding kit, so it's unnecessary to disassemble the old piston.*

7. Remove the secondary piston (it's at the front), and spring by applying air pressure through the front outlet.

8. Make sure that your hands are clean and then use new brake fluid to clean all metal parts thoroughly.

9. Check the cylinder bore for pitting or corrosion. Clean the outlet ports of any dirt and then rewash all parts.

10. Place the parts on a clean rag and allow them to air dry.

NOTE: *Be sure you have the correct rebuilding kit by checking the identification marks on the old secondary piston with those on the new one in the kit.*

11. Install the new secondary piston seals in the grooves of the piston. The seal that is nearest the front end of the piston will have its lip facing toward that end. Be sure that the seal protector is in place. The front seal has the smallest inside diameter.

12. Install the seal retainer and spring seat after the seal is in place.

Location of the brake master cylinder

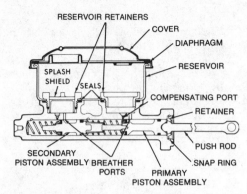

Cross-section of the master cylinder

Bleeder valve location on rear brake

13. Install the seal on the rear of the secondary piston. The seal should face toward the rear of the piston.

14. Use new brake fluid to coat the bore of the master cylinder and the primary and secondary seals of the front piston.

15. Install the secondary piston spring over the nose of the piston and onto the spring seat.

16. Install the primary piston and pushrod and retainer into the cylinder bore. Hold pressure on the pushrod and install the snapring.

17. Fill the master cylinder reservoir with fresh brake fluid and stroke the pushrod several times to bench bleed the cylinder. Snap the retaining bails over the cylinder cover.

18. Install the master cylinder as previously described.

19. Bleed the brakes.

BLEEDING

The hydraulic system must be bled whenever the pedal feels spongy, indicating that compressible air has entered the system. The system must be bled whenever any component has been disconnected or there has been a leak.

Brake fluid sometimes becomes contaminated and loses its original qualities. Old brake fluid should be bled from the system and replaced if any part of the hydraulic system becomes corroded or if the fluid is dirty or discolored.

1. Clean off the top of the master cylinder and remove the cover. Check that the fluid level in each reservoir is within ¼ in. of the top.

2. Attach a 7/32 in. inside diameter hose to the bleeder valve at the first wheel to be bled. Start at the wheel farthest from the master cylinder and work closer. Pour a few inches of brake fluid into a clear container and stick the end of the tube below the surface.

NOTE: *The tube and container of brake fluid are not absolutely necessary, but this is a very sloppy job without them.*

3. Open the bleed valve counterclockwise ⅓ turn. Have a helper slowly depress the pedal.

Close the valve just before the pedal reaches the end of its travel. Have the helper let the pedal back up.

4. Check the fluid level. If the reservoir runs dry, the procedure will have to be restarted from the beginning.

5. Repeat Step 3 until no more bubbles come out the hose.

6. Repeat the bleeding operation, Steps 3 to 5, at the other three wheels.

7. Check the master cylinder level again.

8. If repeated bleeding has no effect, there is an air leak, probably internally in the master cylinder or in one of the wheel cylinders.

Brake Distribution and Warning Switch Assembly

BRAKE WARNING LIGHT CHECKING

1. Disconnect the electrical lead from the switch terminal and use a jumper wire to connect the lead to a good ground.

2. Turn the ignition to the "On" position. The instrument panel warning lamp should light. If it does not light, either the bulb is

Brake distribution switch assembly mounting

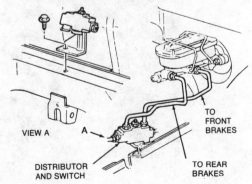

burned out or the circuit is defective. Replace the bulb or repair the circuit as necessary.

3. When the warning lamp lights, turn the ignition off, remove the jumper wire, and connect the electrical lead to the brake line switch.

BRAKE WARNING LIGHT SWITCH TESTING

1. Raise the car on a hoist and attach a bleeder hose to a rear bleed screw. Immerse the other end of the hose in a container partially filled with clean brake fluid. Check the master cylinder reservoir to make sure that it is full.

2. Turn the ignition switch to "On." Open the bleed screw while an assistant applies heavy pressure to the brake pedal. The warning lamp should light. Close the bleed screw before the assistant releases the brake pedal.

3. Repeat Step 2 on the front brake bleed screw. The warning lamp should light again. Turn the ignition off.

4. Lower the car. Check and fill the master cylinder reservoir to the correct level.

NOTE: *If the warning lamp does not light during Steps 2 and 3, but does light when a jumper wire is connected to ground, the warning light switch is defective and must be replaced.*

REMOVAL AND INSTALLATION

The distribution and warning switch assembly is nonadjustable and nonserviceable. It must be replaced if defective.

1. Disconnect the negative battery cable.

2. Clean the switch assembly thoroughly to remove dirt and foreign matter.

3. Disconnect the electrical lead from the switch.

4. Place dry rags below the switch to absorb any brake fluid which may be spilled.

5. Disconnect the hydraulic lines from the switch. If necessary, loosen the lines at the master cylinder to assist removal at the switch. Cover the open lines with clean, lint-free material to prevent the entry of dirt.

6. Remove the mounting screw and remove the switch.

7. Make sure that the new switch is clean and free of dust and lint. If there is any doubt, wash the switch in clean brake fluid and dry with compressed air.

8. Place the switch in its installed position and install its mounting screw. Tighten the mounting screw to 100 in. lbs.

9. Remove the protective covering from the brake lines and connect the lines to the switch. If necessary, tighten the brake lines at the master cylinder. Tighten the brake line nuts at the switch and master cylinder to 150 in. lbs.

10. Connect the electrical lead to the switch.

11. Connect the negative battery cable.

12. Bleed the entire hydraulic system. Fill the master cylinder to within ¼ in. from the top of the reservoir after bleeding. Check for proper brake operation and leaks before moving the car.

FRONT DISC BRAKES

Instead of the traditional expanding brakes that press outward against a circular drum, disc brake systems consist of two cast iron discs with brake pads positioned on either side. Braking action is achieved by the pads squeezing either side of the rotating disc. Dirt and water do not greatly affect braking action since they are thrown off the rotor by centrifugal action or scraped off by the pads. The equal clamping action of the pads tends to ensure uniform, straight stopping. All disc brakes are self-adjusting.

Disc Brake Pads and Caliper

REPLACEMENT

1976–82

1. Siphon off about one half of the brake fluid in the master cylinder. This is necessary because the new, thicker pads will push the caliper pistons in farther and cause the master cylinder to overflow.

2. Jack up the front of the car and support it safely on jackstands. Remove the wheels.

NOTE: *Always replace brake pads on both wheels. Never replace one pair. Replace pads when worn to within ¹⁄₃₂ in. of the metal pad backing.*

3. Mount a 7 in. C-clamp on the caliper with the solid end on the caliper housing and the screw end on the metal back of the outboard shoe (pad). Tighten the C-clamp to bottom the piston in the cylinder bore and remove the clamp.

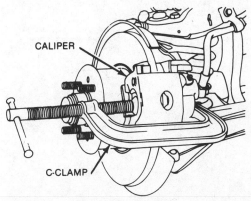

CALIPER

C-CLAMP

A 7 inch or larger C-clamp is necessary for pad replacement—1976–82

4. If the caliper is to be removed for overhaul purposes disconnect the brake hose at the inlet fitting by removing the bolt and washers. If only the shoe and lining are to be replaced do not disconnect the brake hose.

5. Remove the two bracket bolts and remove the caliper from the rotor. Do not remove the socket head bolt which may have a cover on it on later models. Hang the caliper from the front suspension with a chain or heavy wire. Coat hanger wire should be sufficient. Don't let the caliper hang with the brake hose as its support.

6. Remove the old pads. If the shoe retaining spring doesn't come out with the inboard pad, remove it from the piston.

7. Blow any dirt out of the caliper and check that the piston boot isn't damaged or leaking fluid.

8. Install the new pads in the same loca-

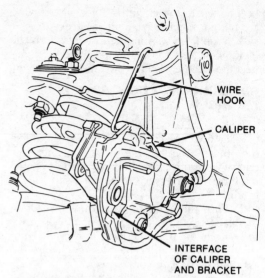

Supporting the caliper assembly from the front suspension—1976–82

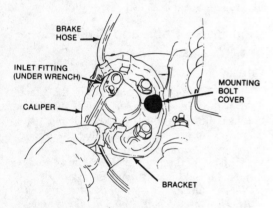

Disconnect the brake hose by removing the bolt at the inlet fitting—1976–82

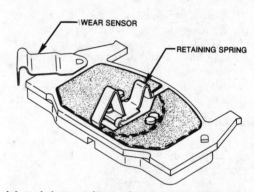

Inboard shoe, retainer and wear sensor—1976–82

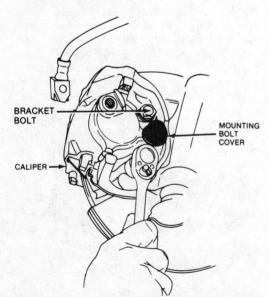

Removing the two bracket bolts. Do not remove the mounting bolt in the center—1976–82

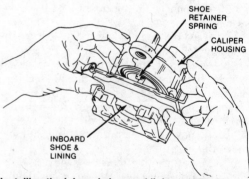

Installing the inboard shoe and lining—1976–82

tions as the old ones. Before installing the inboard pad, be sure that the retaining spring is properly positioned. Push the tab on the single leg end of the spring down into the pad hole, and then snap the other two legs over the edge of the pad notch.

9. Position the caliper over the rotor (disc).

Cinching the brake pad tabs using pliers—1976–82

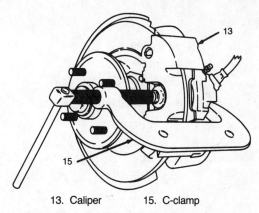

13. Caliper   15. C-clamp

Position a C-clamp to bottom the piston—1983 and later

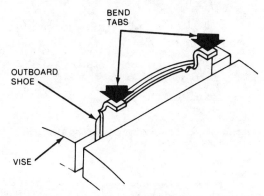

Bending the tabs on the shoe using a vise—1976–82

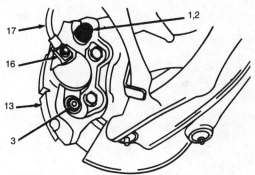

1. Bolt cover	13. Caliper
2. Mounting bolt	16. Inlet fitting
3. Mounting bolt	17. Brake hose

Mounting bolts and inlet fitting bolt—1983 and later

Install the two retaining bolts and tighten them to 70 ft. lbs.

10. Using a large pair of Channel Lock® pliers, clinch the outboard pad to the caliper. Position the lower jaw of the pliers on the bottom edge of the outboard pad. Place the upper jaw of the pliers on the outboard pad tab. Squeeze the pliers firmly to bend the tab. Clinch the other end of the outboard pad the same way. The tabs may also be bent by placing the shoe in a vise and bending slightly. The purpose is to have zero clearance between the shoe and the caliper.

11. Install the wheels and lower the car.

12. Refill the master cylinder with fresh fluid.

13. Pump the brake pedal several times to push the pads in on the rotor. Check the fluid level in the master cylinder after this has been done. Do not move the car until a firm pedal is obtained.

14. Carefully road test the car.

1983–84

1. Remove ⅔ of the brake fluid from the master cylinder assembly.

2. Raise the car and support with jack stands.

3. Mark the relationship of the wheel to the axle, then remove the wheel.

4. Position a C-clamp as shown in the illustration and tighten until the piston bottoms in the bore, then remove the C-clamp.

5. Remove the bolt holding the inlet fitting.

NOTE: *If only the shoe and lining are being replaced, do not remove the inlet fitting.*

6. Remove the two bolt covers and allen head mounting bolts.

NOTE: *If the mounting bolts show signs of corrosion replace them with new ones.*

7. If only the shoe and linings are being replaced, remove the caliper from the rotor and suspend it from the suspension so that there isn't any tension on the brake hose.

8. Remove the shoe and lining assemblies from the caliper. To remove the outboard shoe and lining, use 12 inch channel lock pliers to straighten bent over shoe tabs.

9. Remove the sleeves from the mounting bolt holes.

10. Remove the bushings from the grooves in the mounting bolt holes.

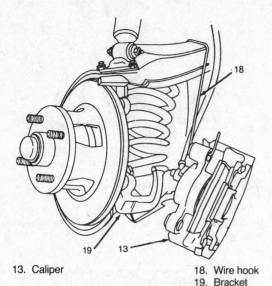

13. Caliper   18. Wire hook
                              19. Bracket

Suspending caliper assembly—1983–84

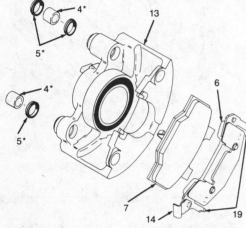

4. Sleeve	7. Inboard shoe & lining
5. Bushing	13. Caliper housing
6. Outboard shoe & lining	14. Wear sensor
	19. Shoe tab

Lubricate the bushings and sleeves with silicone grease before installation—1983–84

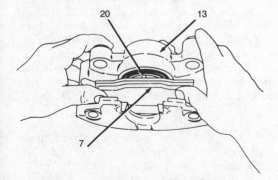

7. Inboard shoe & lining   13. Caliper housing
                                     20. Shoe retainer spring

Installation of the inboard shoe—1983 and later

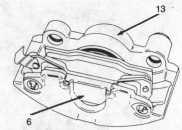

6. Outboard shoe & lining   13. Caliper housing

Installation of the outboard shoe—1983 and later

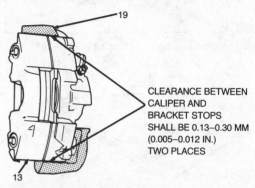

CLEARANCE BETWEEN CALIPER AND BRACKET STOPS SHALL BE 0.13–0.30 MM (0.005–0.012 IN.) TWO PLACES

Check clearance between the caliper and the bracket stops—1983 and later

11. Prior to installation, lubricate and install new bushings and sleeves.

12. Install the inboard shoe and lining positioning the shoe retainer spring into the piston.

13. Install the outboard shoe and lining with the wear sensor at the leading edge of the shoe during forward wheel rotation.

14. Position the caliper over the rotor in the mounting bracket.

15. Coat the threads and shoulder of the mounting bolts with silicone grease. Install the mounting bolts and torque to 21–25 ft. lbs.

16. Check the clearance between the caliper and bracket stops as shown in the illustration and if necessary, file the ends of the bracket to provide the proper clearance.

17. Install the inlet fitting if removed and torque to 18–30 ft. lbs.

18. Cinch the outboard shoe by performing the following steps:

    a. Wedge a prying tool between the outboard shoe flange and the hat section of the rotor to seat the shoe flange in the caliper.

    b. Have an assistant lightly press on the brake pedal to clamp the outboard shoe tightly to the caliper. Maintain pressure on the hydraulic system to keep the tool wedged in place during the remaining steps.

NOTE: *Make sure the master cylinder is filled to the proper level and the cover is in place before performing the previous step.*

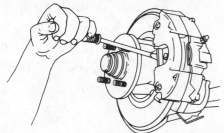

Wedge a large pry tool between the outboard shoe flange and the hat section of the rotor—1983 and later

c. Bend the outboard shoe tabs and cinch the shoe to the caliper by positioning an 8 ounce machinists hammer as shown in the illustration, then striking it with a 16 ounce brass hammer.

d. Check that the shoe tabs are bent to an angle of approximately 45 degrees. After both tabs are bent and hydraulic pressure released, check that the outboard shoe is locked tightly in position. If not, repeat steps a thru c.

CAUTION: *Outboard shoe and linings that have been cinched as described in the pre-*

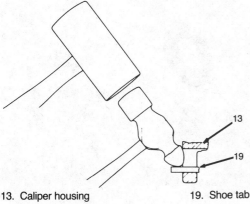

13. Caliper housing   19. Shoe tab

Bending the outboard shoe tabs with a hammer— 1983 and later

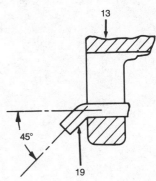

13. Caliper housing   19. Shoe tab

Check the angle of the shoe tabs—1983 and later

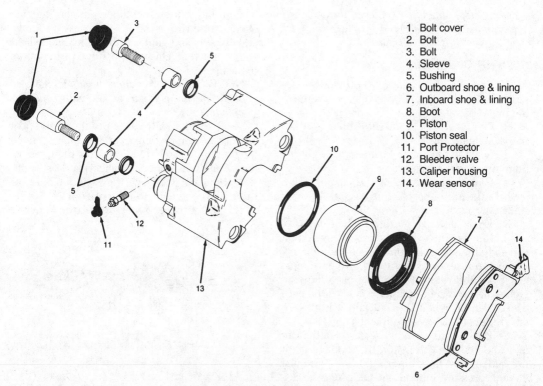

1. Bolt cover
2. Bolt
3. Bolt
4. Sleeve
5. Bushing
6. Outboard shoe & lining
7. Inboard shoe & lining
8. Boot
9. Piston
10. Piston seal
11. Port Protector
12. Bleeder valve
13. Caliper housing
14. Wear sensor

Caliper and shoe assembly—1983 and later

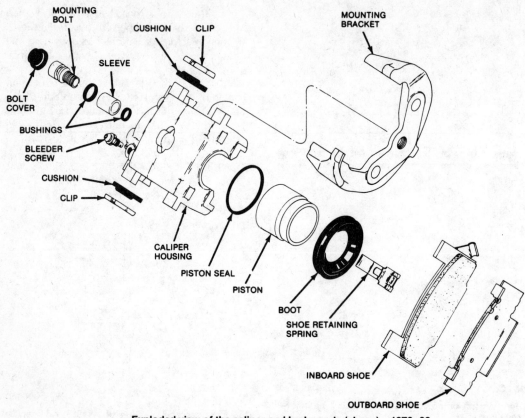

Exploded view of the caliper and brake pads (shoes)—1976–82

ceding steps should be replaced if uncinched for any reason. Bleed the system if the inlet fitting and hose were removed.

CALIPER OVERHAUL

1. Remove the caliper as previously described. Disconnect the brake line and remove the brake pads.

2. Clean all dirt from the brake hose-to-caliper connection.

3. Seal the brake line fitting to prevent dirt from entering the caliper.

4. Clean the outside of the caliper using fresh brake fluid and place it on a clean work surface.

5. Drain all brake fluid from the caliper.

6. Remove the mounting backcover and bolt and slide the mounting bracket off the caliper.

7. Remove the sleeve and two bushings, one from the retainer bolt and one from the groove in the caliper mounting hole. If the clips do not fall off when the bracket is removed, take them off and remove the cushions.

8. Use rags to cushion the inside of the caliper and remove the piston by applying compressed air into the caliper inlet hole. Use just enough pressure to ease out the piston; excessive pressure may cause damage to the piston

when it flies out of the caliper. Another method of removing the piston is to depress the brake pedal slowly and gently with the hydraulic lines still connected. This will push the piston out of the caliper.

NOTE: *Never place your hands in the way of the piston as it can fly out with considerable force.*

9. Use a screwdriver to pry the piston boot out of the caliper being careful not to scratch the housing bore. Extend the screwdriver across the caliper bore, under the boot, and pry it up. Be careful not to gouge the cylinder bore, or the caliper will have to be replaced.

10. Use a piece of wood or plastic (a plastic

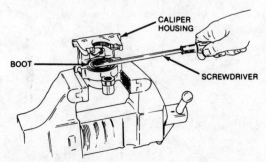

Removing the piston boot

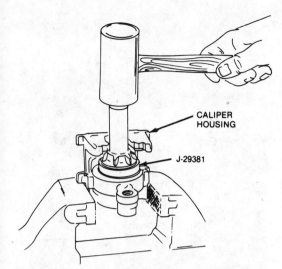

CALIPER
HOUSING

J-29381

Installing the piston and boot into the caliper using a bushing driver. 1976–82 tool shown. Use tool J-29077 for 1983 and later models

knitting needle is perfect), to remove the seal from its groove in the caliper bore. Using a metal tool will damage the bore surface.

11. Remove the bleeder valve from the caliper.

12. Buy a high quality caliper rebuilding kit, preferably original equipment type.

13. Clean all metal parts in fresh brake fluid. Never use other solvents for cleaning, as gasoline or paint thinner will ruin the rubber parts.

14. Inspect all parts for rust or other damage. The caliper bore should be free from corrosion or nicks. Replace any suspect parts. Minor stains or corrosion can be polished out of the caliper bore with *crocus cloth*, but heavily damaged pieces should be discarded.

15. Lubricate the caliper bore and the new piston seal with fresh brake fluid. Position the seal in the caliper bore groove.

16. Lubricate the piston with fresh brake fluid and assemble a new boot into the piston groove so that the fold faces the open end of the piston.

17. Insert the piston into the caliper being careful not to dislodge the seal. Force the piston down to the bottom in the bore. This requires about 50–100 lbs. of force.

18. Place the outside diameter of the boot in the caliper counterbore and seat it with a bushing driver of the same diameter as the boot.

19. Install the bleeder screw.

20. Fit new cushions on the caliper lugs. Stretch the cushions over the lugs, fitting the heavy section in the lug recess, with the saw-tooth edges of the cushions pointing out.

21. Liberally lubricate the sleeve and bushings, inside and out, and the unthreaded portion of the retainer bolt with silicone lubricant.

22. Fit the larger bushing in the caliper mounting hole groove and install the sleeve.

23. Position the smaller bushing in the groove in the retainer bolt.

24. Clamp the caliper in a vise, mounting lug up, across the pad openings. Fit the clips over the cushions and squeeze the mounting bracket down over the clips, lining up the retainer bolt hole.

25. Move the bracket against the retainer boss on the caliper and install the retainer bolt. Tighten the bolt to 28 ft. lbs.

NOTE: *It may be very difficult to squeeze the bracket over the cushions and clips on the caliper. Start with the open end of the bracket over the ends of the clips near the boot and move the bracket towards the closed end of the piston housing.*

26. Install the caliper. Use new copper gaskets on the brake hose connection. Bleed the brakes.

Brake Disc
REMOVAL AND INSTALLATION

1. Jack up the front of the car and support it safely with jackstands.

2. Remove the wheel and tire.

3. Remove the brake caliper as previously described.

4. Remove the hub dust cap, cotter pin, spindle nut and washer, and remove the disc. Do not allow the bearing to fall out of the hub when removing the disc.

5. Remove the outer bearing with the fingers.

6. Remove the inner bearing by prying out the grease seal. Discard the seal.

7. Thoroughly clean all parts in solvent and blow dry.

8. Check the bearings for cracked separators or pitting. Check the races for scoring or pitting.

NOTE: *If it is necessary to replace either the inner or outer bearing it will also be necessary to replace the race for that bearing.*

9. Drive out the old race from the hub with a brass drift inserted behind the race in the notches in the hub.

10. Lubricate the new race with a light film of grease.

11. Use the proper tool to start the race squarely into the hub and carefully seat it.

12. Pack the inner and outer bearings with high melting point wheel bearing grease.

13. Place the inner bearing in the hub and install a new grease seal. The seal should be installed flush with the hub surface. Use a block of wood to seat the seal.

14. Install the disc over the spindle.

15. Press the outer bearing firmly into the hub by hand.

16. Install the spindle washer and nut. Adjust the wheel bearings as outlined in "Front Wheel Bearing Adjustment," following.

17. Install the brake caliper. Tighten the brake caliper mounting bolts to 70 ft. lbs.

18. Install the wheel and tire.

19. Lower the car.

Front Wheel Bearings

INSPECTION

1. Raise the car and support it at the front lower control arm.

2. Spin the wheel to check for unusual noise or roughness.

3. If the bearings are noisy, tight, or excessively loose they should be cleaned, inspected, and relubricated before adjustment.

4. Grip the tire at the top and bottom and move the wheel assembly in and out on the spindle. Measure the movement of the hub, it should be 0.001–0.005 in. If not, adjust the bearings.

ADJUSTMENT

1. Raise the car and support it at the front lower control arm.

2. Remove the hub cap or wheel cover from the wheel. Remove the dust cap from the hub.

3. Remove the cotter pin from the spindle.

4. Spin the wheel forward by hand and

Unbend the cotter pin and remove it from the spindle nut

Hand-tighten (approx. 12 ft lbs), the spindle nut to seat the wheel bearings

tighten the spindle nut to 12 ft. lbs. This will fully seat the bearings.

5. Back off the nut to the "just loose" position.

6. Hand-tighten the spindle nut. Loosen the spindle nut until either hole in the spindle aligns with a slot in the nut, but not more than ½ flat.

7. Install a new cotter pin, bend the ends of the pin against the nut, and cut off any extra length to avoid interference with the dust cap.

Pry the dust cover off with a large, flat-bladed screwdriver

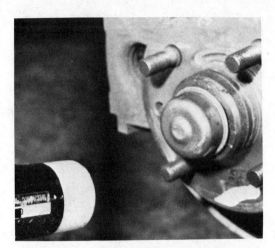

Tap the dustcover back on with a soft-faced hammer

8. Measure the end-play in the hub. Proper bearing adjustment should give 0.001–0.005 in. of end-play.

9. Install the dust cap on the hub and the hub cap or wheel cover on the wheel.

10. Lower the car.

11. Adjust the opposite front wheel bearings in the same manner.

REMOVAL AND INSTALLATION

For wheel bearing removal and installation procedure see "Brake Disc Removal and Installation."

REAR DRUM BRAKES

1976–79

Drum brakes employ two brake shoes mounted on a stationary backing plate. These shoes are positioned inside a circular cast iron drum which rotates with the wheel assembly. The shoes are held in place by springs; this allows them to slide toward the drums (when they are applied) while keeping the linings and drums in alignment. The shoes are actuated by a wheel cylinder which is mounted at the top of the backing plate. When the brakes are applied, hydraulic pressure forces the wheel cylinder's two actuating links outward. Since these links bear directly against the top of the brake shoes, the tops of the shoes are then forced outward against the inner side of the drum. This action forces the bottoms of the two shoes to contact the brake drum by rotating the entire assembly slightly (known as servo action). When pressure within the wheel cylinder is relaxed, return springs pull the shoes back away from the drum.

Most modern drum brakes are designed to self-adjust themselves during application when the vehicle is moving in reverse. This motion causes both shoes to rotate very slightly with the drum, rocking an adjusting lever, thereby causing rotation of the adjusting screw by means of a star wheel.

The duo-servo brake with pin and slot adjusters is a new design used only on the Chevette through 1979.

1980–81

The rear drum brake system introduced in 1980 is a duo-servo and direct torque design. In the duo-servo design the force which the wheel cylinder applies to the shoes is supplemented by the tendency of the shoes to wrap into the drum during braking. With the direct torque design, torque from the brake shoes is transferred directly through the anchor pin to the control arm.

Brake Shoes

REPLACEMENT

1976–79

1. Remove the brake drum.

NOTE: *If the brake drum is stubborn in coming off, rotate the adjusters on the back of the brake toward the axle tube to retract the shoes from the drum.*

2. Loosen the equalizer to let all tension from the parking brake cable.

3. Unhook the parking brake cable from the lever.

4. Use pliers to remove the long shoe pull back spring at the top.

5. Use pliers to remove the shoe hold down springs and retainers from the middle of each shoe.

6. Separate the shoes at the top and remove them.

7. Check that the adjusters work properly; it should take 29–36 ft. lbs. torque to turn the adjusters. The adjusters and backing plate must be replaced as an essembly.

8. Lubricate the shoe contact surfaces on the backing plate and all pivot points with brake lubricant. Lubricate the parking brake cable.

9. Lubricate the pivot end of the parking brake lever and attach the lever to the shoe.

10. Connect the shoes at the bottom with the retaining spring.

11. Place the shoes in position and fasten the front shoe with the hold down spring and retainer. Be sure that the adjuster peg is in the shoe slot.

12. Install the parking brake lever to front shoe strut. Fasten down the rear shoe with the hold down spring and retainer. Be sure that the adjuster peg is in the shoe slot.

13. Install the shoe pull back spring.

Remove the spring washers (arrows) before attempting to remove the drum

Rotate adjuster bolts in direction of arrows to retract shoes

Unhooking the parking brake cable

Removing the hold-down springs and retainers

Removing the brake shoes (linings)

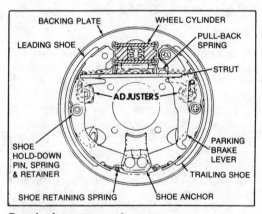

Rear brake components

is firm. Check the fluid level frequently. Adjust the parking brake.

1980–82

REMOVAL

1. Jack up the car and support safely with jack stands.

2. Mark the relationship of the wheel to the axle and remove the wheel.

14. Attach the end of the parking brake cable to the lever.

15. Replace the drum. Adjust the brakes by applying the brake several times until the pedal

3. Mark the relationship of the drum to the axle and remove the drum.

4. Using a suitable tool remove the return springs, hold down springs, lever pivot and hold down pins.

5. Lift up on the actuator lever and remove the actuating link.

6. Remove the actuator lever, actuator pivot and return spring.

7. Remove the parking brake strut and spring by spreading the shoes apart.

8. Spread the shoe and lining assemblies to clear the axle flange. Disconnect the parking brake cable and remove the shoes, connected by a spring from the vehicle.

9. While noting the position of the adjusting spring, remove the adjusting screw and spring.

10. Remove the parking brake lever from the secondary shoe.

INSTALLATION

1. Install the parking brake lever on the new secondary shoe.

2. Install the adjusting screw and spring.

NOTE: *The coils of the spring must not be over the star wheel. Left and right hand springs are different and must not be interchanged.*

3. Spread the shoe and lining assemblies to clear the axle flange and connect the parking brake cable.

4. Install the parking brake strut and spring by spreading the shoes apart.

NOTE: *The end of the strut without the spring engages the parking brake lever. The end with the spring engages the primary shoe.*

5. Install the actuator pivot, lever and return spring.

6. Install the actuating link in the shoe retainer.

7. Lift up on the actuator lever and hook the link onto the lever.

8. Install the hold down pins, lever pivot and hold down springs.

9. Install the shoe return springs.

10. Install the drum and wheel. Adjust the brakes by applying the brake several times until the pedal is firm. Check the fluid level and adjust the parking brake.

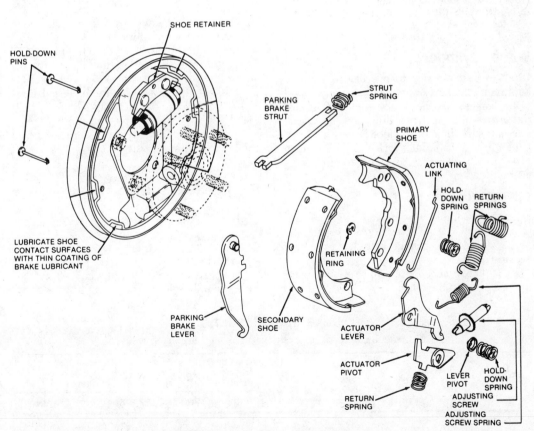

Rear brake assembly—1980 and later

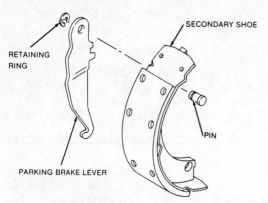

The parking brake lever is connected to secondary shoe by a retaining ring

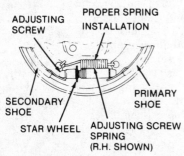

Proper installation of the adjusting screw and spring. Note that the coils of the spring are not over the star wheel

Wheel Cylinders

It is the best practice to overhaul or replace both rear wheel cylinders if either one is found to be leaking. If this is not done, the undisturbed cylinder will probably develop a leak soon after the first repair job. New wheel cylinders are available at a price low enough to make overhaul impractical, except in emergency situations.

OVERHAUL

1. Disassemble the brake system as described under "Brake Shoe Replacement."
2. Unbolt the wheel cylinder from the backing plate.
3. Remove and discard the rubber boots, the pistons, and the cups.

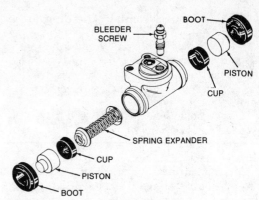

Exploded view of a wheel cylinder

4. Clean all parts in brake fluid or denatured alcohol.
5. If there are any pits or roughness inside the cylinder, it must be replaced. Polish off any discolored area by removing the cylinder around a piece of crocus cloth held by a finger. Do not polish the cylinder in a lengthwise direction. Clean the cylinder again after polishing. Air dry.
6. Replace the piston if it is scratched or damaged in any way.
7. Lubricate the cylinder bore with clean brake fluid and insert the spring and the expanders.
8. Install the new cups with the flat side to the outside. Do not lubricate them.
9. Install the new boot onto the piston and insert the piston into the cylinder with the flat surface towards the center of the cylinder. Do not lubricate the pistons before the installation.
10. Replace the cylinder and tighten the bolts evenly.
11. Reassemble the brake system and bleed the brake hydraulic system.

PARKING BRAKE

Cable

ADJUSTMENT

1. Raise the car.
2. Applying the parking brake 1–3 notches from the fully released position.

Brake Specifications

All measurements in mm, inches are given in parentheses

Year	Model	Master Cylinder Bore	Wheel Cylinder or Caliper Piston Bore		Brake Disc or Drum Diameter	
			Front	Rear	Front	Rear
1976–84	All	19.05 (.750)	47.625 (1.875)	19.05 (.750)	245.87 (9.68)	200.15 (7.88)

NOTE: *Drums cannot be turned more than 0.632 mm (0.025 in.)*

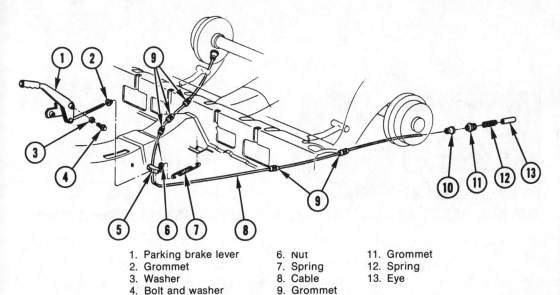

1. Parking brake lever
2. Grommet
3. Washer
4. Bolt and washer
5. Equalizer
6. Nut
7. Spring
8. Cable
9. Grommet
10. Boot
11. Grommet
12. Spring
13. Eye

Parking brake components

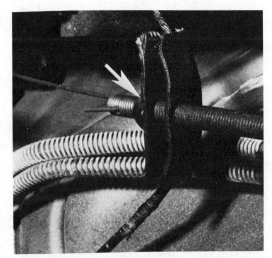

Parking brake cable is adjusted by turning the equalizer nut (arrow) in or out as necessary

3. Tighten the parking brake cable, equalizer adjusting nut until a light drag is felt when the rear wheels are rotated forward. The equalizer adjusting nut should be tightened to 55 in. lbs. at its adjustment point.

4. Fully release the parking brake and rotate the rear wheels. There should be no drag.

5. Lower the car.

REMOVAL AND INSTALLATION

1. Raise the car.

2. Disconnect the parking brake equalizer spring and equalizer.

3. Remove the cable from the underbody mounting brackets.

4. Remove the wheel and brake drum. With the rear brakes exposed, remove the parking brake cable from the parking brake lever.

5. Remove the spring locking clip and push out the cable grommets at the flange plate entry hole and remove the cable.

6. To install, pass the cable end through the flange plate entry hole making sure that the grommets are in place on the flange plate, and install the spring locking clips.

7. Connect the cable end to the parking brake lever.

8. Install the brake drum and the wheel.

9. Install the cable grommets at the underbody mounting brackets. On 1976–77 models, tighten the rear lower control arm bolt to 50 ft. lbs.; the rear control arm bracket to 50 ft. lbs.; the front control arm bracket to 15 ft. lbs. On 1978–80 models, tighten the rear lower control arm bracket to 33 ft. lbs.; the rear control arm bolt to 33 ft. lbs.; the front control arm bracket to 16 ft. lbs.

10. Install the equalizer onto the cable.

11. Install the equalizer over the parking brake lever rod and install the equalizer nut. Install the cable return spring.

12. Pre-stress the cable by applying the parking brake two or three times with heavy handle pressure.

13. Adjust the parking brake as previously described.

14. Lubricate the cable at the equalizer and at all grommets.

15. Lower the car.

Troubleshooting

This section is designed to aid in the quick, accurate diagnosis of automotive problems. While automotive repairs can be made by many people, accurate troubleshooting is a rare skill for the amateur and professional alike.

In its simplest state, troubleshooting is an exercise in logic. It is essential to realize that an automobile is really composed of a series of systems. Some of these systems are interrelated; others are not. Automobiles operate within a framework of logical rules and physical laws, and the key to trouble-shooting is a good understanding of all the automotive systems.

This section breaks the car or truck down into its component systems, allowing the problem to be isolated. The charts and diagnostic road maps list the most common problems and the most probable causes of trouble. Obviously it would be impossible to list every possible problem that could happen along with every possible cause, but it will locate MOST problems and eliminate a lot of unnecessary guesswork. The systematic format will locate problems within a given system, but, because many automotive systems are interrelated, the solution to your particular problem may be found in a number of systems on the car or truck.

USING THE TROUBLESHOOTING CHARTS

This book contains all of the specific information that the average do-it-yourself mechanic needs to repair and maintain his or her car or truck. The troubleshooting charts are designed to be used in conjunction with the specific procedures and information in the text. For instance, troubleshooting a point-type ignition system is fairly standard for all models, but you may be directed to the text to find procedures for troubleshooting an individual type of electronic ignition. You will also have to refer to the specification charts throughout the book for specifications applicable to your car or truck.

TOOLS AND EQUIPMENT

The tools illustrated in Chapter 1 (plus two more diagnostic pieces) will be adequate to troubleshoot most problems. The two other tools needed are a voltmeter and an ohmmeter. These can be purchased separately or in combination, known as a VOM meter.

In the event that other tools are required, they will be noted in the procedures.

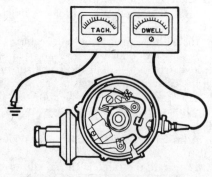

Tach-dwell hooked-up to distributor

Troubleshooting Engine Problems

See Chapters 2, 3, 4 for more information and service procedures.

Index to Systems

System	To Test	Group
Battery	Engine need not be running	1
Starting system	Engine need not be running	2
Primary electrical system	Engine need not be running	3
Secondary electrical system	Engine need not be running	4
Fuel system	Engine need not be running	5
Engine compression	Engine need not be running	6
Engine vacuum	Engine must be running	7
Secondary electrical system	Engine must be running	8
Valve train	Engine must be running	9
Exhaust system	Engine must be running	10
Cooling system	Engine must be running	11
Engine lubrication	Engine must be running	12

Index to Problems

Problem: Symptom	Begin at Specific Diagnosis, Number ____
Engine Won't Start:	
Starter doesn't turn	1.1, 2.1
Starter turns, engine doesn't	2.1
Starter turns engine very slowly	1.1, 2.4
Starter turns engine normally	3.1, 4.1
Starter turns engine very quickly	6.1
Engine fires intermittently	4.1
Engine fires consistently	5.1, 6.1
Engine Runs Poorly:	
Hard starting	3.1, 4.1, 5.1, 8.1
Rough idle	4.1, 5.1, 8.1
Stalling	3.1, 4.1, 5.1, 8.1
Engine dies at high speeds	4.1, 5.1
Hesitation (on acceleration from standing stop)	5.1, 8.1
Poor pickup	4.1, 5.1, 8.1
Lack of power	3.1, 4.1, 5.1, 8.1
Backfire through the carburetor	4.1, 8.1, 9.1
Backfire through the exhaust	4.1, 8.1, 9.1
Blue exhaust gases	6.1, 7.1
Black exhaust gases	5.1
Running on (after the ignition is shut off)	3.1, 8.1
Susceptible to moisture	4.1
Engine misfires under load	4.1, 7.1, 8.4, 9.1
Engine misfires at speed	4.1, 8.4
Engine misfires at idle	3.1, 4.1, 5.1, 7.1, 8.4

Sample Section

Test and Procedure	Results and Indications	Proceed to
4.1—Check for spark: Hold each spark plug wire approximately ¼″ from ground with gloves or a heavy, dry rag. Crank the engine and observe the spark.	→ If no spark is evident:	→ **4.2**
	→ If spark is good in some cases:	→ **4.3**
	→ If spark is good in all cases:	→ **4.6**

Specific Diagnosis

This section is arranged so that following each test, instructions are given to proceed to another, until a problem is diagnosed.

Section 1—Battery

Test and Procedure	Results and Indications	Proceed to
1.1—Inspect the battery visually for case condition (corrosion, cracks) and water level.	If case is cracked, replace battery:	**1.4**
	If the case is intact, remove corrosion with a solution of baking soda and water (**CAUTION**: *do not get the solution into the battery*), and fill with water:	**1.2**

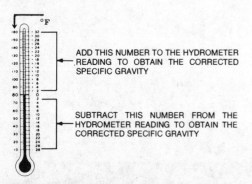

DIRT ON TOP OF BATTERY
CORROSION
PLUGGED VENT
LOOSE CABLE OR POSTS
CRACKS
LOW WATER LEVEL

Inspect the battery case

Test and Procedure	Results and Indications	Proceed to
1.2—Check the battery cable connections: Insert a screwdriver between the battery post and the cable clamp. Turn the headlights on high beam, and observe them as the screwdriver is gently twisted to ensure good metal to metal contact.	If the lights brighten, remove and clean the clamp and post; coat the post with petroleum jelly, install and tighten the clamp:	**1.4**
	If no improvement is noted:	**1.3**

TESTING BATTERY CABLE CONNECTIONS USING A SCREWDRIVER

Test and Procedure	Results and Indications	Proceed to
1.3—Test the state of charge of the battery using an individual cell tester or hydrometer.	If indicated, charge the battery. **NOTE**: *If no obvious reason exists for the low state of charge (i.e., battery age, prolonged storage), proceed to:*	**1.4**

°F

ADD THIS NUMBER TO THE HYDROMETER READING TO OBTAIN THE CORRECTED SPECIFIC GRAVITY

SUBTRACT THIS NUMBER FROM THE HYDROMETER READING TO OBTAIN THE CORRECTED SPECIFIC GRAVITY

Specific Gravity (@ 80° F.)

Minimum	Battery Charge
1.260	100% Charged
1.230	75% Charged
1.200	50% Charged
1.170	25% Charged
1.140	Very Little Power Left
1.110	Completely Discharged

The effects of temperature on battery specific gravity (left) and amount of battery charge in relation to specific gravity (right)

Test and Procedure	Results and Indications	Proceed to
1.4—Visually inspect battery cables for cracking, bad connection to ground, or bad connection to starter.	If necessary, tighten connections or replace the cables:	**2.1**

Section 2—Starting System
See Chapter 3 for service procedures

Test and Procedure	Results and Indications	Proceed to
Note: Tests in Group 2 are performed with coil high tension lead disconnected to prevent accidental starting.		
2.1—Test the starter motor and solenoid: Connect a jumper from the battery post of the solenoid (or relay) to the starter post of the solenoid (or relay).	If starter turns the engine normally:	2.2
	If the starter buzzes, or turns the engine very slowly:	2.4
	If no response, replace the solenoid (or relay).	3.1
	If the starter turns, but the engine doesn't, ensure that the flywheel ring gear is intact. If the gear is undamaged, replace the starter drive.	3.1
2.2—Determine whether ignition override switches are functioning properly (clutch start switch, neutral safety switch), by connecting a jumper across the switch(es), and turning the ignition switch to "start".	If starter operates, adjust or replace switch:	3.1
	If the starter doesn't operate:	2.3
2.3—Check the ignition switch "start" position: Connect a 12V test lamp or voltmeter between the starter post of the solenoid (or relay) and ground. Turn the ignition switch to the "start" position, and jiggle the key.	If the lamp doesn't light or the meter needle doesn't move when the switch is turned, check the ignition switch for loose connections, cracked insulation, or broken wires. Repair or replace as necessary:	3.1
	If the lamp flickers or needle moves when the key is jiggled, replace the ignition switch.	3.3

Checking the ignition switch "start" position

STARTER RELAY
(IF EQUIPPED)

Test and Procedure	Results and Indications	Proceed to
2.4—Remove and bench test the starter, according to specifications in the engine electrical section.	If the starter does not meet specifications, repair or replace as needed:	3.1
	If the starter is operating properly:	2.5
2.5—Determine whether the engine can turn freely: Remove the spark plugs, and check for water in the cylinders. Check for water on the dipstick, or oil in the radiator. Attempt to turn the engine using an 18″ flex drive and socket on the crankshaft pulley nut or bolt.	If the engine will turn freely only with the spark plugs out, and hydrostatic lock (water in the cylinders) is ruled out, check valve timing:	9.2
	If engine will not turn freely, and it is known that the clutch and transmission are free, the engine must be disassembled for further evaluation:	Chapter 3

Section 3—Primary Electrical System

Test and Procedure	Results and Indications	Proceed to
3.1—Check the ignition switch "on" position: Connect a jumper wire between the distributor side of the coil and ground, and a 12V test lamp between the switch side of the coil and ground. Remove the high tension lead from the coil. Turn the ignition switch on and jiggle the key.	If the lamp lights:	**3.2**
	If the lamp flickers when the key is jiggled, replace the ignition switch:	**3.3**
	If the lamp doesn't light, check for loose or open connections. If none are found, remove the ignition switch and check for continuity. If the switch is faulty, replace it:	**3.3**

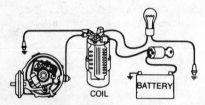

Checking the ignition switch "on" position

3.2—Check the ballast resistor or resistance wire for an open circuit, using an ohmmeter. See Chapter 3 for specific tests.	Replace the resistor or resistance wire if the resistance is zero. **NOTE:** *Some ignition systems have no ballast resistor.*	**3.3**

 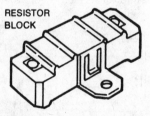

Two types of resistors

3.3—On point-type ignition systems, visually inspect the breaker points for burning, pitting or excessive wear. Gray coloring of the point contact surfaces is normal. Rotate the crankshaft until the contact heel rests on a high point of the distributor cam and adjust the point gap to specifications. On electronic ignition models, remove the distributor cap and visually inspect the armature. Ensure that the armature pin is in place, and that the armature is on tight and rotates when the engine is cranked. Make sure there are no cracks, chips or rounded edges on the armature.	If the breaker points are intact, clean the contact surfaces with fine emery cloth, and adjust the point gap to specifications. If the points are worn, replace them. On electronic systems, replace any parts which appear defective. If condition persists:	**3.4**

Test and Procedure	Results and Indications	Proceed to
3.4—On point-type ignition systems, connect a dwell-meter between the distributor primary lead and ground. Crank the engine and observe the point dwell angle. On electronic ignition systems, conduct a stator (magnetic pickup assembly) test. See Chapter 3.	On point-type systems, adjust the dwell angle if necessary. **NOTE:** *Increasing the point gap decreases the dwell angle and vice-versa.*	**3.6**
	If the dwell meter shows little or no reading;	**3.5**
	On electronic ignition systems, if the stator is bad, replace the stator. If the stator is good, proceed to the other tests in Chapter 3.	

CLOSE   OPEN

NORMAL DWELL

WIDE GAP

SMALL DWELL

INSUFFICIENT DWELL

NARROW GAP

LARGE DWELL

EXCESSIVE DWELL

Dwell is a function of point gap

3.5—On the point-type ignition systems, check the condenser for short: connect an ohmeter across the condenser body and the pigtail lead.	If any reading other than infinite is noted, replace the condenser	**3.6**

OHMMETER

Checking the condenser for short

3.6—Test the coil primary resistance: On point-type ignition systems, connect an ohmmeter across the coil primary terminals, and read the resistance on the low scale. Note whether an external ballast resistor or resistance wire is used. On electronic ignition systems, test the coil primary resistance as in Chapter 3.	Point-type ignition coils utilizing ballast resistors or resistance wires should have approximately 1.0 ohms resistance. Coils with internal resistors should have approximately 4.0 ohms resistance. If values far from the above are noted, replace the coil.	**4.1**

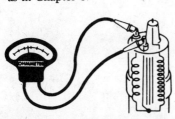

Check the coil primary resistance

Section 4—Secondary Electrical System
See Chapters 2–3 for service procedures

Test and Procedure	Results and Indications	Proceed to
4.1—Check for spark: Hold each spark plug wire approximately ¼″ from ground with gloves or a heavy, dry rag. Crank the engine, and observe the spark.	If no spark is evident:	**4.2**
	If spark is good in some cylinders:	**4.3**
	If spark is good in all cylinders:	**4.6**

Check for spark at the plugs

4.2—Check for spark at the coil high tension lead: Remove the coil high tension lead from the distributor and position it approximately ¼″ from ground. Crank the engine and observe spark. **CAUTION:** *This test should not be performed on engines equipped with electronic ignition.*	If the spark is good and consistent:	**4.3**
	If the spark is good but intermittent, test the primary electrical system starting at 3.3:	**3.3**
	If the spark is weak or non-existent, replace the coil high tension lead, clean and tighten all connections and retest. If no improvement is noted:	**4.4**
4.3—Visually inspect the distributor cap and rotor for burned or corroded contacts, cracks, carbon tracks, or moisture. Also check the fit of the rotor on the distributor shaft (where applicable).	If moisture is present, dry thoroughly, and retest per 4.1:	**4.1**
	If burned or excessively corroded contacts, cracks, or carbon tracks are noted, replace the defective part(s) and retest per 4.1:	**4.1**
	If the rotor and cap appear intact, or are only slightly corroded, clean the contacts thoroughly (including the cap towers and spark plug wire ends) and retest per 4.1:	
	If the spark is good in all cases:	**4.6**
	If the spark is poor in all cases:	**4.5**

Inspect the distributor cap and rotor

Test and Procedure	Results and Indications	Proceed to
4.4—Check the coil secondary resistance: On point-type systems connect an ohmmeter across the distributor side of the coil and the coil tower. Read the resistance on the high scale of the ohmmeter. On electronic ignition systems, see Chapter 3 for specific tests.	The resistance of a satisfactory coil should be between 4,000 and 10,000 ohms. If resistance is considerably higher (i.e., 40,000 ohms) replace the coil and retest per 4.1. **NOTE:** *This does not apply to high performance coils.*	

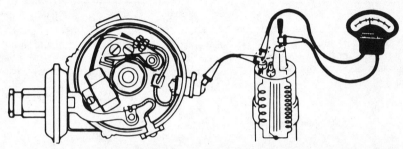

Testing the coil secondary resistance

4.5—Visually inspect the spark plug wires for cracking or brittleness. Ensure that no two wires are positioned so as to cause induction firing (adjacent and parallel). Remove each wire, one by one, and check resistance with an ohmmeter.	Replace any cracked or brittle wires. If any of the wires are defective, replace the entire set. Replace any wires with excessive resistance (over 8000 Ω per foot for suppression wire), and separate any wires that might cause induction firing.	**4.6**

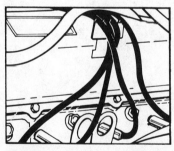

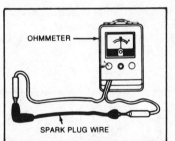

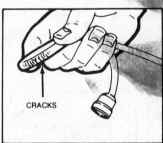

Misfiring can be the result of spark plug leads to adjacent, consecutively firing cylinders running parallel and too close together

On point-type ignition systems, check the spark plug wires as shown. On electronic ignitions, do not remove the wire from the distributor cap terminal; instead, test through the cap

Spark plug wires can be checked visually by bending them in a loop over your finger. This will reveal any cracks, burned or broken insulation. Any wire with cracked insulation should be replaced

4.6—Remove the spark plugs, noting the cylinders from which they were removed, and evaluate according to the color photos in the middle of this book.	See following.	**See following.**

Test and Procedure	Results and Indications	Proceed to
4.7—Examine the location of all the plugs.	The following diagrams illustrate some of the conditions that the location of plugs will reveal.	4.8

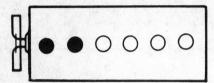

Two adjacent plugs are fouled in a 6-cylinder engine, 4-cylinder engine or either bank of a V-8. This is probably due to a blown head gasket between the two cylinders

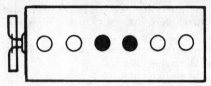

The two center plugs in a 6-cylinder engine are fouled. Raw fuel may be "boiled" out of the carburetor into the intake manifold after the engine is shut-off. Stop-start driving can also foul the center plugs, due to overly rich mixture. Proper float level, a new float needle and seat or use of an insulating spacer may help this problem

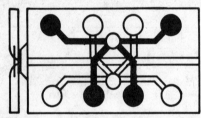

An unbalanced carburetor is indicated. Following the fuel flow on this particular design shows that the cylinders fed by the right-hand barrel are fouled from overly rich mixture, while the cylinders fed by the left-hand barrel are normal

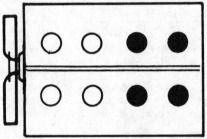

If the four rear plugs are overheated, a cooling system problem is suggested. A thorough cleaning of the cooling system may restore coolant circulation and cure the problem

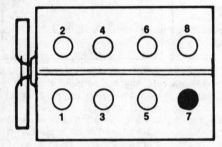

Finding one plug overheated may indicate an intake manifold leak near the affected cylinder. If the overheated plug is the second of two adjacent, consecutively firing plugs, it could be the result of ignition cross-firing. Separating the leads to these two plugs will eliminate cross-fire

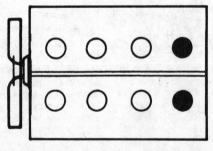

Occasionally, the two rear plugs in large, lightly used V-8's will become oil fouled. High oil consumption and smoky exhaust may also be noticed. It is probably due to plugged oil drain holes in the rear of the cylinder head, causing oil to be sucked in around the valve stems. This usually occurs in the rear cylinders first, because the engine slants that way

Test and Procedure	Results and Indications	Proceed to
4.8—Determine the static ignition timing. Using the crankshaft pulley timing marks as a guide, locate top dead center on the compression stroke of the number one cylinder.	The rotor should be pointing toward the No. 1 tower in the distributor cap, and, on electronic ignitions, the armature spoke for that cylinder should be lined up with the stator.	4.8
4.9—Check coil polarity: Connect a voltmeter negative lead to the coil high tension lead, and the positive lead to ground (**NOTE: *Reverse the hook-up for positive ground systems***). Crank the engine momentarily. **Checking coil polarity**	If the voltmeter reads up-scale, the polarity is correct: If the voltmeter reads down-scale, reverse the coil polarity (switch the primary leads):	5.1 5.1

Section 5—Fuel System
See Chapter 4 for service procedures

Test and Procedure	Results and Indications	Proceed to
5.1—Determine that the air filter is functioning efficiently: Hold paper elements up to a strong light, and attempt to see light through the filter.	Clean permanent air filters in solvent (or manufacturer's recommendation), and allow to dry. Replace paper elements through which light cannot be seen:	5.2
5.2—Determine whether a flooding condition exists: Flooding is identified by a strong gasoline odor, and excessive gasoline present in the throttle bore(s) of the carburetor. **If the engine floods repeatedly, check the choke butterfly flap**	If flooding is not evident: If flooding is evident, permit the gasoline to dry for a few moments and restart. If flooding doesn't recur: If flooding is persistent:	5.3 5.7 5.5
5.3—Check that fuel is reaching the carburetor: Detach the fuel line at the carburetor inlet. Hold the end of the line in a cup (not styrofoam), and crank the engine. **Check the fuel pump by disconnecting the output line (fuel pump-to-carburetor) at the carburetor and operating the starter briefly**	If fuel flows smoothly: If fuel doesn't flow (**NOTE: *Make sure that there is fuel in the tank***), or flows erratically:	5.7 5.4

Test and Procedure	Results and Indications	Proceed to
5.4—Test the fuel pump: Disconnect all fuel lines from the fuel pump. Hold a finger over the input fitting, crank the engine (with electric pump, turn the ignition or pump on); and feel for suction.	If suction is evident, blow out the fuel line to the tank with low pressure compressed air until bubbling is heard from the fuel filler neck. Also blow out the carburetor fuel line (both ends disconnected):	5.7
	If no suction is evident, replace or repair the fuel pump:	5.7
	NOTE: *Repeated oil fouling of the spark plugs, or a no-start condition, could be the result of a ruptured vacuum booster pump diaphragm, through which oil or gasoline is being drawn into the intake manifold (where applicable).*	
5.5—Occasionally, small specks of dirt will clog the small jets and orifices in the carburetor. With the engine cold, hold a flat piece of wood or similar material over the carburetor, where possible, and crank the engine.	If the engine starts, but runs roughly the engine is probably not run enough. If the engine won't start:	5.9
5.6—Check the needle and seat: Tap the carburetor in the area of the needle and seat.	If flooding stops, a gasoline additive (e.g., Gumout) will often cure the problem:	5.7
	If flooding continues, check the fuel pump for excessive pressure at the carburetor (according to specifications). If the pressure is normal, the needle and seat must be removed and checked, and/or the float level adjusted:	5.7
5.7—Test the accelerator pump by looking into the throttle bores while operating the throttle.	If the accelerator pump appears to be operating normally:	5.8
	If the accelerator pump is not operating, the pump must be reconditioned. Where possible, service the pump with the carburetor(s) installed on the engine. If necessary, remove the carburetor. Prior to removal:	5.8

Check for gas at the carburetor by looking down the carburetor throat while someone moves the accelerator

Test and Procedure	Results and Indications	Proceed to
5.8—Determine whether the carburetor main fuel system is functioning: Spray a commercial starting fluid into the carburetor while attempting to start the engine.	If the engine starts, runs for a few seconds, and dies:	5.9
	If the engine doesn't start:	6.1

CHILTON'S
AUTO BODY
REPAIR TIPS

Tools and Materials • Step-by-Step Illustrated Procedures
How To Repair Dents, Scratches and Rust Holes
Spray Painting and Refinishing Tips

With a little practice, basic body repair procedures can be mastered by any do-it-yourself mechanic. The step-by-step repairs shown here can be applied to almost any type of auto body repair.

TOOLS & MATERIALS

You may already have basic tools, such as hammers and electric drills. Other tools unique to body repair — body hammers, grinding attachments, sanding blocks, dent puller, half-round plastic file and plastic spreaders — are relatively inexpensive and can be obtained wherever auto parts or auto body repair parts are sold. Portable air compressors and paint spray guns can be purchased or rented.

Auto Body Repair Kits

The best and most often used products are available to the do-it-yourselfer in kit form, from major manufacturers of auto body repair products. The same manufacturers also merchandise the individual products for use by pros.

Kits are available to make a wide variety of repairs, including holes, dents and scratches and fiberglass, and offer the advantage of buying the materials you'll need for the job. There is little waste or chance of materials going bad from not being used. Many kits may also contain basic body-working tools such as body files, sanding blocks and spreaders. Check the contents of the kit before buying your tools.

BODY REPAIR TIPS

Safety

Many of the products associated with auto body repair and refinishing contain toxic chemicals. Read all labels before opening containers and store them in a safe place and manner.

• Wear eye protection (safety goggles) when using power tools or when performing any operation that involves the removal of any type of material.

• Wear lung protection (disposable mask or respirator) when grinding, sanding or painting.

Sanding

1 Sand off paint before using a dent puller. When using a non-adhesive sanding disc, cover the back of the disc with an overlapping layer or two of masking tape and trim the edges. The disc will last considerably longer.

2 Use the circular motion of the sanding disc to grind *into* the edge of the repair. Grinding or sanding away from the jagged edge will only tear the sandpaper.

3 Use the palm of your hand flat on the panel to detect high and low spots. Do not use your fingertips. Slide your hand slowly back and forth.

WORKING WITH BODY FILLER

Mixing The Filler

Cleanliness and proper mixing and application are extremely important. Use a clean piece of plastic or glass or a disposable artist's palette to mix body filler.

1 Allow plenty of time and follow directions. No useful purpose will be served by adding more hardener to make it cure (set-up) faster. Less hardener means more curing time, but the mixture dries harder; more hardener means less curing time but a softer mixture.

2 Both the hardener and the filler should be thoroughly kneaded or stirred before mixing. Hardener should be a solid paste and dispense like thin toothpaste. Body filler should be smooth, and free of lumps or thick spots.

Getting the proper amount of hardener in the filler is the trickiest part of preparing the filler. Use the same amount of hardener in cold or warm weather. For contour filler (thick coats), a bead of hardener twice the diameter of the filler is about right. There's about a 15% margin on either side, but, if in doubt use less hardener.

3 Mix the body filler and hardener by wiping across the mixing surface, picking the mixture up and wiping it again. Colder weather requires longer mixing times. Do not mix in a circular motion; this will trap air bubbles which will become holes in the cured filler.

Applying The Filler

1 For best results, filler should not be applied over ¼" thick.

Apply the filler in several coats. Build it up to above the level of the repair surface so that it can be sanded or grated down.

The first coat of filler must be pressed on with a firm wiping motion.

Apply the filler in one direction only. Working the filler back and forth will either pull it off the metal or trap air bubbles.

REPAIRING DENTS

Before you start, take a few minutes to study the damaged area. Try to visualize the shape of the panel before it was damaged. If the damage is on the left fender, look at the right fender and use it as a guide. If there is access to the panel from behind, you can reshape it with a body hammer. If not, you'll have to use a dent puller. Go slowly and work the metal a little at a time. Get the panel as straight as possible before applying filler.

1 This dent is typical of one that can be pulled out or hammered out from behind. Remove the headlight cover, headlight assembly and turn signal housing.

2 Drill a series of holes ½ the size of the end of the dent puller along the stress line. Make some trial pulls and assess the results. If necessary, drill more holes and try again. Do not hurry.

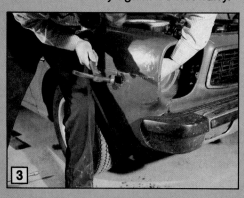

3 If possible, use a body hammer and block to shape the metal back to its original contours. Get the metal back as close to its original shape as possible. Don't depend on body filler to fill dents.

4 Using an 80-grit grinding disc on an electric drill, grind the paint from the surrounding area down to bare metal. Use a new grinding pad to prevent heat buildup that will warp metal.

5 The area should look like this when you're finished grinding. Knock the drill holes in and tape over small openings to keep plastic filler out.

6 Mix the body filler (see Body Repair Tips). Spread the body filler evenly over the entire area (see Body Repair Tips). Be sure to cover the area completely.

7 Let the body filler dry until the surface can just be scratched with your fingernail. Knock the high spots from the body filler with a body file ("Cheese-grater"). Check frequently with the palm of your hand for high and low spots.

8 Check to be sure that trim pieces that will be installed later will fit exactly. Sand the area with 40-grit paper.

9 If you wind up with low spots, you may have to apply another layer of filler.

10 Knock the high spots off with 40-grit paper. When you are satisfied with the contours of the repair, apply a thin coat of filler to cover pin holes and scratches.

11 Block sand the area with 40-grit paper to a smooth finish. Pay particular attention to body lines and ridges that must be well-defined.

12 Sand the area with 400 paper and then finish with a scuff pad. The finished repair is ready for priming and painting (see Painting Tips).

Materials and photos courtesy of Ritt Jones Auto Body, Prospect Park, PA.

REPAIRING RUST HOLES

There are many ways to repair rust holes. The fiberglass cloth kit shown here is one of the most cost efficient for the owner because it provides a strong repair that resists cracking and moisture and is relatively easy to use. It can be used on large and small holes (with or without backing) and can be applied over contoured areas. Remember, however, that short of replacing an entire panel, no repair is a guarantee that the rust will not return.

1 Remove any trim that will be in the way. Clean away all loose debris. Cut away all the rusted metal. But be sure to leave enough metal to retain the contour or body shape.

2 Grind away all traces of rust with a 24-grit grinding disc. Be sure to grind back 3-4 inches from the edge of the hole down to bare metal and be sure all traces of paint, primer and rust are removed.

3 Block sand the area with 80 or 100 grit sandpaper to get a clear, shiny surface and feathered paint edge. Tap the edges of the hole inward with a ball peen hammer.

4 If you are going to use release film, cut a piece about 2-3" larger than the area you have sanded. Place the film over the repair and mark the sanded area on the film. Avoid any unnecessary wrinkling of the film.

5 Cut 2 pieces of fiberglass matte to match the shape of the repair. One piece should be about 1" smaller than the sanded area and the second piece should be 1" smaller than the first. Mix enough filler and hardener to saturate the fiberglass material (see Body Repair Tips).

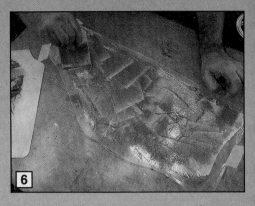

6 Lay the release sheet on a flat surface and spread an even layer of filler, large enough to cover the repair. Lay the smaller piece of fiberglass cloth in the center of the sheet and spread another layer of filler over the fiberglass cloth. Repeat the operation for the larger piece of cloth.

7 Place the repair material over the repair area, with the release film facing outward. Use a spreader and work from the center outward to smooth the material, following the body contours. Be sure to remove all air bubbles.

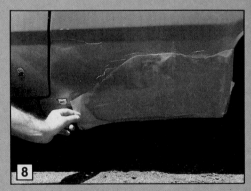

8 Wait until the repair has dried tack-free and peel off the release sheet. The ideal working temperature is 60°-90° F. Cooler or warmer temperatures or high humidity may require additional curing time. Wait longer, if in doubt.

9

9 Sand and feather-edge the entire area. The initial sanding can be done with a sanding disc on an electric drill if care is used. Finish the sanding with a block sander. Low spots can be filled with body filler; this may require several applications.

10

10 When the filler can just be scratched with a fingernail, knock the high spots down with a body file and smooth the entire area with 80-grit. Feather the filled areas into the surrounding areas.

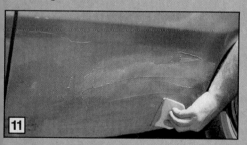

11

11 When the area is sanded smooth, mix some topcoat and hardener and apply it directly with a spreader. This will give a smooth finish and prevent the glass matte from showing through the paint.

12

12 Block sand the topcoat smooth with finishing sandpaper (200 grit), and 400 grit. The repair is ready for masking, priming and painting (see Painting Tips).

Materials and photos courtesy Marson Corporation, Chelsea, Massachusetts

PAINTING TIPS

Preparation

1 SANDING — Use a 400 or 600 grit wet or dry sandpaper. Wet-sand the area with a 1/4 sheet of sandpaper soaked in clean water. Keep the paper wet while sanding. Sand the area until the repaired area tapers into the original finish.

2 CLEANING — Wash the area to be painted thoroughly with water and a clean rag. Rinse it thoroughly and wipe the surface dry until you're sure it's completely free of dirt, dust, fingerprints, wax, detergent or other foreign matter.

3 MASKING — Protect any areas you don't want to overspray by covering them with masking tape and newspaper. Be careful not get fingerprints on the area to be painted.

4 PRIMING — All exposed metal should be primed before painting. Primer protects the metal and provides an excellent surface for paint adhesion. When the primer is dry, wet-sand the area again with 600 grit wet-sandpaper. Clean the area again after sanding.

4

Painting Techniques

P aint applied from either a spray gun or a spray can (for small areas) will provide good results. Experiment on an old piece of metal to get the right combination before you begin painting.

SPRAYING VISCOSITY (SPRAY GUN ONLY) — Paint should be thinned to spraying viscosity according to the directions on the can. Use only the recommended thinner or reducer and the same amount of reduction regardless of temperature.

AIR PRESSURE (SPRAY GUN ONLY) — This is extremely important. Be sure you are using the proper recommended pressure.

TEMPERATURE — The surface to be painted should be approximately the same temperature as the surrounding air. Applying warm paint to a cold surface, or vice versa, will completely upset the paint characteristics.

THICKNESS — Spray with smooth strokes. In general, the thicker the coat of paint, the longer the drying time. Apply several thin coats about 30 seconds apart. The paint should remain wet long enough to flow out and no longer; heavier coats will only produce sags or wrinkles. Spray a light (fog) coat, followed by heavier color coats.

DISTANCE — The ideal spraying distance is 8"-12" from the gun or can to the surface. Shorter distances will produce ripples, while greater distances will result in orange peel, dry film and poor color match and loss of material due to overspray.

OVERLAPPING — The gun or can should be kept at right angles to the surface at all times. Work to a wet edge at an even speed, using a 50% overlap and direct the center of the spray at the lower or nearest edge of the previous stroke.

RUBBING OUT (BLENDING) FRESH PAINT — Let the paint dry thoroughly. Runs or imperfections can be sanded out, primed and repainted.

Don't be in too big a hurry to remove the masking. This only produces paint ridges. When the finish has dried for at least a week, apply a small amount of fine grade rubbing compound with a clean, wet cloth. Use lots of water and blend the new paint with the surrounding area.

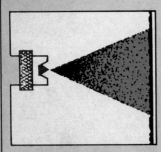

WRONG

Thin coat. Stroke too fast, not enough overlap, gun too far away.

CORRECT

Medium coat. Proper distance, good stroke, proper overlap.

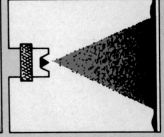

WRONG

Heavy coat. Stroke too slow, too much overlap, gun too close.

Test and Procedure	Results and Indications	Proceed to
5.9—Uncommon fuel system malfunctions: See below:	If the problem is solved: If the problem remains, remove and recondition the carburetor.	6.1

Condition	Indication	Test	Prevailing Weather Conditions	Remedy
Vapor lock	Engine will not restart shortly after running.	Cool the components of the fuel system until the engine starts. Vapor lock can be cured faster by draping a wet cloth over a mechanical fuel pump.	Hot to very hot	Ensure that the exhaust manifold heat control valve is operating. Check with the vehicle manufacturer for the recommended solution to vapor lock on the model in question.
Carburetor icing	Engine will not idle, stalls at low speeds.	Visually inspect the throttle plate area of the throttle bores for frost.	High humidity, 32–40° F.	Ensure that the exhaust manifold heat control valve is operating, and that the intake manifold heat riser is not blocked.
Water in the fuel	Engine sputters and stalls; may not start.	Pump a small amount of fuel into a glass jar. Allow to stand, and inspect for droplets or a layer of water.	High humidity, extreme temperature changes.	For droplets, use one or two cans of commercial gas line anti-freeze. For a layer of water, the tank must be drained, and the fuel lines blown out with compressed air.

Section 6—Engine Compression
See Chapter 3 for service procedures

6.1—Test engine compression: Remove all spark plugs. Block the throttle wide open. Insert a compression gauge into a spark plug port, crank the engine to obtain the maximum reading, and record.	If compression is within limits on all cylinders: If gauge reading is extremely low on all cylinders: If gauge reading is low on one or two cylinders: (If gauge readings are identical and low on two or more adjacent cylinders, the head gasket must be replaced.)	7.1 6.2 6.2

Checking compression

6.2—Test engine compression (wet): Squirt approximately 30 cc. of engine oil into each cylinder, and retest per 6.1.	If the readings improve, worn or cracked rings or broken pistons are indicated: If the readings do not improve, burned or excessively carboned valves or a jumped timing chain are indicated: NOTE: *A jumped timing chain is often indicated by difficult cranking.*	See Chapter 3 7.1

Section 7—Engine Vacuum

See Chapter 3 for service procedures

Test and Procedure	Results and Indications	Proceed to
7.1—Attach a vacuum gauge to the intake manifold beyond the throttle plate. Start the engine, and observe the action of the needle over the range of engine speeds.	See below.	**See below**

INDICATION: normal engine in good condition

Proceed to: 8.1

Normal engine
Gauge reading: steady, from 17–22 in./Hg.

INDICATION: sticking valves or ignition miss

Proceed to: 9.1, 8.3

Sticking valves
Gauge reading: intermittent fluctuation at idle

INDICATION: late ignition or valve timing, low compression, stuck throttle valve, leaking carburetor or manifold gasket

Proceed to: 6.1

Incorrect valve timing
Gauge reading: low (10–15 in./Hg) but steady

INDICATION: improper carburetor adjustment or minor intake leak.

Proceed to: 7.2

Carburetor requires adjustment
Gauge reading: drifting needle

INDICATION: ignition miss, blown cylinder head gasket, leaking valve or weak valve spring

Proceed to: 8.3, 6.1

Blown head gasket
Gauge reading: needle fluctuates as engine speed increases

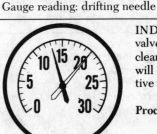

INDICATION: burnt valve or faulty valve clearance. Needle will fall when defective valve operates

Proceed to: 9.1

Burnt or leaking valves
Gauge reading: steady needle, but drops regularly

INDICATION: choked muffler, excessive back pressure in system

Proceed to: 10.1

Clogged exhaust system
Gauge reading: gradual drop in reading at idle

INDICATION: worn valve guides

Proceed to: 9.1

Worn valve guides
Gauge reading: needle vibrates excessively at idle, but steadies as engine speed increases

---

White pointer = steady gauge hand   Black pointer = fluctuating gauge hand

Test and Procedure	Results and Indications	Proceed to
7.2—Attach a vacuum gauge per 7.1, and test for an intake manifold leak. Squirt a small amount of oil around the intake manifold gaskets, carburetor gaskets, plugs and fittings. Observe the action of the vacuum gauge.	If the reading improves, replace the indicated gasket, or seal the indicated fitting or plug: If the reading remains low:	**8.1** **7.3**
7.3—Test all vacuum hoses and accessories for leaks as described in 7.2. Also check the carburetor body (dashpots, automatic choke mechanism, throttle shafts) for leaks in the same manner.	If the reading improves, service or replace the offending part(s): If the reading remains low:	**8.1** **6.1**

Section 8—Secondary Electrical System
See Chapter 2 for service procedures

Test and Procedure	Results and Indications	Proceed to
8.1—Remove the distributor cap and check to make sure that the rotor turns when the engine is cranked. Visually inspect the distributor components.	Clean, tighten or replace any components which appear defective.	**8.2**
8.2—Connect a timing light (per manufacturer's recommendation) and check the dynamic ignition timing. Disconnect and plug the vacuum hose(s) to the distributor if specified, start the engine, and observe the timing marks at the specified engine speed.	If the timing is not correct, adjust to specifications by rotating the distributor in the engine: (Advance timing by rotating distributor opposite normal direction of rotor rotation, retard timing by rotating distributor in same direction as rotor rotation.)	**8.3**
8.3—Check the operation of the distributor advance mechanism(s): To test the mechanical advance, disconnect the vacuum lines from the distributor advance unit and observe the timing marks with a timing light as the engine speed is increased from idle. If the mark moves smoothly, without hesitation, it may be assumed that the mechanical advance is functioning properly. To test vacuum advance and/or retard systems, alternately crimp and release the vacuum line, and observe the timing mark for movement. If movement is noted, the system is operating.	If the systems are functioning: If the systems are not functioning, remove the distributor, and test on a distributor tester:	**8.4** **8.4**
8.4—Locate an ignition miss: With the engine running, remove each spark plug wire, one at a time, until one is found that doesn't cause the engine to roughen and slow down.	When the missing cylinder is identified:	**4.1**

Section 9—Valve Train
See Chapter 3 for service procedures

Test and Procedure	Results and Indications	Proceed to
9.1—Evaluate the valve train: Remove the valve cover, and ensure that the valves are adjusted to specifications. A mechanic's stethoscope may be used to aid in the diagnosis of the valve train. By pushing the probe on or near push rods or rockers, valve noise often can be isolated. A timing light also may be used to diagnose valve problems. Connect the light according to manufacturer's recommendations, and start the engine. Vary the firing moment of the light by increasing the engine speed (and therefore the ignition advance), and moving the trigger from cylinder to cylinder. Observe the movement of each valve.	Sticking valves or erratic valve train motion can be observed with the timing light. The cylinder head must be disassembled for repairs.	**See Chapter 3**
9.2—Check the valve timing: Locate top dead center of the No. 1 piston, and install a degree wheel or tape on the crankshaft pulley or damper with zero corresponding to an index mark on the engine. Rotate the crankshaft in its direction of rotation, and observe the opening of the No. 1 cylinder intake valve. The opening should correspond with the correct mark on the degree wheel according to specifications.	If the timing is not correct, the timing cover must be removed for further investigation.	**See Chapter 3**

Section 10—Exhaust System

Test and Procedure	Results and Indications	Proceed to
10.1—Determine whether the exhaust manifold heat control valve is operating: Operate the valve by hand to determine whether it is free to move. If the valve is free, run the engine to operating temperature and observe the action of the valve, to ensure that it is opening.	If the valve sticks, spray it with a suitable solvent, open and close the valve to free it, and retest. If the valve functions properly: If the valve does not free, or does not operate, replace the valve:	 **10.2** **10.2**
10.2—Ensure that there are no exhaust restrictions: Visually inspect the exhaust system for kinks, dents, or crushing. Also note that gases are flowing freely from the tailpipe at all engine speeds, indicating no restriction in the muffler or resonator.	Replace any damaged portion of the system:	**11.1**

Section 11—Cooling System
See Chapter 3 for service procedures

Test and Procedure	Results and Indications	Proceed to
11.1—Visually inspect the fan belt for glazing, cracks, and fraying, and replace if necessary. Tighten the belt so that the longest span has approximately ½″ play at its mid-point under thumb pressure (see Chapter 1).	Replace or tighten the fan belt as necessary:	**11.2**

Checking belt tension

Test and Procedure	Results and Indications	Proceed to
11.2—Check the fluid level of the cooling system.	If full or slightly low, fill as necessary:	**11.5**
	If extremely low:	**11.3**
11.3—Visually inspect the external portions of the cooling system (radiator, radiator hoses, thermostat elbow, water pump seals, heater hoses, etc.) for leaks. If none are found, pressurize the cooling system to 14–15 psi.	If cooling system holds the pressure:	**11.5**
	If cooling system loses pressure rapidly, reinspect external parts of the system for leaks under pressure. If none are found, check dipstick for coolant in crankcase. If no coolant is present, but pressure loss continues:	**11.4**
	If coolant is evident in crankcase, remove cylinder head(s), and check gasket(s). If gaskets are intact, block and cylinder head(s) should be checked for cracks or holes.	
	If the gasket(s) is blown, replace, and purge the crankcase of coolant:	**12.6**
	NOTE: *Occasionally, due to atmospheric and driving conditions, condensation of water can occur in the crankcase. This causes the oil to appear milky white. To remedy, run the engine until hot, and change the oil and oil filter.*	
11.4—Check for combustion leaks into the cooling system: Pressurize the cooling system as above. Start the engine, and observe the pressure gauge. If the needle fluctuates, remove each spark plug wire, one at a time, noting which cylinder(s) reduce or eliminate the fluctuation.	Cylinders which reduce or eliminate the fluctuation, when the spark plug wire is removed, are leaking into the cooling system. Replace the head gasket on the affected cylinder bank(s).	

Pressurizing the cooling system

Test and Procedure	Results and Indications	Proceed to
11.5—Check the radiator pressure cap: Attach a radiator pressure tester to the radiator cap (wet the seal prior to installation). Quickly pump up the pressure, noting the point at which the cap releases.	If the cap releases within ± 1 psi of the specified rating, it is operating properly:	**11.6**
	If the cap releases at more than ± 1 psi of the specified rating, it should be replaced:	**11.6**

Checking radiator pressure cap

Test and Procedure	Results and Indications	Proceed to
11.6—Test the thermostat: Start the engine cold, remove the radiator cap, and insert a thermometer into the radiator. Allow the engine to idle. After a short while, there will be a sudden, rapid increase in coolant temperature. The temperature at which this sharp rise stops is the thermostat opening temperature.	If the thermostat opens at or about the specified temperature:	**11.7**
	If the temperature doesn't increase: (If the temperature increases slowly and gradually, replace the thermostat.)	**11.7**
11.7—Check the water pump: Remove the thermostat elbow and the thermostat, disconnect the coil high tension lead (to prevent starting), and crank the engine momentarily.	If coolant flows, replace the thermostat and retest per 11.6:	**11.6**
	If coolant doesn't flow, reverse flush the cooling system to alleviate any blockage that might exist. If system is not blocked, and coolant will not flow, replace the water pump.	

Section 12—Lubrication
See Chapter 3 for service procedures

Test and Procedure	Results and Indications	Proceed to
12.1—Check the oil pressure gauge or warning light: If the gauge shows low pressure, or the light is on for no obvious reason, remove the oil pressure sender. Install an accurate oil pressure gauge and run the engine momentarily.	If oil pressure builds normally, run engine for a few moments to determine that it is functioning normally, and replace the sender.	—
	If the pressure remains low:	**12.2**
	If the pressure surges:	**12.3**
	If the oil pressure is zero:	**12.3**
12.2—Visually inspect the oil: If the oil is watery or very thin, milky, or foamy, replace the oil and oil filter.	If the oil is normal:	**12.3**
	If after replacing oil the pressure remains low:	**12.3**
	If after replacing oil the pressure becomes normal:	—

Test and Procedure	Results and Indications	Proceed to
12.3—Inspect the oil pressure relief valve and spring, to ensure that it is not sticking or stuck. Remove and thoroughly clean the valve, spring, and the valve body.	If the oil pressure improves: If no improvement is noted:	— **12.4**
12.4—Check to ensure that the oil pump is not cavitating (sucking air instead of oil): See that the crankcase is neither over nor underfull, and that the pickup in the sump is in the proper position and free from sludge.	Fill or drain the crankcase to the proper capacity, and clean the pickup screen in solvent if necessary. If no improvement is noted:	**12.5**
12.5—Inspect the oil pump drive and the oil pump:	If the pump drive or the oil pump appear to be defective, service as necessary and retest per 12.1:	**12.1**
	If the pump drive and pump appear to be operating normally, the engine should be disassembled to determine where blockage exists:	**See Chapter 3**
12.6—Purge the engine of ethylene glycol coolant: Completely drain the crankcase and the oil filter. Obtain a commercial butyl cellosolve base solvent, designated for this purpose, and follow the instructions precisely. Following this, install a new oil filter and refill the crankcase with the proper weight oil. The next oil and filter change should follow shortly thereafter (1000 miles).		

TROUBLESHOOTING EMISSION CONTROL SYSTEMS

See Chapter 4 for procedures applicable to individual emission control systems used on specific combinations of engine/transmission/model.

TROUBLESHOOTING THE CARBURETOR
See Chapter 4 for service procedures

Carburetor problems cannot be effectively isolated unless all other engine systems (particularly ignition and emission) are functioning properly and the engine is properly tuned.

Condition	Possible Cause
Engine cranks, but does not start	1. Improper starting procedure 2. No fuel in tank 3. Clogged fuel line or filter 4. Defective fuel pump 5. Choke valve not closing properly 6. Engine flooded 7. Choke valve not unloading 8. Throttle linkage not making full travel 9. Stuck needle or float 10. Leaking float needle or seat 11. Improper float adjustment
Engine stalls	1. Improperly adjusted idle speed or mixture **Engine hot** 2. Improperly adjusted dashpot 3. Defective or improperly adjusted solenoid 4. Incorrect fuel level in fuel bowl 5. Fuel pump pressure too high 6. Leaking float needle seat 7. Secondary throttle valve stuck open 8. Air or fuel leaks 9. Idle air bleeds plugged or missing 10. Idle passages plugged **Engine Cold** 11. Incorrectly adjusted choke 12. Improperly adjusted fast idle speed 13. Air leaks 14. Plugged idle or idle air passages 15. Stuck choke valve or binding linkage 16. Stuck secondary throttle valves 17. Engine flooding—high fuel level 18. Leaking or misaligned float
Engine hesitates on acceleration	1. Clogged fuel filter 2. Leaking fuel pump diaphragm 3. Low fuel pump pressure 4. Secondary throttle valves stuck, bent or misadjusted 5. Sticking or binding air valve 6. Defective accelerator pump 7. Vacuum leaks 8. Clogged air filter 9. Incorrect choke adjustment (engine cold)
Engine feels sluggish or flat on acceleration	1. Improperly adjusted idle speed or mixture 2. Clogged fuel filter 3. Defective accelerator pump 4. Dirty, plugged or incorrect main metering jets 5. Bent or sticking main metering rods 6. Sticking throttle valves 7. Stuck heat riser 8. Binding or stuck air valve 9. Dirty, plugged or incorrect secondary jets 10. Bent or sticking secondary metering rods. 11. Throttle body or manifold heat passages plugged 12. Improperly adjusted choke or choke vacuum break.
Carburetor floods	1. Defective fuel pump. Pressure too high. 2. Stuck choke valve 3. Dirty, worn or damaged float or needle valve/seat 4. Incorrect float/fuel level 5. Leaking float bowl

Condition	Possible Cause
Engine idles roughly and stalls	1. Incorrect idle speed 2. Clogged fuel filter 3. Dirt in fuel system or carburetor 4. Loose carburetor screws or attaching bolts 5. Broken carburetor gaskets 6. Air leaks 7. Dirty carburetor 8. Worn idle mixture needles 9. Throttle valves stuck open 10. Incorrectly adjusted float or fuel level 11. Clogged air filter
Engine runs unevenly or surges	1. Defective fuel pump 2. Dirty or clogged fuel filter 3. Plugged, loose or incorrect main metering jets or rods 4. Air leaks 5. Bent or sticking main metering rods 6. Stuck power piston 7. Incorrect float adjustment 8. Incorrect idle speed or mixture 9. Dirty or plugged idle system passages 10. Hard, brittle or broken gaskets 11. Loose attaching or mounting screws 12. Stuck or misaligned secondary throttle valves
Poor fuel economy	1. Poor driving habits 2. Stuck choke valve 3. Binding choke linkage 4. Stuck heat riser 5. Incorrect idle mixture 6. Defective accelerator pump 7. Air leaks 8. Plugged, loose or incorrect main metering jets 9. Improperly adjusted float or fuel level 10. Bent, misaligned or fuel-clogged float 11. Leaking float needle seat 12. Fuel leak 13. Accelerator pump discharge ball not seating properly 14. Incorrect main jets
Engine lacks high speed performance or power	1. Incorrect throttle linkage adjustment 2. Stuck or binding power piston 3. Defective accelerator pump 4. Air leaks 5. Incorrect float setting or fuel level 6. Dirty, plugged, worn or incorrect main metering jets or rods 7. Binding or sticking air valve 8. Brittle or cracked gaskets 9. Bent, incorrect or improperly adjusted secondary metering rods 10. Clogged fuel filter 11. Clogged air filter 12. Defective fuel pump

TROUBLESHOOTING FUEL INJECTION PROBLEMS

Each fuel injection system has its own unique components and test procedures, for which it is impossible to generalize. Refer to Chapter 4 of this Repair & Tune-Up Guide for specific test and repair procedures, if the vehicle is equipped with fuel injection.

TROUBLESHOOTING ELECTRICAL PROBLEMS

See Chapter 5 for service procedures

For any electrical system to operate, it must make a complete circuit. This simply means that the power flow from the battery must make a complete circle. When an electrical component is operating, power flows from the battery to the component, passes through the component causing it to perform its function (lighting a light bulb), and then returns to the battery through the ground of the circuit. This ground is usually (but not always) the metal part of the car or truck on which the electrical component is mounted.

Perhaps the easiest way to visualize this is to think of connecting a light bulb with two wires attached to it to the battery. If one of the two wires attached to the light bulb were attached to the negative post of the battery and the other were attached to the positive post of the battery, you would have a complete circuit. Current from the battery would flow to the light bulb, causing it to light, and return to the negative post of the battery.

The normal automotive circuit differs from this simple example in two ways. First, instead of having a return wire from the bulb to the battery, the light bulb returns the current to the battery through the chassis of the vehicle. Since the negative battery cable is attached to the chassis and the chassis is made of electrically conductive metal, the chassis of the vehicle can serve as a ground wire to complete the circuit. Secondly, most automotive circuits contain switches to turn components on and off as required.

Every complete circuit from a power source must include a component which is using the power from the power source. If you were to disconnect the light bulb from the wires and touch the two wires together (don't do this) the power supply wire to the component would be grounded before the normal ground connection for the circuit.

Because grounding a wire from a power source makes a complete circuit—less the required component to use the power—this phenomenon is called a short circuit. Common causes are: broken insulation (exposing the metal wire to a metal part of the car or truck), or a shorted switch.

Some electrical components which require a large amount of current to operate also have a relay in their circuit. Since these circuits carry a large amount of current, the thickness of the wire in the circuit (gauge size) is also greater. If this large wire were connected from the component to the control switch on the instrument panel, and then back to the component, a voltage drop would occur in the circuit. To prevent this potential drop in voltage, an electromagnetic switch (relay) is used. The large wires in the circuit are connected from the battery to one side of the relay, and from the opposite side of the relay to the component. The relay is normally open, preventing current from passing through the circuit. An additional, smaller, wire is connected from the relay to the control switch for the circuit. When the control switch is turned on, it grounds the smaller wire from the relay and completes the circuit. This closes the relay and allows current to flow from the battery to the component. The horn, headlight, and starter circuits are three which use relays.

It is possible for larger surges of current to pass through the electrical system of your car or truck. If this surge of current were to reach an electrical component, it could burn it out. To prevent this, fuses, circuit breakers or fusible links are connected into the current supply wires of most of the major electrical systems. When an electrical current of excessive power passes through the component's fuse, the fuse blows out and breaks the circuit, saving the component from destruction.

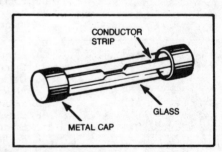

Typical automotive fuse

A circuit breaker is basically a self-repairing fuse. The circuit breaker opens the circuit the same way a fuse does. However, when either the short is removed from the circuit or the surge subsides, the circuit breaker resets itself and does not have to be replaced as a fuse does.

A fuse link is a wire that acts as a fuse. It is normally connected between the starter relay and the main wiring harness. This connection is usually under the hood. The fuse link (if installed) protects all the

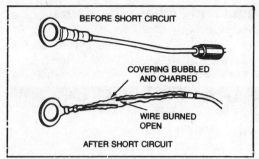

BEFORE SHORT CIRCUIT

COVERING BUBBLED AND CHARRED

WIRE BURNED OPEN

AFTER SHORT CIRCUIT

Most fusible links show a charred, melted insulation when they burn out

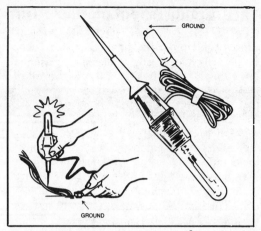

GROUND

GROUND

The test light will show the presence of current when touched to a hot wire and grounded at the other end

chassis electrical components, and is the probable cause of trouble when none of the electrical components function, unless the battery is disconnected or dead.

Electrical problems generally fall into one of three areas:

1. The component that is not functioning is not receiving current.

2. The component itself is not functioning.

3. The component is not properly grounded.

The electrical system can be checked with a test light and a jumper wire. A test light is a device that looks like a pointed screwdriver with a wire attached to it and has a light bulb in its handle. A jumper wire is a piece of insulated wire with an alligator clip attached to each end.

If a component is not working, you must follow a systematic plan to determine which of the three causes is the villain.

1. Turn on the switch that controls the inoperable component.

2. Disconnect the power supply wire from the component.

3. Attach the ground wire on the test light to a good metal ground.

4. Touch the probe end of the test light to the end of the power supply wire that was disconnected from the component. If the component is receiving current, the test light will go on.

NOTE: *Some components work only when the ignition switch is turned on.*

If the test light does not go on, then the problem is in the circuit between the battery and the component. This includes all the switches, fuses, and relays in the system. Follow the wire that runs back to the battery. The problem is an open circuit between the

battery and the component. If the fuse is blown and, when replaced, immediately blows again, there is a short circuit in the system which must be located and repaired. If there is a switch in the system, bypass it with a jumper wire. This is done by connecting one end of the jumper wire to the power supply wire into the switch and the other end of the jumper wire to the wire coming out of the switch. If the test light lights with the jumper wire installed, the switch or whatever was bypassed is defective.

NOTE: *Never substitute the jumper wire for the component, since it is required to use the power from the power source.*

5. If the bulb in the test light goes on, then the current is getting to the component that is not working. This eliminates the first of the three possible causes. Connect the power supply wire and connect a jumper wire from the component to a good metal ground. Do this with the switch which controls the component turned on, and also the ignition switch turned on if it is required for the component to work. If the component works with the jumper wire installed, then it has a bad ground. This is usually caused by the metal area on which the component mounts to the chassis being coated with some type of foreign matter.

6. If neither test located the source of the trouble, then the component itself is defective. Remember that for any electrical system to work, all connections must be clean and tight.

Troubleshooting Basic Turn Signal and Flasher Problems
See Chapter 5 for service procedures

Most problems in the turn signals or flasher system can be reduced to defective flashers or bulbs, which are easily replaced. Occasionally, the turn signal switch will prove defective.

F = Front   R = Rear   ● = Lights off   ○ = Lights on

Condition		Possible Cause
Turn signals light, but do not flash	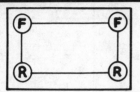	Defective flasher
No turn signals light on either side	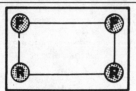	Blown fuse. Replace if defective. Defective flasher. Check by substitution. Open circuit, short circuit or poor ground.
Both turn signals on one side don't work	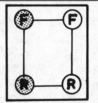	Bad bulbs. Bad ground in both (or either) housings.
One turn signal light on one side doesn't work	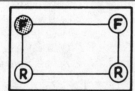	Defective bulb. Corrosion in socket. Clean contacts. Poor ground at socket.
Turn signal flashes too fast or too slowly	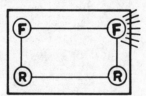	Check any bulb on the side flashing too fast. A heavy-duty bulb is probably installed in place of a regular bulb. Check the bulb flashing too slowly. A standard bulb was probably installed in place of a heavy-duty bulb. Loose connections or corrosion at the bulb socket.
Indicator lights don't work in either direction		Check if the turn signals are working. Check the dash indicator lights. Check the flasher by substitution.
One indicator light doesn't light		On systems with one dash indicator: See if the lights work on the same side. Often the filaments have been reversed in systems combining stoplights with taillights and turn signals. Check the flasher by substitution. On systems with two indicators: Check the bulbs on the same side. Check the indicator light bulb. Check the flasher by substitution.

Troubleshooting Lighting Problems

See Chapter 5 for service procedures

Condition	Possible Cause
One or more lights don't work, but others do	1. Defective bulb(s) 2. Blown fuse(s) 3. Dirty fuse clips or light sockets 4. Poor ground circuit
Lights burn out quickly	1. Incorrect voltage regulator setting or defective regulator 2. Poor battery/alternator connections
Lights go dim	1. Low/discharged battery 2. Alternator not charging 3. Corroded sockets or connections 4. Low voltage output
Lights flicker	1. Loose connection 2. Poor ground. (Run ground wire from light housing to frame) 3. Circuit breaker operating (short circuit)
Lights "flare"—Some flare is normal on acceleration—If excessive, see "Lights Burn Out Quickly"	High voltage setting
Lights glare—approaching drivers are blinded	1. Lights adjusted too high 2. Rear springs or shocks sagging 3. Rear tires soft

Troubleshooting Dash Gauge Problems

Most problems can be traced to a defective sending unit or faulty wiring. Occasionally, the gauge itself is at fault. See Chapter 5 for service procedures.

Condition	Possible Cause
COOLANT TEMPERATURE GAUGE	
Gauge reads erratically or not at all	1. Loose or dirty connections 2. Defective sending unit. 3. Defective gauge. To test a bi-metal gauge, remove the wire from the sending unit. Ground the wire for an instant. If the gauge registers, replace the sending unit. To test a magnetic gauge, disconnect the wire at the sending unit. With ignition ON gauge should register COLD. Ground the wire; gauge should register HOT.
AMMETER GAUGE—TURN HEADLIGHTS ON (DO NOT START ENGINE). NOTE REACTION	
Ammeter shows charge Ammeter shows discharge Ammeter does not move	1. Connections reversed on gauge 2. Ammeter is OK 3. Loose connections or faulty wiring 4. Defective gauge

Condition	Possible Cause

OIL PRESSURE GAUGE

Condition	Possible Cause
Gauge does not register or is inaccurate	1. On mechanical gauge, Bourdon tube may be bent or kinked. 2. Low oil pressure. Remove sending unit. Idle the engine briefly. If no oil flows from sending unit hole, problem is in engine. 3. Defective gauge. Remove the wire from the sending unit and ground it for an instant with the ignition ON. A good gauge will go to the top of the scale. 4. Defective wiring. Check the wiring to the gauge. If it's OK and the gauge doesn't register when grounded, replace the gauge. 5. Defective sending unit.

ALL GAUGES

Condition	Possible Cause
All gauges do not operate All gauges read low or erratically All gauges pegged	1. Blown fuse 2. Defective instrument regulator 3. Defective or dirty instrument voltage regulator 4. Loss of ground between instrument voltage regulator and frame 5. Defective instrument regulator

WARNING LIGHTS

Condition	Possible Cause
Light(s) do not come on when ignition is ON, but engine is not started Light comes on with engine running	1. Defective bulb 2. Defective wire 3. Defective sending unit. Disconnect the wire from the sending unit and ground it. Replace the sending unit if the light comes on with the ignition ON. 4. Problem in individual system 5. Defective sending unit

Troubleshooting Clutch Problems

It is false economy to replace individual clutch components. The pressure plate, clutch plate and throwout bearing should be replaced as a set, and the flywheel face inspected, whenever the clutch is overhauled. See Chapter 6 for service procedures.

Condition	Possible Cause
Clutch chatter	1. Grease on driven plate (disc) facing 2. Binding clutch linkage or cable 3. Loose, damaged facings on driven plate (disc) 4. Engine mounts loose 5. Incorrect height adjustment of pressure plate release levers 6. Clutch housing or housing to transmission adapter misalignment 7. Loose driven plate hub
Clutch grabbing	1. Oil, grease on driven plate (disc) facing 2. Broken pressure plate 3. Warped or binding driven plate. Driven plate binding on clutch shaft
Clutch slips	1. Lack of lubrication in clutch linkage or cable (linkage or cable binds, causes incomplete engagement) 2. Incorrect pedal, or linkage adjustment 3. Broken pressure plate springs 4. Weak pressure plate springs 5. Grease on driven plate facings (disc)

Troubleshooting Clutch Problems (cont.)

Condition	Possible Cause
Incomplete clutch release	1. Incorrect pedal or linkage adjustment or linkage or cable binding 2. Incorrect height adjustment on pressure plate release levers 3. Loose, broken facings on driven plate (disc) 4. Bent, dished, warped driven plate caused by overheating
Grinding, whirring grating noise when pedal is depressed	1. Worn or defective throwout bearing 2. Starter drive teeth contacting flywheel ring gear teeth. Look for milled or polished teeth on ring gear.
Squeal, howl, trumpeting noise when pedal is being released (occurs during first inch to inch and one-half of pedal travel)	Pilot bushing worn or lack of lubricant. If bushing appears OK, polish bushing with emery cloth, soak lube wick in oil, lube bushing with oil, apply film of chassis grease to clutch shaft pilot hub, reassemble. NOTE: Bushing wear may be due to misalignment of clutch housing or housing to transmission adapter
Vibration or clutch pedal pulsation with clutch disengaged (pedal fully depressed)	1. Worn or defective engine transmission mounts 2. Flywheel run out. (Flywheel run out at face not to exceed 0.005″) 3. Damaged or defective clutch components

Troubleshooting Manual Transmission Problems
See Chapter 6 for service procedures

Condition	Possible Cause
Transmission jumps out of gear	1. Misalignment of transmission case or clutch housing. 2. Worn pilot bearing in crankshaft. 3. Bent transmission shaft. 4. Worn high speed sliding gear. 5. Worn teeth or end-play in clutch shaft. 6. Insufficient spring tension on shifter rail plunger. 7. Bent or loose shifter fork. 8. Gears not engaging completely. 9. Loose or worn bearings on clutch shaft or mainshaft. 10. Worn gear teeth. 11. Worn or damaged detent balls.
Transmission sticks in gear	1. Clutch not releasing fully. 2. Burred or battered teeth on clutch shaft, or sliding sleeve. 3. Burred or battered transmission mainshaft. 4. Frozen synchronizing clutch. 5. Stuck shifter rail plunger. 6. Gearshift lever twisting and binding shifter rail. 7. Battered teeth on high speed sliding gear or on sleeve. 8. Improper lubrication, or lack of lubrication. 9. Corroded transmission parts. 10. Defective mainshaft pilot bearing. 11. Locked gear bearings will give same effect as stuck in gear.
Transmission gears will not synchronize	1. Binding pilot bearing on mainshaft, will synchronize in high gear only. 2. Clutch not releasing fully. 3. Detent spring weak or broken. 4. Weak or broken springs under balls in sliding gear sleeve. 5. Binding bearing on clutch shaft, or binding countershaft. 6. Binding pilot bearing in crankshaft. 7. Badly worn gear teeth. 8. Improper lubrication. 9. Constant mesh gear not turning freely on transmission mainshaft. Will synchronize in that gear only.

Condition	Possible Cause
Gears spinning when shifting into gear from neutral	1. Clutch not releasing fully. 2. In some cases an extremely light lubricant in transmission will cause gears to continue to spin for a short time after clutch is released. 3. Binding pilot bearing in crankshaft.
Transmission noisy in all gears	1. Insufficient lubricant, or improper lubricant. 2. Worn countergear bearings. 3. Worn or damaged main drive gear or countergear. 4. Damaged main drive gear or mainshaft bearings. 5. Worn or damaged countergear anti-lash plate.
Transmission noisy in neutral only	1. Damaged main drive gear bearing. 2. Damaged or loose mainshaft pilot bearing. 3. Worn or damaged countergear anti-lash plate. 4. Worn countergear bearings.
Transmission noisy in one gear only	1. Damaged or worn constant mesh gears. 2. Worn or damaged countergear bearings. 3. Damaged or worn synchronizer.
Transmission noisy in reverse only	1. Worn or damaged reverse idler gear or idler bushing. 2. Worn or damaged mainshaft reverse gear. 3. Worn or damaged reverse countergear. 4. Damaged shift mechanism.

TROUBLESHOOTING AUTOMATIC TRANSMISSION PROBLEMS

Keeping alert to changes in the operating characteristics of the transmission (changing shift points, noises, etc.) can prevent small problems from becoming large ones. If the problem cannot be traced to loose bolts, fluid level, misadjusted linkage, clogged filters or similar problems, you should probably seek professional service.

Transmission Fluid Indications

The appearance and odor of the transmission fluid can give valuable clues to the overall condition of the transmission. Always note the appearance of the fluid when you check the fluid level or change the fluid. Rub a small amount of fluid between your fingers to feel for grit and smell the fluid on the dipstick.

If the fluid appears:	It indicates:
Clear and red colored	Normal operation
Discolored (extremely dark red or brownish) or smells burned	Band or clutch pack failure, usually caused by an overheated transmission. Hauling very heavy loads with insufficient power or failure to change the fluid often result in overheating. Do not confuse this appearance with newer fluids that have a darker red color and a strong odor (though not a burned odor).
Foamy or aerated (light in color and full of bubbles)	1. The level is too high (gear train is churning oil) 2. An internal air leak (air is mixing with the fluid). Have the transmission checked professionally.
Solid residue in the fluid	Defective bands, clutch pack or bearings. Bits of band material or metal abrasives are clinging to the dipstick. Have the transmission checked professionally.
Varnish coating on the dipstick	The transmission fluid is overheating

TROUBLESHOOTING DRIVE AXLE PROBLEMS

First, determine when the noise is most noticeable.

Drive Noise: Produced under vehicle acceleration.

Coast Noise: Produced while coasting with a closed throttle.

Float Noise: Occurs while maintaining constant speed (just enough to keep speed constant) on a level road.

External Noise Elimination

It is advisable to make a thorough road test to determine whether the noise originates in the rear axle or whether it originates from the tires, engine, transmission, wheel bearings or road surface. Noise originating from other places cannot be corrected by servicing the rear axle.

ROAD NOISE

Brick or rough surfaced concrete roads produce noises that seem to come from the rear axle. Road noise is usually identical in Drive or Coast and driving on a different type of road will tell whether the road is the problem.

TIRE NOISE

Tire noise can be mistaken as rear axle noise, even though the tires on the front are at fault. Snow tread and mud tread tires or tires worn unevenly will frequently cause vibrations which seem to originate elsewhere; *temporarily, and for test purposes only,* inflate the tires to 40–50 lbs. This will significantly alter the noise produced by the tires, but will not alter noise from the rear axle. Noises from the rear axle will normally cease at speeds below 30 mph on coast, while tire noise will continue at lower tone as speed is decreased. The rear axle noise will usually change from drive conditions to coast conditions, while tire noise will not. Do not forget to lower the tire pressure to normal after the test is complete.

ENGINE/TRANSMISSION NOISE

Determine at what speed the noise is most pronounced, then stop in a quiet place. With the transmission in Neutral, run the engine through speeds corresponding to road speeds where the noise was noticed. Noises produced with the vehicle standing still are coming from the engine or transmission.

FRONT WHEEL BEARINGS

Front wheel bearing noises, sometimes confused with rear axle noises, will not change when comparing drive and coast conditions. While holding the speed steady, lightly apply the footbrake. This will often cause wheel bearing noise to lessen, as some of the weight is taken off the bearing. Front wheel bearings are easily checked by jacking up the wheels and spinning the wheels. Shaking the wheels will also determine if the wheel bearings are excessively loose.

REAR AXLE NOISES

Eliminating other possible sources can narrow the cause to the rear axle, which normally produces noise from worn gears or bearings. Gear noises tend to peak in a narrow speed range, while bearing noises will usually vary in pitch with engine speeds.

Noise Diagnosis

The Noise Is:	Most Probably Produced By:
1. Identical under Drive or Coast	Road surface, tires or front wheel bearings
2. Different depending on road surface	Road surface or tires
3. Lower as speed is lowered	Tires
4. Similar when standing or moving	Engine or transmission
5. A vibration	Unbalanced tires, rear wheel bearing, unbalanced driveshaft or worn U-joint
6. A knock or click about every two tire revolutions	Rear wheel bearing
7. Most pronounced on turns	Damaged differential gears
8. A steady low-pitched whirring or scraping, starting at low speeds	Damaged or worn pinion bearing
9. A chattering vibration on turns	Wrong differential lubricant or worn clutch plates (limited slip rear axle)
10. Noticed only in Drive, Coast or Float conditions	Worn ring gear and/or pinion gear

Troubleshooting Steering & Suspension Problems

Condition	Possible Cause
Hard steering (wheel is hard to turn)	1. Improper tire pressure 2. Loose or glazed pump drive belt 3. Low or incorrect fluid 4. Loose, bent or poorly lubricated front end parts 5. Improper front end alignment (excessive caster) 6. Bind in steering column or linkage 7. Kinked hydraulic hose 8. Air in hydraulic system 9. Low pump output or leaks in system 10. Obstruction in lines 11. Pump valves sticking or out of adjustment 12. Incorrect wheel alignment
Loose steering (too much play in steering wheel)	1. Loose wheel bearings 2. Faulty shocks 3. Worn linkage or suspension components 4. Loose steering gear mounting or linkage points 5. Steering mechanism worn or improperly adjusted 6. Valve spool improperly adjusted 7. Worn ball joints, tie-rod ends, etc.
Veers or wanders (pulls to one side with hands off steering wheel)	1. Improper tire pressure 2. Improper front end alignment 3. Dragging or improperly adjusted brakes 4. Bent frame 5. Improper rear end alignment 6. Faulty shocks or springs 7. Loose or bent front end components 8. Play in Pitman arm 9. Steering gear mountings loose 10. Loose wheel bearings 11. Binding Pitman arm 12. Spool valve sticking or improperly adjusted 13. Worn ball joints
Wheel oscillation or vibration transmitted through steering wheel	1. Low or uneven tire pressure 2. Loose wheel bearings 3. Improper front end alignment 4. Bent spindle 5. Worn, bent or broken front end components 6. Tires out of round or out of balance 7. Excessive lateral runout in disc brake rotor 8. Loose or bent shock absorber or strut
Noises (see also "Troubleshooting Drive Axle Problems")	1. Loose belts 2. Low fluid, air in system 3. Foreign matter in system 4. Improper lubrication 5. Interference or chafing in linkage 6. Steering gear mountings loose 7. Incorrect adjustment or wear in gear box 8. Faulty valves or wear in pump 9. Kinked hydraulic lines 10. Worn wheel bearings
Poor return of steering	1. Over-inflated tires 2. Improperly aligned front end (excessive caster) 3. Binding in steering column 4. No lubrication in front end 5. Steering gear adjusted too tight
Uneven tire wear (see "How To Read Tire Wear")	1. Incorrect tire pressure 2. Improperly aligned front end 3. Tires out-of-balance 4. Bent or worn suspension parts

HOW TO READ TIRE WEAR

The way your tires wear is a good indicator of other parts of the suspension. Abnormal wear patterns are often caused by the need for simple tire maintenance, or for front end alignment.

Excessive wear at the center of the tread indicates that the air pressure in the tire is consistently too high. The tire is riding on the center of the tread and wearing it prematurely. Occasionally, this wear pattern can result from outrageously wide tires on narrow rims. The cure for this is to replace either the tires or the wheels.

This type of wear usually results from consistent under-inflation. When a tire is under-inflated, there is too much contact with the road by the outer treads, which wear prematurely. When this type of wear occurs, and the tire pressure is known to be consistently correct, a bent or worn steering component or the need for wheel alignment could be indicated.

Feathering is a condition when the edge of each tread rib develops a slightly rounded edge on one side and a sharp edge on the other. By running your hand over the tire, you can usually feel the sharper edges before you'll be able to see them. The most common causes of feathering are incorrect toe-in setting or deteriorated bushings in the front suspension.

When an inner or outer rib wears faster than the rest of the tire, the need for wheel alignment is indicated. There is excessive camber in the front suspension, causing the wheel to lean too much putting excessive load on one side of the tire. Misalignment could also be due to sagging springs, worn ball joints, or worn control arm bushings. Be sure the vehicle is loaded the way it's normally driven when you have the wheels aligned.

Cups or scalloped dips appearing around the edge of the tread almost always indicate worn (sometimes bent) suspension parts. Adjustment of wheel alignment alone will seldom cure the problem. Any worn component that connects the wheel to the suspension can cause this type of wear. Occasionally, wheels that are out of balance will wear like this, but wheel imbalance usually shows up as bald spots between the outside edges and center of the tread.

Second-rib wear is usually found only in radial tires, and appears where the steel belts end in relation to the tread. It can be kept to a minimum by paying careful attention to tire pressure and frequently rotating the tires. This is often considered normal wear but excessive amounts indicate that the tires are too wide for the wheels.

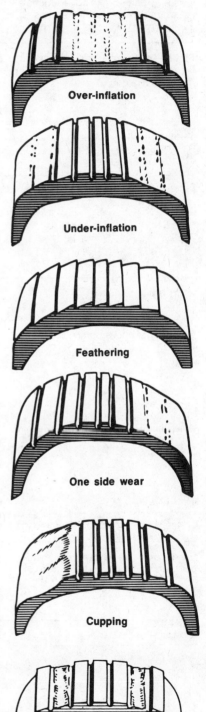

Over-inflation

Under-inflation

Feathering

One side wear

Cupping

Second-rib wear

Troubleshooting Disc Brake Problems

Condition	Possible Cause
Noise—groan—brake noise emanating when slowly releasing brakes (creep-groan)	Not detrimental to function of disc brakes—no corrective action required. (This noise may be eliminated by slightly increasing or decreasing brake pedal efforts.)
Rattle—brake noise or rattle emanating at low speeds on rough roads, (front wheels only).	1. Shoe anti-rattle spring missing or not properly positioned. 2. Excessive clearance between shoe and caliper. 3. Soft or broken caliper seals. 4. Deformed or misaligned disc. 5. Loose caliper.
Scraping	1. Mounting bolts too long. 2. Loose wheel bearings. 3. Bent, loose, or misaligned splash shield.
Front brakes heat up during driving and fail to release	1. Operator riding brake pedal. 2. Stop light switch improperly adjusted. 3. Sticking pedal linkage. 4. Frozen or seized piston. 5. Residual pressure valve in master cylinder. 6. Power brake malfunction. 7. Proportioning valve malfunction.
Leaky brake caliper	1. Damaged or worn caliper piston seal. 2. Scores or corrosion on surface of cylinder bore.
Grabbing or uneven brake action— Brakes pull to one side	1. Causes listed under "Brakes Pull". 2. Power brake malfunction. 3. Low fluid level in master cylinder. 4. Air in hydraulic system. 5. Brake fluid, oil or grease on linings. 6. Unmatched linings. 7. Distorted brake pads. 8. Frozen or seized pistons. 9. Incorrect tire pressure. 10. Front end out of alignment. 11. Broken rear spring. 12. Brake caliper pistons sticking. 13. Restricted hose or line. 14. Caliper not in proper alignment to braking disc. 15. Stuck or malfunctioning metering valve. 16. Soft or broken caliper seals. 17. Loose caliper.
Brake pedal can be depressed without braking effect	1. Air in hydraulic system or improper bleeding procedure. 2. Leak past primary cup in master cylinder. 3. Leak in system. 4. Rear brakes out of adjustment. 5. Bleeder screw open.
Excessive pedal travel	1. Air, leak, or insufficient fluid in system or caliper. 2. Warped or excessively tapered shoe and lining assembly. 3. Excessive disc runout. 4. Rear brake adjustment required. 5. Loose wheel bearing adjustment. 6. Damaged caliper piston seal. 7. Improper brake fluid (boil). 8. Power brake malfunction. 9. Weak or soft hoses.

Troubleshooting Disc Brake Problems (cont.)

Condition	Possible Cause
Brake roughness or chatter (pedal pumping)	1. Excessive thickness variation of braking disc. 2. Excessive lateral runout of braking disc. 3. Rear brake drums out-of-round. 4. Excessive front bearing clearance.
Excessive pedal effort	1. Brake fluid, oil or grease on linings. 2. Incorrect lining. 3. Frozen or seized pistons. 4. Power brake malfunction. 5. Kinked or collapsed hose or line. 6. Stuck metering valve. 7. Scored caliper or master cylinder bore. 8. Seized caliper pistons.
Brake pedal fades (pedal travel increases with foot on brake)	1. Rough master cylinder or caliper bore. 2. Loose or broken hydraulic lines/connections. 3. Air in hydraulic system. 4. Fluid level low. 5. Weak or soft hoses. 6. Inferior quality brake shoes or fluid. 7. Worn master cylinder piston cups or seals.

Troubleshooting Drum Brakes

Condition	Possible Cause
Pedal goes to floor	1. Fluid low in reservoir. 2. Air in hydraulic system. 3. Improperly adjusted brake. 4. Leaking wheel cylinders. 5. Loose or broken brake lines. 6. Leaking or worn master cylinder. 7. Excessively worn brake lining.
Spongy brake pedal	1. Air in hydraulic system. 2. Improper brake fluid (low boiling point). 3. Excessively worn or cracked brake drums. 4. Broken pedal pivot bushing.
Brakes pulling	1. Contaminated lining. 2. Front end out of alignment. 3. Incorrect brake adjustment. 4. Unmatched brake lining. 5. Brake drums out of round. 6. Brake shoes distorted. 7. Restricted brake hose or line. 8. Broken rear spring. 9. Worn brake linings. 10. Uneven lining wear. 11. Glazed brake lining. 12. Excessive brake lining dust. 13. Heat spotted brake drums. 14. Weak brake return springs. 15. Faulty automatic adjusters. 16. Low or incorrect tire pressure.

Condition	Possible Cause
Squealing brakes	1. Glazed brake lining. 2. Saturated brake lining. 3. Weak or broken brake shoe retaining spring. 4. Broken or weak brake shoe return spring. 5. Incorrect brake lining. 6. Distorted brake shoes. 7. Bent support plate. 8. Dust in brakes or scored brake drums. 9. Linings worn below limit. 10. Uneven brake lining wear. 11. Heat spotted brake drums.
Chirping brakes	1. Out of round drum or eccentric axle flange pilot.
Dragging brakes	1. Incorrect wheel or parking brake adjustment. 2. Parking brakes engaged or improperly adjusted. 3. Weak or broken brake shoe return spring. 4. Brake pedal binding. 5. Master cylinder cup sticking. 6. Obstructed master cylinder relief port. 7. Saturated brake lining. 8. Bent or out of round brake drum. 9. Contaminated or improper brake fluid. 10. Sticking wheel cylinder pistons. 11. Driver riding brake pedal. 12. Defective proportioning valve. 13. Insufficient brake shoe lubricant.
Hard pedal	1. Brake booster inoperative. 2. Incorrect brake lining. 3. Restricted brake line or hose. 4. Frozen brake pedal linkage. 5. Stuck wheel cylinder. 6. Binding pedal linkage. 7. Faulty proportioning valve.
Wheel locks	1. Contaminated brake lining. 2. Loose or torn brake lining. 3. Wheel cylinder cups sticking. 4. Incorrect wheel bearing adjustment. 5. Faulty proportioning valve.
Brakes fade (high speed)	1. Incorrect lining. 2. Overheated brake drums. 3. Incorrect brake fluid (low boiling temperature). 4. Saturated brake lining. 5. Leak in hydraulic system. 6. Faulty automatic adjusters.
Pedal pulsates	1. Bent or out of round brake drum.
Brake chatter and shoe knock	1. Out of round brake drum. 2. Loose support plate. 3. Bent support plate. 4. Distorted brake shoes. 5. Machine grooves in contact face of brake drum (Shoe Knock). 6. Contaminated brake lining. 7. Missing or loose components. 8. Incorrect lining material. 9. Out-of-round brake drums. 10. Heat spotted or scored brake drums. 11. Out-of-balance wheels.

Troubleshooting Drum Brakes (cont.)

Condition	Possible Cause
Brakes do not self adjust	1. Adjuster screw frozen in thread. 2. Adjuster screw corroded at thrust washer. 3. Adjuster lever does not engage star wheel. 4. Adjuster installed on wrong wheel.
Brake light glows	1. Leak in the hydraulic system. 2. Air in the system. 3. Improperly adjusted master cylinder pushrod. 4. Uneven lining wear. 5. Failure to center combination valve or proportioning valve.

Mechanic's Data

General Conversion Table

Multiply By	To Convert	To	
	LENGTH		
2.54	Inches	Centimeters	.3937
25.4	Inches	Millimeters	.03937
30.48	Feet	Centimeters	.0328
.304	Feet	Meters	3.28
.914	Yards	Meters	1.094
1.609	Miles	Kilometers	.621
	VOLUME		
.473	Pints	Liters	2.11
.946	Quarts	Liters	1.06
3.785	Gallons	Liters	.264
.016	Cubic inches	Liters	61.02
16.39	Cubic inches	Cubic cms.	.061
28.3	Cubic feet	Liters	.0353
	MASS (Weight)		
28.35	Ounces	Grams	.035
.4536	Pounds	Kilograms	2.20
—	To obtain	From	Multiply by

Multiply By	To Convert	To	
	AREA		
.645	Square inches	Square cms.	.155
.836	Square yds.	Square meters	1.196
	FORCE		
4.448	Pounds	Newtons	.225
.138	Ft./lbs.	Kilogram/meters	7.23
1.36	Ft./lbs.	Newton-meters	.737
.112	In./lbs.	Newton-meters	8.844
	PRESSURE		
.068	Psi	Atmospheres	14.7
6.89	Psi	Kilopascals	.145
	OTHER		
1.104	Horsepower (DIN)	Horsepower (SAE)	.9861
.746	Horsepower (SAE)	Kilowatts (KW)	1.34
1.60	Mph	Km/h	.625
.425	Mpg	Km/1	2.35
—	To obtain	From	Multiply by

Tap Drill Sizes

National Coarse or U.S.S.

Screw & Tap Size	Threads Per Inch	Use Drill Number
No. 5	40	39
No. 6	32	36
No. 8	32	29
No. 10	24	25
No. 12	24	17
1/4	20	8
5/16	18	F
3/8	16	5/16
7/16	14	U
1/2	13	27/64
9/16	12	31/64
5/8	11	17/32
3/4	10	21/32
7/8	9	49/64

National Coarse or U.S.S.

Screw & Tap Size	Threads Per Inch	Use Drill Number
1	8	7/8
1 1/8	7	63/64
1 1/4	7	1 7/64
1 1/2	6	1 11/32

National Fine or S.A.E.

Screw & Tap Size	Threads Per Inch	Use Drill Number
No. 5	44	37
No. 6	40	33
No. 8	36	29
No. 10	32	21

National Fine or S.A.E.

Screw & Tap Size	Threads Per Inch	Use Drill Number
No. 12	28	15
1/4	28	3
5/16	24	1
3/8	24	Q
7/16	20	W
1/2	20	29/64
9/16	18	33/64
5/8	18	37/64
3/4	16	11/16
7/8	14	13/16
1 1/8	12	1 3/64
1 1/4	12	1 11/64
1 1/2	12	1 27/64

Drill Sizes In Decimal Equivalents

Inch	Decimal	Wire	mm
1/64	.0156		.39
	.0157		.4
	.0160	78	
	.0165		.42
	.0173		.44
	.0177		.45
	.0180	77	
	.0181		.46
	.0189		.48
	.0197		.5
	.0200	76	
	.0210	75	
	.0217		.55
	.0225	74	
	.0236		.6
	.0240	73	
	.0250	72	
	.0256		.65
	.0260	71	
	.0276		.7
	.0280	70	
	.0292	69	
	.0295		.75
	.0310	68	
1/32	.0312		.79
	.0315		.8
	.0320	67	
	.0330	66	
	.0335		.85
	.0350	65	
	.0354		.9
	.0360	64	
	.0370	63	
	.0374		.95
	.0380	62	
	.0390	61	
	.0394		1.0
	.0400	60	
	.0410	59	
	.0413		1.05
	.0420	58	
	.0430	57	
	.0433		1.1
	.0453		1.15
	.0465	56	
3/64	.0469		1.19
	.0472		1.2
	.0492		1.25
	.0512		1.3
	.0520	55	
	.0531		1.35
	.0550	54	
	.0551		1.4
	.0571		1.45
	.0591		1.5
	.0595	53	
	.0610		1.55
1/16	.0625		1.59
	.0630		1.6
	.0635	52	
	.0650		1.65
	.0669		1.7
	.0670	51	
	.0689		1.75
	.0700	50	
	.0709		1.8
	.0728		1.85

Inch	Decimal	Wire	mm
	.0730	49	
	.0748		1.9
	.0760	48	
	.0768		1.95
5/64	.0781		1.98
	.0785	47	
	.0787		2.0
	.0807		2.05
	.0810	46	
	.0820	45	
	.0827		2.1
	.0846		2.15
	.0860	44	
	.0866		2.2
	.0886		2.25
	.0890	43	
	.0906		2.3
	.0925		2.35
	.0935	42	
3/32	.0938		2.38
	.0945		2.4
	.0960	41	
	.0965		2.45
	.0980	40	
	.0981		2.5
	.0995	39	
	.1015	38	
	.1024		2.6
	.1040	37	
	.1063		2.7
	.1065	36	
	.1083		2.75
7/64	.1094		2.77
	.1100	35	
	.1102		2.8
	.1110	34	
	.1130	33	
	.1142		2.9
	.1160	32	
	.1181		3.0
	.1200	31	
	.1220		3.1
1/8	.1250		3.17
	.1260		3.2
	.1280		3.25
	.1285	30	
	.1299		3.3
	.1339		3.4
	.1360	29	
	.1378		3.5
	.1405	28	
9/64	.1406		3.57
	.1417		3.6
	.1440	27	
	1457		3.7
	.1470	26	
	.1476		3.75
	.1495	25	
	.1496		3.8
	.1520	24	
	.1535		3.9
	.1540	23	
5/32	.1562		3.96
	.1570	22	
	.1575		4.0
	.1590	21	
	.1610	20	

Inch	Decimal	Wire & Letter	mm
	.1614		4.1
	.1654		4.2
	.1660	19	
	.1673		4.25
	.1693		4.3
	.1695	18	
11/64	.1719		4.36
	.1730	17	
	.1732		4.4
	.1770	16	
	.1772		4.5
	.1800	15	
	.1811		4.6
	.1820	14	
	.1850	13	
	.1850		4.7
	.1870		4.75
3/16	.1875		4.76
	.1890	12	
	.1890		4.8
	.1910	11	
	.1929		4.9
	.1935	10	
	.1960	9	
	.1969		5.0
	.1990	8	
	.2008		5.1
	.2010	7	
13/64	.2031		5.16
	.2040	6	
	.2047		5.2
	.2055	5	
	.2067		5.25
	.2087		5.3
	.2090	4	
	.2126		5.4
	.2130	3	
	.2165		5.5
7/32	.2188		5.55
	.2205		5.6
	.2210	2	
	.2244		5.7
	.2264		5.75
	.2280	1	
	.2283		5.8
	.2323		5.9
	.2340	A	
15/64	.2344		5.95
	.2362		6.0
	.2380	B	
	.2402		6.1
	.2420	C	
	.2441		6.2
	.2460	D	
	.2461		6.25
	.2480		6.3
1/4	.2500	E	6.35
	.2520		6.
	.2559		6.5
	.2570	F	
	.2598		6.6
	.2610	G	
	.2638		6.7
17/64	.2656		6.74
	.2657		6.75
	.2660	H	
	.2677		6.8

Inch	Decimal	Letter	mm
	.2717		6.9
	.2720	I	
	.2756		7.0
	.2770	J	
	.2795		7.1
	.2810	K	
9/32	.2812		7.14
	.2835		7.2
	.2854		7.25
	.2874		7.3
	.2900	L	
	.2913		7.4
	.2950	M	
	.2953		7.5
19/64	.2969		7.54
	.2992		7.6
	.3020	N	
	.3031		7.7
	.3051		7.75
	.3071		7.8
	.3110		7.9
5/16	.3125		7.93
	.3150		8.0
	.3160	O	
	.3189		8.1
	.3228		8.2
	.3230	P	
	.3248		8.25
	.3268		8.3
21/64	.3281		8.33
	.3307		8.4
	.3320	Q	
	.3346		8.5
	.3386		8.6
	.3390	R	
	.3425		8.7
11/32	.3438		8.73
	.3445		8.75
	.3465		8.8
	.3480	S	
	.3504		8.9
	.3543		9.0
	.3580	T	
	.3583		9.1
23/64	.3594		9.12
	.3622		9.2
	.3642		9.25
	.3661		9.3
	.3680	U	
	.3701		9.4
	.3740		9.5
3/8	.3750		9.52
	.3770	V	
	.3780		9.6
	.3819		9.7
	.3839		9.75
	.3858		9.8
	.3860	W	
	.3898		9.9
25/64	.3906		9.92
	.3937		10.0
	.3970	X	
	.4040	Y	
13/32	.4062		10.31
	.4130	Z	
	.4134		10.5
27/64	.4219		10.71

Inch	Decimal	mm
	.4331	11.0
7/16	.4375	11.11
	.4528	11.5
29/64	.4531	11.51
15/32	.4688	11.90
	.4724	12.0
31/64	.4844	12.30
	.4921	12.5
1/2	.5000	12.70
	.5118	13.0
33/64	.5156	13.09
17/32	.5312	13.49
	.5315	13.5
35/64	.5469	13.89
	.5512	14.0
9/16	.5625	14.28
	.5709	14.5
37/64	.5781	14.68
	.5906	15.0
19/32	.5938	15.08
39/64	.6094	15.47
	.6102	15.5
5/8	.6250	15.87
	.6299	16.0
41/64	.6406	16.27
	.6496	16.5
21/32	.6562	16.66
	.6693	17.0
43/64	.6719	17.06
11/16	.6875	17.46
	.6890	17.5
45/64	.7031	17.85
	.7087	18.0
23/32	.7188	18.25
	.7283	18.5
47/64	.7344	18.65
	.7480	19.0
3/4	.7500	19.05
49/64	.7656	19.44
	.7677	19.5
25/32	.7812	19.84
	.7874	20.0
51/64	.7969	20.24
	.8071	20.5
13/16	.8125	20.63
	.8268	21.0
53/64	.8281	21.03
27/32	.8438	21.43
	.8465	21.5
55/64	.8594	21.82
	.8661	22.0
7/8	.8750	22.22
	.8858	22.5
57/64	.8906	22.62
	.9055	23.0
29/32	.9062	23.01
59/64	.9219	23.41
	.9252	23.5
15/16	.9375	23.81
	.9449	24.0
61/64	.9531	24.2
	.9646	24.5
31/32	.9688	24.6
	.9843	25.0
63/64	.9844	25.0
1	1.0000	25.4

Index